MARKETING
AND
INFORMATION
TECHNOLOGY

MARKETING AND INFORMATION TECHNOLOGY

The Strategy, Application and Implementation of IT in Marketing

JOHN O'CONNOR

EAMONN GALVIN

PITMAN PUBLISHING

London • Hong Kong • Johannesburg • Melbourne • Singapore • Washington DC

To the women in our lives:
Margaret, Sheila, Ciara and Louise

PITMAN PUBLISHING
128 Long Acre, London WC2E 9AN
Tel: +44 (0)171 447 2000
Fax: +44 (0)171 240 5771

A Division of Pearson Professional Limited

First published in Great Britain in 1997

© Pearson Professional Limited 1997

The right of John O'Connor and Eamonn Galvin to be identified
as authors of this work has been asserted by them in accordance
with the Copyright, Designs and Patents Act 1988.

ISBN 0 273 62644 2

British Library Cataloguing in Publication Data
A CIP catalogue record for this book can be obtained from the British Library

10 9 8 7 6 5 4 3 2 1

Typeset by M Rules
Printed and bound in Great Britain by Redwood Books, Trowbridge, Wiltshire

The Publishers' policy is to use paper manufactured from sustainable forests.

CONTENTS

PREFACE

Our views on marketing

Marketing is about customers, and customers are the only reason we get out of bed each morning and make our way to work. Marketing is the heart and soul of the organisation; the very reason for its existence. Information technology (IT) is so powerful in marketing because it is enabling organisations to build powerful personal relationships with their customers and to understand their needs. Marketing is being driven more and more by technological advances, for two reasons. First, information technology really does have the potential to make marketing management more effective than it currently is. Second, and more important, information technology is being widely utilised by consumers: the increasing use of personal computers at work and at home, the proliferation of mobile telephones, the explosion of the Internet and so on. To stay one step ahead and to anticipate the changing ways in which consumers choose to live their lives and purchase services and products, marketing managers need to embrace information technology with even more vigour than the consumer.

Our views on information technology

As you read this textbook, keep a couple of thoughts in mind. First, technology in all its forms has a tendency to take longer to mature and commercialise than its supporters estimate. The first workable videocassette recorder was developed in 1959, yet it was not until the late 1970s that the Japanese developed a commercial market for the VCR. Second, when a major technology finally matures, its impact invariably exceed all expectations. When the first modern computer was invented, the experts' (IBM's) view was that the market for such machines was no more than half a dozen worldwide. Yet today's dishwashers and washing machines have more computing power than those early computers. The software and processing power in today's desktop computers are greater than those of Mission Control when the first man was placed on the moon in 1969. And so it goes on. Who knows what technology will be doing for us in another 30 years?

Our views on marketing and IT research

In researching this book, we have used a wide variety of reference sources as well as trawling our own minds and those of our colleagues and clients. In the process, we have confirmed a strong suspicion that we have harboured for some time – that many articles on the combined subject of marketing and information technology completely miss the mark. Most articles appear to be written either by marketers who have a limited understanding of IT or those with an IT perspective who fail to relate to the realities of business, sales or marketing. In the first category are journal articles where most of the references date from the 1980s, or possibly even the 1970s. As the first personal computer (PC) only peered out from its shrinkwrapped box in 1981 in an era where comments like 'a terminal on everybody's desk' seemed as realistic as 'beam me up, Scottie', such articles have limited relevance. Yet articles on marketing systems continue to refer to this historic age. We will make a bold, and somewhat bald, assertion that any article written before 1990 on the subject of IT in marketing is outdated. There are clearly some exceptions to this assertion, but that is exactly what they are – exceptions rather than the norm. You will not find many in this book!

Our thanks

The writers of any book owe a debt of gratitude to people who help them in their endeavours. This book is no exception. First and foremost, to Pradeep Jethi for persuading us to write it; to Professor Martin Evans and other reviewers for proving that the term 'constructive criticism' is not an oxymoron; to Richard O'Reilly, Sue, Rachel, Petrina and Colette for helping us along the way; to Annette McFadyen and Jane Powell at Pitman for their encouragement; and finally special thanks to June for her expert advice.

Readers' comments

Regis McKenna wrote an article entitled 'Real-time marketing' in the *Harvard Business Review* (after 1990!) in which he exhorted marketers to involve the customer in the process of designing products and services. In a similar vein, we would like to invite you to comment on this book. Send your comments, good, bad and indifferent, to:

john.r.o'connor@ac.com
eamonn.galvin@ac.com

We can assure you that they will be taken into account in any future editions of this book.
   Enjoy!

John O'Connor
Eamonn Galvin

May 1997

Part I

INFORMATION FOR MARKETING

Part I of this book provides an overview of the strategic use of information within the field of marketing. It contains five chapters:

1 Recent trends in marketing

2 Management information and decision making

3 Marketing information systems (MkIS)

4 Customer information and customer databases

5 Database marketing

1

RECENT TRENDS IN MARKETING

■ What is marketing?
■ The changing role of marketing
■ Marketing at a crossroads
■ The new marketing organisation
■ The strategic role of information technology

OBJECTIVES

After studying this chapter, you will be able to:

☐ Define the term 'marketing' and offer different interpretations of its meaning and scope

☐ Describe the typical activities performed by the marketing department and the marketing manager

☐ Explain how marketing has changed in recent years and offer reasons for these changes

☐ Provide a view on how marketing will continue to evolve and adapt in the future

WHAT IS MARKETING?

■ Marketing defined

The purpose of this book is to explore and describe the use of information technology within marketing. Let us begin with some definitions of marketing and marketing management. According to Kotler (1994),[1] marketing management is a process which:

> 'consists of analysing market opportunities, researching and selecting target markets, developing marketing strategies, planning marketing tactics, and implementing and controlling the marketing effort.'

In 1954 Peter Drucker, a leading business writer, published a book called *The Practice of Management*.[2] In the book, Drucker took a holistic view of marketing by describing it as:

> 'the distinguishing, the unique function of business . . . It is the whole business seen from the point of view of its final result, that is, from the customer's point of view.'

Drucker's definition fell on willing ears, coming as it did during the consumer boom that followed the end of the Second World War. Six years later, Theodore Levitt wrote an article entitled 'Marketing myopia'[3] in which he claimed that certain industries were in decline not because of any downturns in the economy but because they were product oriented rather than customer oriented.

Baker[4] (1976) described marketing as an enigma, the enigma relating to the fact that it is one of humanity's oldest activities and yet it is regarded as one of the most recent of the business disciplines. Nearly 20 years after the first comment, Baker[5] made the statement that:

> *'in a truly marketing-orientated organisation the need for a specialised marketing function is probably far less than it is in a sales- or production-dominated company.'*

Baker's latter comment reflects a view, which we share, that marketing really is a management philosophy which needs to be at the heart of every organisation, rather than confined to the marketing department. In line with this broad definition of marketing as a management philosophy, the contents of this book are as relevant to general managers as they are to marketing specialists.

■ The central role of the customer

The central role of marketing is its ability to identify and satisfy customer needs. Therefore, marketing can be defined very simply as: 'finding a customer need and filling it'. Indeed, when we look at what marketing people do, we can see how much of their activity is taken up with customers (*see* Exhibit 1.1).

Throughout this book we will return to the theme of the central role of the customer. Many of the IT innovations which we explore later, such as database marketing, relationship marketing, data mining and computer-integrated manufacturing, enable organisations to identify and serve these customers' needs more effectively. IT is not an end in itself and should always link back to customer needs and desires.

We will now discuss how marketing has changed and examine how increasing customer sophistication, product proliferation, brand extensions and new channels have redefined the role of marketing. We will also discuss some of the criticisms which have been made of marketing and some likely future changes to the role of marketing.

THE CHANGING ROLE OF MARKETING

■ Customer sophistication

One of the fundamental changes which have taken place in the past quarter of a century has been that customers have become more sophisticated. Nowadays, customers are more demanding, less loyal and less willing to forgive companies whose products and services do not meet their high standards. The main reason for the recent trends towards customer loyalty programmes and relationship marketing is the fact that customers have become progressively more disloyal and more likely to switch from one product to another. The main trends in customers' lifestyles and attitudes include the following:

- *Cash rich, time poor.* Many people have more disposable income today but find themselves with less and less time to do the things they can now afford. Such people are

Exhibit 1.1

SO WHAT DO MARKETING PEOPLE REALLY DO?

The main activities of marketing are:

- defining markets that fall within the firm's business
- finding out what those in the market want (or potentially might want)
- if those in the market want different things, to group them into segments according to what they seek
- selecting those customer segments whose wants and needs can be better met by the firm than by rival organisations
- determining the offering (product, price, promotion and distribution) that meets the want
- making the offer available
- informing prospective or actual customers about the offering and where it might be obtained
- deciding on a continuous basis what offerings to add, subtract, modify and upgrade to meet changing wants and circumstances, and
- co-operating with other functions of the business and external organisations to secure the resources needed to implement marketing plans.

The above are the activities involved in marketing and which are typically carried out by a marketing department. However, some marketing departments do not have responsibility for all these activities or have even wider responsibilities including dealing with an organisation's suppliers. In any case, marketing as a subject area is involved with the total configuration of features/benefits (that is, the offering) sought by customers and provided by the producer.

Source: O'Shaughnessy (1995).[6]

looking for convenience and speed and are comfortable doing business over the phone.

- *Increased leisure time.* Many other consumers are moving to a 35-hour week while maintaining or increasing their levels of disposable income. These changes are reflected in the growing popularity of eating out, watching videos and a variety of other lifestyle changes.
- *Technology ownership.* The ownership rates of telephone, videocassette recorders (VCRs), television and personal computers have risen rapidly over the years. Although many parents may still rely on their children to set the VCR for them, there is an increasing familiarity with technology in people's lives!

The other changes, which we will examine in the following pages, are a response to this fundamental change in customer sophistication. Customers are demanding better products and quicker introduction of new features – hence the proliferation of products and the shortening of product life cycles. The demand for greater flexibility in the purchase of goods and services is leading to a proliferation of distribution channels and customers. One of the drivers for global brands is the fact that customers seek out similar goods, values and standards of service as they travel abroad.

■ Product proliferation and brand extensions

During the 1980s, fast-moving consumer goods (FMCG) companies had the choice of launching new products or extending their existing brands. The costs and risks of designing, testing and launching a new product were high and many companies already had a brand-management structure in place which made brand extensions easier to manage. The result was an explosion of brand extensions and new variations on existing brands.

Nestlé, for example, launched 120 new product lines in France in 1993, of which 115 were extensions of existing brands. The same company's brands in the UK instant coffee market now include Nescafé, Gold Blend, Blend 37, Alta Rica, Cap Colombie, Nescafé Decaffeinated, Gold Blend Decaffeinated, Alta Rica Decaffeinated, Fine Blend, Nescafé Cappuccino, Unsweetened Cappuccino and Espresso[7] – a fine combination of product proliferation and brand extension. Although it may seem a bewildering array of products with little distinction between any two, it is one of the reasons for Nestlé holding more than half of the UK's £500 million instant coffee market.

Corstjens and Corstjens (1995) refer to this issue as a debate over whether brands are like rice fields and are perpetually self-renewing resources, or more like rain forests which provide magnificent returns only while being depleted. If brands are like rice fields, then companies can continue to exploit them with little risk to the underlying asset value of the brand. If they are like rain forests, the brand equity is devalued or destroyed as it is extended. The general consensus is that we are coming to the point where consumers are no longer willing to put up with an ever-increasing number of products when the level of differentiation is minimal (*see* Exhibit 1.2). In the FMCG market in particular, manufacturers are losing control to retailers who are finding it easier to promote own-label products in an environment where brand extensions have begun to compromise the quality of the original brand.

Exhibit 1.2

LESS CHOICE PLEASE: WE'RE BRITISH

Consumers are becoming 'irritated and bewildered' by the vast amount of product choice in the shops . . . Far from appreciating the variety of consumer goods available in stores, shoppers bitterly resent the time it takes to 'wade through acres of virtually identical products'. They complain that retailers and manufacturers are over-stocking shelves with 'me-too' lines and accuse marketers of making ordinary shopping trips far too complicated. In the US, eight in 10 of the 2,000 shoppers polled by market pollsters FBC Research International said that many 'new' products both look and perform the same as existing lines. Seven in 10 of those aged 40 and over were nostalgic for the days when there were fewer decisions to be made over such prosaic items as lavatory paper or shampoo.

British shoppers have similar misgivings, according to leading market researchers, particularly over the sudden proliferation of yoghurts, spreads, lager beers, detergents, toiletries and pet foods. An estimated 1,000 new consumer products reach British supermarket shelves every month; J. Sainsbury alone introduced 1,500 new lines in 1994. Yet the success rate of new consumer items is notoriously low with around nine in 10 failing within the first six months. More than 100 washing powder products are now estimated to be available in the UK, with each of the leading brands available in up to 15 variants including colour wash and standard, biological or non-bio, powder or liquid, low temperature or suds and a variety of pack sizes and refills. According to the Leatherhead Food RA, there were 1,524 food and drink launches in 1986, but by last year, that figure had almost doubled to 3,303. In 1986, manufacturers launched 157 new varieties of yoghurt and 43 new sauces and pickles. In 1994 alone, supermarket shelves groaned under the weight of 312 new yoghurts and a staggering 375 new sauces and pickles. Can there really be such a thing as too much choice?

Source: Financial Times (30 November 1995).[8]

New distribution channels

New methods of distributing products have also emerged, many of which are technology driven. In financial services, the automated teller machine (ATM) has replaced the branch visit for many routine financial transactions. Building societies which never offered current accounts are now doing so and customers can phone insurance companies for loans. All these changes have had a major impact on European banks and the number of bank branches is falling across Europe. In the UK, the major banks have been on a rationalisation programme throughout the 1990s which has seen hundreds of branches disappear from the high street.[9]

Dell and Gateway 2000 are two US manufacturers of personal computers that sell directly to the public by telephone. Both companies have set up major telephone call centre operations in Ireland from which they sell to the whole of Europe. Indeed, countries such as The Netherlands, Ireland and the UK have been vying for the position as the most attractive call centre location in Europe, not just for selling PCs but also for hotel reservations, customer care operations and so on. These changes are the result of an increasing willingness on the part of customers to use the telephone for purchasing goods and services and improvements in payment mechanisms (*see* Exhibit 1.3). Freephone numbers and the increasingly sophisticated use of telephone call centre technology are changing the way in which marketers and advertisers go to market. Today, 0800 and 0345 numbers, introduced in the UK in 1985, and the more recent introduction by Mercury of its 0500 Freecall service, are widely accepted by advertisers and consumers alike. To underline this shift in consumer behaviour, one recent survey in the UK found that 35 per cent of respondents claimed to have made telephone calls in response to newspaper or television advertisements.[10]

Shortening product life cycles

Over the past decade, many companies have both cut the average time to bring a product to market and shortened the corresponding life cycle of the product. One computer manufacturing company decreased its product development cycle by two-thirds

> **Exhibit 1.3**
>
> **THAT WILL DO NICELY**
>
> Changes in the way people shop is an aspect of market behaviour which greatly influenced the growth of direct marketing. In particular, the move from transactions based only on cash to increased use of credit and debit cards has facilitated the growth of non-store retailing. Now transactions can take place, either via mail, telephone or fax. Direct response advertising is particularly well placed to effect an immediate purchase from consumers from the comfort of their home. Whereas traditional TV advertising was concerned with image building and providing information, direct response can provide short-term incentives to bring about a purchase at the point of sale – in the home. This would not be possible without widespread use of non-cash payment methods.
>
> *Source:* Evans *et al.* (1995).[11]

between 1967 and 1990.[12] Pharmaceutical companies such as Eli Lilly are attempting to halve the time it takes to test a new drug[13] and this phenomenon is not confined to products in the high-tech or pharmaceutical industries. The same has been seen in the automobile industry, the consumer goods industry – in fact, in almost every industry. The impact on the marketing function has been no less dramatic, with demand for more and more revenues in shorter and shorter timescales.

■ Globalisation of markets and products

The world is indeed becoming a global village as more and more companies are looking at extending their markets beyond their immediate geographic boundaries. And yet there is still considerable room for truly global brands to be created. Of the top 100 brands in the FMCG market in Europe, the US and Japan, only seven are common to all three[14] (*see* Figure 1.1).

Even within Europe, the story is the same. Global brands from the major FMCG manufacturers like Unilever and Procter & Gamble, as well as 'megabrands' such as Coca-Cola*, are popular across the continent. However, many of the 'Top 10' FMCG products in these countries are still relatively unknown outside their own national boundaries (*see* Table 1.1, p. 10).

Simon (1992)[15] carried out an interesting analysis of the success of Germany's small and medium-sized companies, where he examined low-profile companies such as Krones, Korber/Hauni, Weinig, Webasto and TetraWerke. None of these companies is a well-known global organisation, yet they have world market shares between 70 and 90 per cent in markets as diverse as automatic woodworking moulding machines, cigarette machines, tropical fish food and car sunroofs. As Simon puts it:

> *'The hidden champions consistently follow a strategy that combines technical excellence with worldwide marketing and sales . . . they leverage their product-specialisation across broad geographic markets. Globalisation of marketing and sales provides sufficient scale to recover R&D expenses and to keep costs within range.'*

---

*'Coca-Cola' and 'Coke' are registered trade marks of The Coca-Cola Company. This reference (and others in this book) is reproduced with kind permission from The Coca-Cola Company.

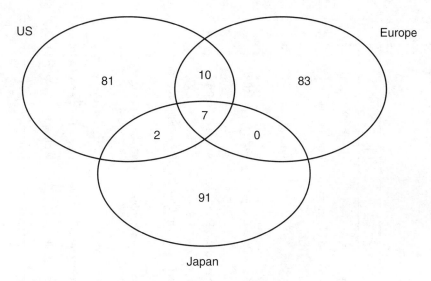

Fig 1.1   Extent of overlap of top 100 FMCG brands in US, Europe and Japan
Source: Corstjens & Corstjens (1995).

MARKETING AT A CROSSROADS

■ Marketing's mid-life crisis

If modern marketing was born in the 1950s during the post-war boom period and, if we measure age in purely human terms, marketing can now be said to have reached middle age. Since then, marketing has developed and undergone many changes. As Brown (1995)[16] has described it:

> *'Marketing's hairline may be receding, its eyesight and hearing may be imperfect, a wrinkle or two may be discernible, and cosmetic surgery may well be necessary, but there's life in the old dog yet!'*

But there are many others who offer a less positive diagnosis and much of the recent commentary has been very critical. If we take the widest definition of marketing, there are examples of major marketing failures in recent years. One study[17] of 432 large companies in the US found that, in many cases, value was being destroyed rather than being created. In the decade from 1980 to 1990, the investments made by General Motors generated a paltry return and in the process the group destroyed over $100 billion in shareholder value. During the same period, Ford destroyed nearly $25 billion, while British Petroleum was not very far behind.

In a 1993 survey of 100 leading companies in the UK,[18] the accounting and consultancy firm Coopers & Lybrand declared that the marketing department was critically ill and that it had been outflanked by other disciplines, most notably finance and manufacturing. They claimed that marketing directors overestimated their own contribution to the business and that their marketing departments suffered from a series of ills, including:

Table 1.1 Top 10 FMCG brands in the five major European markets

	Germany	Spain	France	Italy	UK
1	Coca-Cola	Coca-Cola	Danone Yoghurt	Barilla Pasta	Coca-Cola
2	Lagnese Ice Cream (Unilever)	Danone Yoghurt	Café Jacobs (Jacobs Suchard)	Moulin Blanc Biscuits	Persil (Unilever)
3	Jacobs Coffee (Jacobs Suchard)	Carbonell Oil (Carbonal y Cia)	Coca-Cola	Coca-Cola	Ariel (Procter & Gamble)
4	Pepsodent Toothpaste (Unilever)	Ariel (Procter & Gamble)	Pampers (Procter & Gamble)	Algida Ice Cream (Unilever)	Nescafé (Nestlé)
5	Iglo frozen vegetables (Unilever)	Danone Deserts	Le Biscuits (Danone)	Grandapadano Parmesan	Andrex (Scott)
6	Persil (Henkel)	La Casera soft drinks	Chambourcy Yoghurts (Nestlé)	Findus frozen fish (Nestlé)	Silver Spoon sugar
7	Milka Chocolate (Jacobs Suchard)	Fanta (Coca-Cola)	Ariel (Procter & Gamble)	Iglo frozen vegetables (Unilever)	Whiskas (Pedigree Petfoods)
8	Fanta (Coca-Cola)	Pesconova frozen meals	Yoplait Yoghurt	Lavazza Coffee	Flora (Van Den Bergs)
9	Ariel (Procter & Gamble)	Koipe oil	Panzani Pasta	Dash (Procter & Gamble)	Dash (Procter & Gamble)
10	Barenmark condensed milk (Nestlé)	Nescafé (Nestlé)	Nestlé Chocolate	Parmalat Milk	Walker's Crisps (PepsiCo)

Source: L'Expansion, No. 463, November 1993.

- undertaking an ill-defined mixture of activities
- being short-sighted and missing business opportunities
- lacking clearly defined responsibilities and accountability
- rarely leading the drive to enhance business performance
- being marginalised in their organisations.

On this last point, Piercy (1995)[19] describes the marginalisation as follows:

'It is relatively, and probably increasingly, rare in real organisations to encounter the integration of all marketing activities under a single all-powerful marketing director and organisation. For example, the evidence suggests that decisions like advertising spend and allocation are decided in the boardroom not the marketing department. Frequently, the main movers on price are accountants and chief executives, not marketing executives. Distribution (and often customer service) decisions are made elsewhere in the company. Issues of quality and service often exclude marketing "specialists", particularly if key account management operates outside the marketing area.'

Other sources, including marketing practitioners,[20] academics[21] and management consultancies[22] have made similar pronouncements. The attacks that have been made on modern marketing are varied and are neatly summed up in Exhibit 1.4.

Exhibit 1.4

THE MARGINALISATION OF MODERN MARKETING

Indeed, such is the current unease about marketing – the 1993 Academy of Marketing Science conference devoted a special session, featuring some of America's foremost marketing scholars, to the issue. A European conference entitled 'Rethinking Marketing' was also considered necessary – and so prominent are the practitioners, consultants and academics concerned, that even the staunchest defenders of modern marketing seem prepared to concede that the field is facing a crisis of representation:

- Piercy[23] maintains that the traditional marketing concept 'assumes and relies on the existence of a world which is alien and unrecognisable to many of the executives who actually have to manage marketing for real'.
- Gummesson[24] states that 'the present marketing concept . . . is unrealistic and needs to be replaced'.
- Nilson[25] contends that 'a revision of the marketing concept is necessary'.
- Rapp and Collins[26] suggest that 'the traditional methods . . . simply aren't working as well anymore'.
- Brownlie and Saren[27] argue that 'it is questionable whether the marketing concept as it has been propagated can provide the basis for successful business at the end of the twentieth century'.
- McKenna[28] concludes that 'there is less and less reason to believe that the traditional approach can keep up with real customer wishes and demands or with the rigors of competition'.
- Professor Michael Thomas,[29] one of the most respected marketing academics in Britain, has recently made the frank, and frankly astonishing, confession that after 30 years of propagating the marketing message, he is having serious doubts about its continuing efficacy.

Source: Brown (1995).

In our view, the most serious criticisms of marketing are the following five which we will explore in greater depth:

1 Existing customers are continually short-changed.
2 Promotional resources continue to be squandered needlessly.
3 The traditional brand-management system can no longer cope.
4 Marketing departments are not coming up with new ideas.
5 Marketing fails to leverage the strengths of the company.

■ Existing customers are continually short-changed

A key objective in any company is to generate new sales, yet all too often this is inter-preted as winning new customers. Once a new customer is on board, the salespeople move onto the next prospect. In too many companies, a game of 'pass the parcel' is played with existing customers. Do they belong to operations? Or customer service? All too often they don't belong to anybody, least of all the marketing department.

A considerable amount of analysis has been done to calculate the cost of customer acquisition and the lifetime value of customers. The logic of such analysis is quite com-pelling, as customers can take several years to become profitable because of the high costs of acquiring them. Companies that have reduced customer defection rates have seen their profits soar. Existing customers are also easier to sell to than new customers. While some companies have taken these messages on board, many fail to follow it through. In the UK, some of the worst examples have come from financial services com-panies. Banks still use existing mortgage-holders to subsidise special low interest rate, introductory offers for new homeowners. The message to the existing consumer runs something like this:

> 'Thank you for taking a loan from us and meeting your repayments for the last number of years. In reward for this we are charging you a higher rate of interest than we charge a new customer with no track record who walks in off the street. In addition we have built in exit fees for solicitors and property valuations such that it is uneconomic for you to express your dissatisfaction and move to another institution.'

Life assurance companies have only recently been forced by legislation to re-examine the entire commission system for life and investment products which previously encour-aged their salesforces to deliver unwanted products and poor value for money to customers. This failure to look after existing customers while employing sharp tactics to attract new ones has resulted in a dramatic loss of consumer trust, an erosion of cus-tomer loyalty and the promotion of a system which encourages consumers to switch. Banks and assurance companies are now paying a heavy price in advertising and pro-motion revenues just to watch their customers play musical chairs with each other.

Credit card companies have also consistently used the profits of their most valuable customers – those who fail to pay off their balance in full each month – to provide free credit for those who do. The only way that most credit card marketing (and finance) departments felt that this situation could be sustained was to levy consistently high interest rates on the profitable customers. As customers became aware of the monthly interest charge, the number of people paying off their balances increased. In order to maintain profitability, the credit card companies in the UK were forced to levy an annual charge for the use of their cards and promptly lost a large number of customers. Perhaps they were happy to lose many of these customers – those who rarely used their card, for example – but the episode could hardly qualify as a marketing success.

■ Promotional resources continue to be squandered needlessly

Sheth and Sisodia (1995)[30] cite the many instances of questionable returns on the promotional expenditure of US companies. In 1993, FMCG manufacturers spent $6.1 billion on more than 300 billion coupons, 98 per cent of which were never redeemed. Of the five billion coupons that were redeemed, an estimated 80 per cent were accounted for by shoppers who would have purchased the promoted product in any case. Of the remaining 20 per cent, an unquantified but considerable proportion was redeemed by shoppers whose purchases are based purely on the fact that there was an incentive. Stop the incentive – no further sales.

In a similar vein, in-store supermarket promotions in the US have an equally dubious record, costing the industry an estimated $20 billion a year. Who takes up the offers? Evidence suggests that it is simply existing shoppers who are engaging in forward buying and that, once the promotion ends, sales drop to below the pre-promotion level and do not return to normal levels for up to three months. From the retailer's point of view, there is some merit in all of this as most retailers have to attract customers into their stores on the basis of price. But from the manufacturer's point of view, it is money down the drain. It may help the marketing and sales staff to achieve short-term targets, but its impact on long-term demand is questionable. Advertising and promotion are most effective when there is a strong product or service to market in the first place; and yet evidence suggests that marketing expenditure is often highest where companies attempt to prop up weaker products with little to differentiate them from the competition. Propping up weak products provides a very low return on marketing investment which could be better spent on reinforcing stronger products or dealing with the root cause of the product or service being weak in the first place. The real problem that marketing departments face is that it is extremely difficult to measure the impact of marketing activity. Nonetheless, as pressure mounts to keep costs under control, it also increases on marketing to become more accountable for expenditure.

■ The traditional brand management system can no longer cope

The marketing strategies employed by FMCG companies from the 1950s through to the early 1980s achieved spectacular results. Good brand management was the source of consistently high returns for companies such as Procter & Gamble and Lever Brothers. Perhaps the best example of the value generated by the brand managers was the takeover of Kraft by Philip Morris in the US in 1988. The asset value of Kraft at the time of the takeover was roughly $2 billion. Yet Philip Morris spent $13 billion to buy the company. The reason? Over the years, the brand managers had added $11 billion of value to the company by building up the brand equities of the various Kraft brands. In the UK, Rowntree's takeover by Nestlé in 1988 underscored the hidden value locked away in Kit-Kats, Smarties and After Eights – five times the asset value of the company. The value of brand equity even threw the accounting profession into commotion and for a while discussion raged over whether brands should be capitalised on a company's balance sheet.

But the love affair with traditional brand management began to go sour from the mid-1980s onwards. It stopped delivering the goods for the chief executive officer (CEO) and, more importantly, it stopped delivering for the customer. Product proliferation and the seemingly endless brand extensions became sources of irritation rather than choice. As customer dissatisfaction grew, CEOs began to look to other areas of their organisations for profits. In addition, the traditional role of the brand manager has been downgraded significantly over the past two decades. With a dizzying array of products to be managed and the day-to-day tactics of promotions and markdowns to be administered, the job has been given to younger, less experienced people who now do not have the time, the cross-functional skills or the in-depth market knowledge to carry out the tasks of the brand managers of old.

■ Marketing departments are not coming up with new ideas

One of the paradoxes of recent years is the success that German and Japanese companies have had in manufacturing compared to their British counterparts, despite the low profile that the marketing department has in these countries. Britain's manufacturing companies have been in decline for decades and now account for less that 20 per cent of GDP, compared to a figure of more than 30 per cent in Germany where labour costs are higher. In one study[31] of the marketing strategies of 40 British and German machine tool manufacturers, the following conclusions were drawn:

- German companies place greater emphasis on longer term customer-oriented strategies than on short-term financial gains.
- The marketing strategies of German companies seek competitive advantage through product quality and reliability.
- German companies give a higher priority to the product element of the marketing mix, whereas British companies compete on the basis of price.

Just under half of the British manufacturers did not appear to understand the importance of identifying market segments according to customer needs. The marketing director of one British company had a very clear view on segmentation: 'We don't need to segment our market.' The German response? 'The British do not represent serious competition.' Another interesting observation from this study was that the majority of British products had been developed over 20 years previously with little recent modification. This compared with nearly three-quarters of German participants whose machine tools had been developed or significantly modified in the previous 10 years.

It is arguable whether the marketing departments in many companies are capable of leveraging the power of new channels of distribution and promotion such as the Internet and home shopping to develop new business opportunities.

■ Marketing fails to leverage the strengths of the company

In 1986, an article appeared in the *Harvard Business Review* entitled 'What's your excuse for not using JIT?'[32] The just-in-time (JIT) revolution had just begun to take off outside Japan as it captured the imagination of executives and production managers. In the decade that followed, manufacturing and production groups in the West embarked on a campaign of implementing demand-led manufacturing. Inventory levels were slashed from an average of two months' worth of production in 1982 to 1.4 months' a decade later. As a result, the companies in the vanguard of this revolution increased their ability to react quickly to changes in the marketplace. Set-up times and lead times plummeted and products no longer had to be made in large batches. New production systems allowed them to be manufactured in much smaller lots.

And what was marketing's reaction to this new-found flexibility? Rather muted, in fact. Companies continued to use quarterly or half-yearly sales forecasts to drive production. That would not have been so bad if it were not for the fact that the forecasts were notoriously inaccurate. Furthermore, once the forecasts were agreed within a company, they were pursued at all costs. If demand was not as high as marketing had predicted three or six months previously, then additional advertising, merchandising, promotions, price cuts and other weapons in marketing's arsenal would be deployed to achieve the sales targets. If demand was more buoyant, the targets were easier to meet. Because marketing continued to be forecast led rather than demand driven, it might take weeks for an increase in consumer demand to work its way through to the factory where production could be increased. Critics talked about just-in-time manufacturing and just-in-case marketing. The fact of the matter was that marketing was being left behind and was failing to take advantage of the flexibility of modern production systems.

In many organisations expensive internal sales channels are favoured over the more efficient use of third-party distribution channels. As technology costs plummet and more customer data becomes available for use in marketing, most companies are still incapable of utilising this information effectively. Rapid response marketing capabilities using electronic point-of-sale (EPoS) data systems are still being ignored by some marketing managers. Despite the success of brand management in the past, we still have very few brands that can be considered international, let alone global. Marketing is still carried out and managed along geographical lines rather than by customer group or product group.

THE NEW MARKETING ORGANISATION

■ The reinvention of the marketing organisation

Faced with these challenges, the traditional marketing organisation has been forced to change or 'reinvent itself'. The scope of the new marketing organisation, for many companies, now extends far beyond those areas with which its predecessors dealt. Companies such as Unilever and AT&T have abolished the position of chief marketing executive and replaced it with a variety of different structures, such as business groups, customer development teams and customer focus teams.[33] Other examples include the creation of pan-European customer service, marketing and brand strategies now being implemented by companies such as Microsoft. Some organisations have gone much further and developed various types of network organisation to implement inter-organisational collaborations and partnerships. For example, the Astra/Merck sales organisation was formed from a licensing agreement between the US pharmaceutical company, Merck & Co, and Astra of Sweden. The 325 salespeople in this new organisation have been equipped with computerised sales tools and operate a very lean and flat organisation structure.[34]

■ Marketing as orchestrators and integrators

During the early 1990s, many organisations embarked on major projects to reengineer their businesses. The results have been mixed and, in many instances, the reengineered processes lack some of the key links that are needed to hold them together. Marketing can deliver that missing coherence because it can address such issues as:[35]

- What kinds of customers do we want to attract?
- What is most important to those customers?
- How can we best reach and serve them?
- How will this bring sustainable competitive advantage and high shareholder returns?

There is a role for marketing to change from 'functional expert' to the more facilitative role of 'orchestrator'[36] or 'integrator'[37] (*see* Exhibit 1.5). In order to fulfil this role, marketing managers need to have a wider understanding of business problems, a pragmatic approach to resolving these issues and a very clear understanding of how information technology can be used to dominate its chosen market.

Exhibit 1.5

CRAFTY INTEGRATORS

Kraft, the US packaged goods company, found that it could not keep up with the fast-growing Hispanics market under its traditional brand management system. Developing Hispanic programmes was always the fifteenth marketing priority of every brand manager, as well as the first area to get cut when budgets were in trouble. So, when Kraft finally decided to get serious about serving this important segment, it made one of its senior marketing managers responsible for developing integrated programmes to serve Hispanics in each local market.

Chemical Bank has also reorganised its retail marketing function around income-based consumer segments in an attempt to do away with the product-based organisation structures that have long prevented it from effectively cross-selling products that appeal to the same markets.

Source: George, Freeling and Court (1994).[37]

THE STRATEGIC ROLE OF INFORMATION TECHNOLOGY

■ The value of IT

Organisations put forward a number of reasons why they have invested in information technology. The most common reasons include the need to sustain and improve competitive position; increase revenue; reduce costs; or improve flexibility and responsiveness. While these are important, many organisations are driven simply by the need to survive in a highly competitive marketplace. Thus, while it could be argued that banks installed automated teller machines (ATMs) to increase customer service, the reality is that, once one bank had installed ATMs, competitors were left with little choice but to match that investment. The use of information technology has become increasingly strategic for a number of reasons:

■ IT significantly increases the choice of options available to a company and plays an important role in the effective implementation of every element of a marketing strategy. In particular, it has the power to gather and use information about customers: who they are, what they like, how they purchase and so on. We will discuss the management and use of customer information in detail in Chapter 4.

■ IT affects the process of marketing strategy development as it provides more information to managers through the use of decision support systems (DSS). We will examine these, and other information systems for marketing management and decision making, in Chapters 2 and 3.

■ IT has the potential to integrate different parts of the organisation and provide more information to managers. Executive information systems (EIS), for example, affect the vertical flow of information through an organisation. Top management has greater access to information and a reduced reliance on middle management to source that information. Telecommunications networks allow information to flow easily and quickly between different departments and divisions.

■ IT also affects the organisation's interfaces with the external environment, such as customers and suppliers. Inter-organisational systems, facilitated by electronic data interchange (EDI) for instance, create closer links between organisations and their suppliers, facilitate more efficient inventory management and allow a just-in-time approach to reordering.

There is a key role for marketing in understanding and utilising the enormous potential of IT to market goods and services more effectively. The issue of how IT should be used has become too important to be left to the technologists to resolve.

CONCLUSION

Marketing is one of the oldest professions in the world even though, in its modern reincarnation, it has been with us for less than half a century. It is fundamental to any organisation and should not be seen as a separate, isolated department where highly educated and highly paid people plan the future products and services of the company. Rather, marketing should be seen as a philosophy which permeates the organisation and as the prime function of the senior management of that organisation. The role of marketing has changed significantly over the past couple of decades. More products and more brand extensions have been created which have certainly given the customer more choice, but the ever-increasing choice may now be leading to confusion and irritation. This is only one of a number of criticisms laid at the door of traditional marketing management. Brand management and the entire marketing function are at a crossroads. However, new approaches are being adopted to meet these challenges. Information technology has its part to play here. Direct marketing, database marketing, telemarketing and other technology-enabled aspects of marketing are helping to change the way in which companies market their products and services.

ASSIGNMENT QUESTIONS

1 Marketing is a philosophy. Discuss.

2 Brands are rice fields, not rain forests. Discuss.

3 What are the major challenges facing marketing as it approaches the millennium?

4 Why has the role of IT become more strategic?

5 Comment on the central role of marketing in an organisation.

References

1 Kotler, P. (1994). *Marketing Management: Analysis, Planning, Implementation and Control*. 8th edn, New Jersey: Prentice-Hall.
2 Drucker, P. (1954). *The Practice of Management*. Oxford: Butterworth-Heinemann.
3 Levitt, T. (1960). 'Marketing myopia', *Harvard Business Review*, July–August.
4 Baker, M.J. (1976). *Marketing: Theory and Practice*. London: Macmillan.
5 Baker, M.J. (1994). 'One more time – what is marketing?' in Baker, M.J. (ed.) *The Marketing Book*. 3rd edn, Oxford: Butterworth-Heinemann.
6 O'Shaughnessy, J. (1995). *Competitive Marketing: A Strategic Approach*. 3rd edn, London: Routledge.
7 Corstjens, J. and Corstjens, M. (1995). *Store Wars: The Battle for Mindspace and Shelfspace*. Chichester: John Wiley.
8 Matthews, V. (1995). 'Not so much choice please', *Financial Times*, 30 November.
9 Kelly, S. (1996). 'Branches face chop as virtual banking grows', *Computer Weekly*, 6 June.
10 Young, M. (1994). 'Direct response television', *Journal of Targeting, Measurement and Analysis*, Vol. 2, No. 2.
11 Evans, M., O'Malley, L. and Patterson, M. (1995). 'Direct marketing: rise and rise or rise and fall?', *Marketing Intelligence and Planning*, Vol. 3, No. 6.
12 Cespedes, F.V. (1994). 'Industrial marketing: managing new requirements', *Sloan Management Review*, Spring.
13 Taylor, P. (1996). 'Increasingly crucial role', *Financial Times*, 10 June.
14 Corstjens, J. and Corstjens, M. (1995). Op. cit.
15 Simon, H. (1991). 'Lessons from Germany's mid-sized giants', *Harvard Business Review*, January–February.
16 Brown, S. (1995). 'Life begins at 40? Further thoughts on marketing's "mid-life crisis"', *Marketing Intelligence and Planning*, Vol. 13, No. 1.
17 The Economist (1995). 'Another victory for myopia', *The Economist*, 2 December.
18 Coopers & Lybrand (1993). *Marketing at the Crossroads – A Survey on the Role of Marketing*. London: Coopers & Lybrand.
19 Piercy, N.F. (1995). 'Marketing and strategy fit together (in spite of what some management educators seem to think!)', *Management Decision*, Vol. 33, No. 1.
20 Casey, J. (1995). 'Business needs to focus on its markets and its basic needs', *Irish Times*, 17 November.
21 McDonald, M.H.B. (1994). 'Marketing – a mid-life crisis?', *Marketing Business*, Vol. 30, May.
22 Brady, J. and Davis, I. (1993). 'Marketing's mid-life crisis', *McKinsey Quarterly*, Vol. 2.
23 Piercy, N. (1992). *Market Led Strategic Change*. Oxford: Butterworth-Heinemann.
24 Gummesson, E. (1987). 'The new marketing: developing long-term interactive relationships', *Long Range Planning*, Vol. 20, No. 4.
25 Nilson, T.H. (1992). *Value-added Marketing: Marketing Management for Superior Results*. Maidenhead: McGraw-Hill.
26 Rapp, S. and Collins, T.L. (1990). *The Great Marketing Turnaround: The Age of the Individual and How to Profit from it*. New Jersey: Prentice-Hall.
27 Brownlie, D. and Saren, M. (1992). 'The four Ps of the marketing concept: prescriptive, polemical, permanent and problematical', *European Journal of Marketing*, Vol. 26, No. 4.
28 McKenna, R. (1991). 'Marketing is everything', *Harvard Business Review*, January–February.
29 Thomas, M.J. (1993). 'Marketing – in chaos or transition?'. In Brownlie, D. *et al.* (eds) *Rethinking Marketing*. Warwick: Warwick Business School Research Bureau.

[30] Sheth, J.N. and Sisodia, R.S. (1995). 'Symptoms of marketing malaise', *Marketing Management*, Vol. 4, No. 2, Fall.

[31] Shaw, V. (1994). 'The marketing strategies of British and German companies', *European Journal of Marketing*, Vol. 28, No. 7.

[32] Walleigh, R.C. (1986). 'What's your excuse for not using JIT?', *Harvard Business Review*, March–April.

[33] Piercy, N.F. and Cravens, D.W. (1995). 'The network paradigm and the marketing organisation: developing a new management agenda', *European Journal of Marketing*, Vol. 29, No. 3.

[34] Harrer, G. (1994). 'Pills 'n' pads no more', *Forbes*, 6 June.

[35] Leemon, D.O. (1995). 'Marketing's core role in strategic reengineering', *Planning Review*, Vol. 23, No. 2.

[36] Planning Review (1995). 'The process view: how marketing needs to change', *Planning Review*, Vol. 23, No. 2.

[37] George, M., Freeling, A. and Court, D. (1994). 'Reinventing the marketing organisation', *McKinsey Quarterly*, Vol. 4.

2

MANAGEMENT INFORMATION AND DECISION MAKING

- Management information systems (MIS)
- Decision support systems (DSS)
- New developments in management information
- Creating a 'knowledge organisation'

OBJECTIVES

After studying this chapter, you will be able to:

- Understand the key role of management information
- Explain the differences between management information systems (MIS), decision support systems (DSS) and executive information systems (EIS)
- Define what is meant by the phrases 'data warehouse', 'data mart' and 'data mining'
- Describe what a knowledge organisation is and how one can be achieved through the use of information technology
- Understand how information technology is used to link different parts of the same organisation

MANAGEMENT INFORMATION SYSTEMS (MIS)

■ The need for management information

Managers have always needed information to help them manage. Such information can be gathered through a *formal* reporting system or through *informal* means – the so-called management by walking around. Formalised management information systems were available to managers even before the modern computer was invented. The Ford Motor Company built and marketed cars and oil companies such as Shell and Exxon built business empires in the early part of the twentieth century using management reports which were created without the use of computers. One of the first steps that Alfred Sloan took when he became chief executive of General Motors in 1921 was to install a comprehensive system of formal reports. Centuries earlier, the great trading companies carved out their own trading empires across the globe, again without a computer in sight. While the advent of computers made it easier to process large amounts of performance and financial information to help manage companies, business management, or marketing management, did not begin in 1948 when the first computer was invented.

■ Management information systems

By the 1960s, the concept and usage of computer-based management information systems (MIS) had begun to take hold. Today, the use of computers for gathering and disseminating management information is commonplace, even if it is still supplemented by traditional informal means.

Because computers make so much information available, management must prioritise which information is most important to running the business when designing and using an MIS (*see* Exhibit 2.1).

Exhibit 2.1

AS SIMPLE AS ABC!

It's remarkable how the computer has enriched our ability to master our managerial capabilities. The geometric growth of hardware, software and especially our own comfort with systems has helped us replace complicated guesswork with fact-based analysis. We don't even call them computers any more – now they are 'Management Information Systems' (MIS). . . .

The problem is that we are unconsciously becoming report administrators and computer experts rather than strategic business managers. Is your desk and floor littered with reports? How many of those reports – even the good ones – really get examined? Here are three tips to improve your reporting system:

- define the critical indicators for your business
- report by exception
- use A-B-C reporting

'A' items are those that account for 50 percent of your volume. Typically, this is a very limited number of items. However, they require the greatest focus and most frequent attention by management because they account for such a significant amount of the volume. 'B' items then account for the next 30 percent of total volume. This group still requires fairly regular review, but perhaps not quite as frequently as the 'A' items. Finally, 'C' items account for the last 20 percent of total volume. Invariably, this group contains the largest number of items by a wide margin. But because each item contributes such a proportionally small amount to the total picture, they should not receive the same amount of attention as the 'A' and 'B' groups.

Source: Direct Marketing (June 1992).[2]

Handy (1985)[1] describes four different types of management information and provides a description of the kind of information processed by each:

- *Planning.* The bringing together of information to prepare strategic, tactical or immediate action programmes, e.g. a weekly production schedule or a two-year investment programme.

■ *Logistics*. The flow of information to link different parts of the organisation, to allow certain specific actions to happen or to stop others occurring, e.g. inventory management.

■ *Monitoring and control*. Information to monitor the work of an organisation, to point out requirements for corrective action or opportunities for improvement, e.g. variance analysis or monthly sales reports.

■ *Motivation*. Information used to allow individuals or groups more involvement or motivation, e.g. targets and objectives, general information regarding the organisation.

DECISION SUPPORT SYSTEMS (DSS)

■ What are decision support systems?

We can define decision support systems as a subset of the broader category of MIS used by people in managerial and executive positions (*see* Figure 2.1). DSS refer to the support tools that help managers deal with problems where computer-based analysis is used to complement the manager's own judgement.

The range of computerised tools and PC database systems available to managers for analysis and decision making has increased dramatically in the past ten years. The most common DSS are the spreadsheet packages such as *Excel* and *Lotus 1-2-3* which are available on almost all managers' PCs. Later in this chapter we will examine some of the newer developments in DSS, including data mining and neural networks.

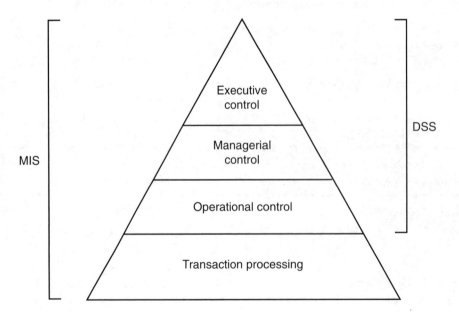

Fig 2.1   DSS versus MIS

■ Executive information systems (EIS)

If we refer back to Figure 2.1, we notice that the top layer of management information systems are for 'executive control'. In the 1980s, software companies such as Comshare and Holos were at the forefront of computerised systems known as executive information systems (EIS), which provided up-to-date information to senior executives in a clear, understandable format. These EIS were positioned as an even more distinct subset of management information systems. Since then, many other companies have moved into the EIS market and the distinction between EIS, DSS and even MIS has become blurred. However, the term EIS is still generally used to describe a category of decision support systems used exclusively by senior managers (*see* Exhibit 2.2).

Exhibit 2.2

'IF THEY'VE GOT TO READ THE USER GUIDE, I'VE FAILED'

A senior executive from the Wellcome Foundation, the UK pharmaceuticals group recently acquired by Glaxo, found a note in his desk late in February. It introduced him to the executive information system (EIS) that had just been installed on his computer. It explained that although a user guide to the system was available, 'we don't expect you to read it'. The note's author was Roger Shaw, corporate EIS manager at Wellcome, among whose tasks is implementing an international board level information system that will provide rapid access to analytical data. The 60 top people for whom Wellcome's corporate EIS was designed have better things to do than delve into manuals – 'if they've got to read the user guide, I've failed', he admits.

The process began three years ago when the drugs company identified the need to make the provision of information to its top personnel more effective. Shaw conducted interviews with 45 executives in the US and UK. They were asked a series of oblique questions intended to establish what kind of information they were not getting. Shaw distilled this research into a checklist of critical data types, including areas such as market performance, share prices and R&D, a function that has driven Wellcome.

The EIS has been implemented in Germany, and Wellcome has been planning to link up executives shortly in the rest of Europe and the US. Shaw sees the EIS as a natural reaction to traditional difficulties in extracting pertinent and comprehensible data from larger mainframe computer systems. 'Rapid access to analytical information is paramount and it's highly regarded. These people haven't got the time to wait for a traditional report to be cranked out by a computer.'

Source: Financial Times (1 March 1995).[3]

NEW DEVELOPMENTS IN MANAGEMENT INFORMATION

■ Data overload

In the 1980s and early 1990s, many large organisations were examining the way in which management information was reported and used. The oversupply of data, and the undersupply of good management information, prompted these companies to investigate how technology could be used to provide better decision-making information. One of the main reasons that DSS applications have not reached their full potential in the past is because the data has either been of very poor quality or has been difficult to access (*see* Exhibit 2.3).

Exhibit 2.3

DEATH BY DATA

The difference between data and information was strikingly forced upon my attention when serving in ICI. Initially, every quarter, we used to receive a massive book, giving the detailed financial accounts of all our businesses, but these gave us very little feeling of the actual dynamics of the business. We found that each of us was spending long hours trying to interpret it, and realised that things would have to change. Imaginative pictorial computer programs projected the same data to all of us simultaneously, but it was presented in a wide variety of ways. Not only did these presentations save us tremendous amounts of work, but they also gave us a far better 'feel' of the events that were unfolding before us. This enabled us to contrast the actions of one business with those of another, and to understand the underlying causes and reasons why the cosy patterns of theory were not actually developing in practice.

During the *Troubleshooter* series, I normally worked from the accounts of whatever organisation I was visiting. I was shaken when I visited one of the National Health Authorities to receive mountains of data but no information. Information works in almost inverse ratio to the quantity of paper that is transferred.

We need a sort of smorgasbord of information from which individuals can pick, but which is also backed by broad, dynamic and constantly changing pictures of the totality of the scene, analysed and simplified down so that the major trends are immediately discernible.

Source: Harvey-Jones (1993).[4]

■ Data warehouses

A solution proposed in recent years is the data warehouse, which is a very large database that holds operational, historical and customer data and makes it available for decision-making purposes. It is the foundation of many large DSS applications and is designed to help users make better decisions by analysing summarised snapshots of corporate performance. The retail industry, which uses large amounts of bar-code data from checkouts to provide accurate purchasing information, provides one of the best examples of the data-warehousing concept in action (*see* Exhibit 2.4). Many supermarket chains have integrated their entire ordering, stocking and replenishment systems with their checkout systems, enabling them to maintain a high degree of data integrity. When all this data is integrated with reliable customer information in data warehouses, data mining (which we will discuss below) becomes feasible. Few other industries have reached the same degree of integration or sophistication as the retail trade.

Despite the high costs involved, data warehouses have proved successful in several aspects of the marketing function; notable proponents in the UK include Tesco, British

Exhibit 2.4

NAPPIES AND BEER

There is a strange story about nappies – diapers in North America – and beer that concerns the use of an 'information warehouse' by a US retailer. In trawling through some historical data and analysing it, the manager in a large US retailer noticed a distinct correlation between the sale of nappies and beer, just after work hours, which was particularly marked on a Friday. Further research confirmed the explanation: the man of the family was stopping off on his way home to pick up nappies for the baby – and a six-pack for himself. The retailer responded by merchandising nappies closer to the beer section and was rewarded by an increase in sales of both items.

The information warehouse (also known as the data warehouse) is all about using corporate information for business decisions. Retailing has pioneered the technique: an example in the UK is WH Smith's swift response to the downturn in the pre-Christmas market for computer games. But the potential is as great in finance and other businesses. A financial example might be the insurance actuary who needs historical data to create new products.

Andy Smith, marketing director of database company Informix in the UK, confirms that the beer and nappies story is true. It originated with Wal-Mart, one of the largest proponents of data warehousing in the US, which uses an Informix-based data warehouse. 'The big retailers are the people driving data warehousing, because the competitive pressures are so great', he says.

Source: Financial Times (1 March 1995).[5]

Airways, Barclays Bank and Bulmer[6] (*see* Exhibit 2.5). The US company Datapro[7] cites several examples of successful data warehouse initiatives:

- *Category management.* Data warehouses can help retail product managers gain a better understanding of consumer buying patterns and consumer response to their promotions.

- *Claims analysis.* Insurance and healthcare firms use data-warehousing applications to control costs and provide better customer service.

- *Fraud detection.* Fraud detection is one of the more popular applications of data warehousing, especially in the healthcare and insurance industries.

- *Financial and market planning.* Many organisations gather and collate financial data from different sources in order to carry out product costing and customer-profitability analysis.

- *Rate management.* Telecommunications companies use data warehouses in their efforts to determine the most profitable and competitive rates for cellular, local and long-distance calls.

- *Customer profiling.* Customer profiling and other applications such as demand forecasting and micro-marketing are used in the telecommunications, utility and other industries.

Exhibit 2.5

GOING TO THE MART

Bulmer, the cider company based in Hereford, has set up a data warehouse and three data marts. Dr Martin Wynn, Bulmer's information technology director, says: 'Since 1990, we have been going through a major systems replacement programme costing £20 million a year. In five years we replaced all the old systems and added new ones.' Bulmer decided to introduce a data warehouse to smooth the transition between old and new technology. Dr Wynn says: 'Old and new systems are different not only in the technology they use but in the way they define things such as products, supplies and customers. As we switched over we wanted to draw data from both systems. The warehouse gave us information in a meaningful form that we could not get otherwise.' . . .

Dr Wynn says: 'We can see how information changes from day to day, week to week and month to month. It helps us direct our sales effort.' Staff have been trained, with the 35 national account managers going through a two year programme that has transformed the way they use computers. The warehouse has broken down barriers between departments, so that finance and sales staff look at the same data and understand each other's problems.

Source: The Times (5 June 1996).

In general, data warehouses are appropriate for companies exhibiting the following characteristics:[8]

- an information-based approach to management
- involvement in highly competitive, rapidly changing markets
- a large, diverse customer base
- data stored in different systems
- the same data represented differently in different systems
- data stored in highly technical, difficult-to-decipher formats.

Creating a data warehouse

Data-warehousing systems are not off-the-shelf products but are usually built to meet the specific requirements of individual organisations. They are usually expensive and a typical data-warehousing project can cost up to $10 million over a five-year implementation period.[9] The technologies involved in data warehousing are varied and the skills to create them successfully in organisations are still limited (*see* Exhibit 2.6).

Exhibit 2.6

ACME DATA WAREHOUSE, BATTERIES INCLUDED

Maybe someday, you'll place an order with Wile E. Coyote's favourite supplier, and you'll receive a big wooden crate with 'ACME Data Warehouse' stencilled on the side. Everything you need in one box, batteries included. Maybe someday. But today, data warehouse products couldn't be much further from the ideal of 'one call does it all'. Today you have very little choice but to buy bits and pieces of very complex stuff from a number of vendors. You've got to put it all together and make it work.

Source: Datamation (15 May 1996).[10]

■ Data marts

Given the high costs and long timescales involved in building a data warehouse, many companies question whether the marketing and operational benefits are sufficient to justify the cost. According to one UK insurance company[11] which has already invested heavily in building a data warehouse for decision-making purposes: 'We are still getting the data into our warehouse, rather than pulling it out.'

One solution is to scale down the scope and coverage, confining the activities to, say, a single department with less data and less complexity, rather than the entire enterprise.[12] Data warehouses that are built on a relatively small scale are termed 'data marts', while one company even refers to its mini-versions of such a warehouse as 'data sheds'![13] A data mart cannot do everything a data warehouse can, but it can be implemented at a fraction of the cost.[14] Rather than gathering all the company's information into a single warehouse, a small, cleaned-up subset of data is held, often at a summary level. Typically a data mart is designed for a smaller number of users, which reduces the implementation costs and means that it can be built using off-the-shelf computer packages.

■ On-line analytical processing (OLAP)

It is important at this point to make the distinction between *operational systems* and *analytical systems*.[15] Operational systems support the everyday activities of a business. They are designed for entering and recording transactions, maintaining the integrity of data and providing quick responses to operational queries. For example, if you call into your local bank branch to check the balance in your account, the operational system that the customer service representative (CSR) uses should provide the balance within a few seconds, once you have supplied your name or account number. The balance that you receive may even include the £100 that you withdrew from the ATM this morning, so the information in an operational system is constantly changing as new transactions are recorded on the system.

On the other hand, a data warehouse is an analytical system where the information is a snapshot at a particular point in time. Analytical systems are specifically designed to handle and analyse very large volumes of data and to present findings in a way that is easily understood by users. When we discuss the use of data warehouses, we are referring to the creation of a major infrastructure for decision support rather than for operational purposes.[16] Indeed, the term DSS is now being superseded by the term OLAP (on-line analytical processing).

■ Data mining

With the aid of a good database of information (a data warehouse) and some good analytical tools (DSS or OLAP) with which to query the database, companies can 'mine' for hidden information which can be used for marketing purposes (*see* Exhibit 2.7). Companies which mine their data are looking for new correlations that may help them gain some insights into customer behaviour and competitive advantage in the marketplace. In insurance, for example, it has long been recognised that female drivers are a lower risk than their male counterparts and can be offered cheaper car insurance premiums. Data mining is used to find further subsegments of female drivers with different price and risk profiles.[17] Instead of providing a standard premium to women in the same age category, insurers can now price differently in order to retain their most profitable customers or encourage customers who are likely to be unprofitable to go elsewhere.

Exhibit 2.7

MINING FOR A FEW GOLDEN NUGGETS

Too much information can be a worse problem than not having enough. In the field of marketing, there are now myriad ways of finding out about customers and targeting them. Marketing data comes from many sources – almost too many. Data from external sources such as a census, postcodes and demographic systems have to be dovetailed with internal point of sale, accounting records and all sorts of other systems. So-called expert or intelligent systems can help make sense of such amalgamated data. In the technique known as 'trending' or 'data mining', users can set a piece of software on to the job. The so-called 'intelligent agent' searches the data, looking for a particular pattern.

First, users have to know what they are looking for: a pattern of behaviour, a certain set of criteria, or a set of characteristics which suggest a certain likelihood or outcome. The other term used for intelligent systems, 'neural network', suggests an ability to make connections in the same way as human intelligence. In fact, when a computer makes connections, it is not intuitive, but a matter of searching vast amounts of data and making matches.

One element in the search is speed and efficiency. The other is the ability to 'learn' by correlation of one fact with another to create a third assumption or suggestion. The system can bring something to a user's attention this way, but human judgement on the facts is what matters.

Source: Financial Times (6 December 1995).[18]

Conventional mainframe computers are usually not capable of conducting the levels of analysis that are required to carry out data mining effectively.[19] Instead, computers known as 'massively parallel processors' or 'supercomputers' are required which can work their way through very large numbers of calculations using very large amounts of data (*see* Exhibit 2.8).

While fast computing, efficient databases and high-speed networks are important elements of the data-mining infrastructure, a variety of non-technical factors must be put in place as well. These include:

■ methods for identifying, locating and extracting good-quality, relevant data for analysis

■ tools and techniques for identifying patterns and relationships in the data

■ statisticians and analysts to prepare the data, carry out the analysis and interpret the results

■ the presentation of relevant relationships mined from the data so that management and marketing decisions can be taken.

The other pre-requisite for effective data mining is high-quality data. This is often a

Exhibit 2.8

A WAY TO LOOSEN THE DATA GRIDLOCK

A new generation of technology called 'data mining' is giving companies like American Express, Fingerhut, American Airlines, Royal Caribbean Cruises Ltd. and First Bank System in Minneapolis, a way to loosen the data gridlock. The new approach can help businesses profit by improving distribution, narrowing direct-mail targets, and developing a new view of customers. Data mining uses parallel supercomputers that wire together hundreds of standard microchips from personal computers. The machines run relational database programs which cut data into smaller pieces of information.

American Express is testing supercomputers which they hope will reveal how card holders shop and spend, and which stores, restaurants, and hotels they prefer. An example of how they might use this information is to offer a discount on shoes at Saks Fifth Avenue to a woman who buys most of her dresses at Saks. American Express hopes that customers like this will then charge more purchases and the store will handle more American Express business.

Fingerhut is hoping to discover which of its customers bought outdoor patio furniture and thus might respond to a pitch for a gas barbecue grill.

Source: Adapted from the *Wall Street Journal* (16 August 1994).[20]

limiting factor for many organisations who do not have the processes in place to ensure that high-quality data is held in the data warehouse.

Users of data mining

The subject of data mining, and the techniques employed within the field, are still somewhat immature. The high investment required, combined with the technique's relative immaturity, make data mining an initiative to be undertaken only by large organisations that are not adverse to risk. However, despite the drawbacks, some early adopters in the retail, financial and medical sectors have already claimed considerable success with data mining.[21] In the financial services industry, banks such as Citibank and Bank of America use data-mining techniques for fraud prevention, credit scoring, cross-selling opportunities and marketing campaigns.[22] The availability of large amounts of transaction data on credit card usage, again captured at EPoS terminals, make data mining and the use of neural networks (the subject of the next section) a feasible option to help them detect fraud patterns.

■ Artificial intelligence and neural network technology

Artificial intelligence (AI) systems have been used in the scientific community for many years and during the 1980s some successful attempts were made to commercialise these systems and use them for other purposes such as marketing. By the 1990s, the technology had advanced to a stage where it was more reliable and cheaper to use and it has now found applications in several areas of marketing. The term *neural network technology* has gradually replaced *artificial intelligence* (*see* Exhibit 2.9).

The fundamental concept behind neural network technology is that a computer can be 'trained' to solve a problem in a similar fashion to a human brain, by recognising

---

Exhibit 2.9

LIES, DAMN LIES AND NEURAL NETWORKS

A type of software which may be regarded as complementary to statistical and modelling packages is the emerging technology of neural networks. This is a branch of what used to be called artificial intelligence, until the label fell into disrepute. Leading statistical software vendors have moved into providing neural network applications along with their other products.

Source: Financial Times (3 April 1996).[23]

---

familiar patterns. While conventional computers have to be programmed with very specific instructions, neural computers do not require the same explicit instructions. Instead, they adapt their responses based on previous problems and solutions that are given to them. The systems 'learn' from these problems and, after a sufficient 'training' period, can offer a solution to a new problem. At present, the most commonly used applications of neural networks are the areas of micro-marketing, risk management and fraud detection (*see* Exhibit 2.10).

Exhibit 2.10

TRAWLING BACKWARDS THROUGH THE DATA

Neural network technology has been moving out of the scientific world into commercial applications for a number of years. The technology has been improved, simplified and downsized. In applications such as fraud detection and micro-marketing, there are now quantifiable results available which confirm the low cost and improved performance of neural systems. Neural networking is a modelling technique. However, unlike other statistical techniques, it does not require that causal relationships are fully understood. Neural computing systems are able to find these relationships by trawling backwards through huge quantities of data and looking for them.

Source: Banking Technology (December 1995/January 1996).[24]

A good example of the use of neural network technology for micro-marketing in the UK comes from the insurance company Sun Alliance, which uses the technology to increase the response rate from its direct marketing campaigns.[25, 26] Sun Alliance found that by mailing just 20 per cent of its target database (the prospective customers are selected using neural network technology), it still achieved a very high number of responses. Neural network technology helped increase the response rate dramatically and, in the process, saved Sun Alliance considerable costs in paper and postage.

VISA International, described in a case study at the end of this chapter, uses neural network technology to detect credit card fraud. The system, which cost the organisation $2 million to build, has already paid its way, according to the developers of the system. Bank of America is said to have saved $4.4 million alone over a 16-month period in 1994, thanks to the system. The same system is now in use in the UK, France, Italy and Germany, with similar results. Another example of the use of neural network technology is depicted in Exhibit 2.11.

Exhibit 2.11

SAUSAGES AND WHITE BREAD

Retailers now have another weapon in their armoury of customer analysis techniques: neural networks. Already data warehousing technology has been deployed by many supermarkets as a means of searching through all the information gained from loyalty schemes introduced by retailers such as Tesco. By analysing the information, retailers can identify shopping trends and so better market products within a store.

In tests, the neural network software has identified patterns that retailers might not think of looking for. The system picked up the fact that people who buy sausages tend to buy white bread, for example. Armed with this information supermarkets can make customers aware of a special offer on a white loaf as they pick up their sausages.

The software can also predict individual buying habits, by searching through information gained from a store's loyalty scheme, and so identify which customers are likely to take up an offer and then continue to buy the product. With this knowledge the retailer can tailor its promotions and save money by only targeting those customers that are likely to provide a long-term gain.

Source: Sunday Business Computer Age (12 May 1996).[27]

CREATING A 'KNOWLEDGE ORGANISATION'

■ The knowledge organisation

The loss of corporate knowledge and the creation of corporate memory are being recognised as major management, and marketing, issues. It is more topical in the US than in Europe, but it is moving up the management agenda on this side of the Atlantic. The reason for the concern stems from the fact that managers are spending fewer years with the same company before moving on to their next job or career (*see* Exhibit 2.12).

Exhibit 2.12

CORPORATE ALZHEIMER'S

Having spent the 1990s in the throes of restructuring, re-engineering and downsizing, American companies are worrying about corporate amnesia. There was a time when air travellers in search of timely take-offs and sterling service would fly with Delta Air Lines. That was before Delta embarked on a cost-cutting and re-engineering programme, that has shrunk its workforce by about a sixth, or 12,000 jobs. Somewhere along the way, Delta seemed to 'forget' that service was what gave it an edge, and the loyalty of many customers. That firms should have 'memories' – and that these are strategically important – is not as whimsical as it sounds. John Challenger, executive vice-president of Challenger, Grey & Christmas, a consultancy based in Chicago, thinks that shrinking companies are at risk of 'corporate Alzheimer's'. He argues that the success of a firm depends not only on its skills and knowledge but also on its collective business experiences, successes and failures, culture, vision and numerous other intangible qualities.

Adapted from: The Economist (20 April 1996).[28]

According to Pencorp,[29] the number of UK managers who have more than six years tenure with their current company has decreased from more than 60 per cent in the 1950s and 1960s to less than 20 per cent in the 1990s. With so few long-term employees in our organisations today, it is little wonder that senior managers are looking for new methods of capturing vital knowledge even when the original source of the knowledge has moved on to another job or another company. Exhibit 2.13 provides a couple of additional examples of where companies have attempted to capture this knowledge and improve the long-term memory of their organisations.

Exhibit 2.13

FT

LONG-TERM MEMORIES

At Kraft, food arm of Philip Morris, the US cigarette, beer and foods group, the company's oral history archive has been used to fashion a new marketing approach to an old product. Towards the end of the 1980s one of the company's brands, Cracker Barrel cheese, was not selling well. Linda Crowder, the brand's manager, used the oral tapes to delve into the brand's origins in 1953 in order to shape a new marketing strategy. By reading the transcripts of interviews, she was able to gain the insights of Med Connelly, national sales manager of cheese products from 1959 to 1962, the period when the brands sales began to take off: 'He gave us a perspective we just couldn't get anywhere else', she says. 'Our research gave us a sense of what the theory was when Cracker Barrel was first introduced, and what we told consumers about the brand in the beginning.'

In the UK, the oral interview technique was used recently by a merchant bank ahead of the departure of a senior corporate director. NM Rothschild's decision to use an exit interview came when John Antcliffe, director of corporate affairs, decided to leave the company before a successor could be appointed. The merchant bank was conscious of the need for job continuity and of the fact that a key employee was leaving with a wealth of experience which could be lost forever. In Rothschild's case, the exit interview was conducted by an independent researcher two weeks before Antcliffe's departure. Antcliffe says: 'It fleshed out areas I would not have thought of mentioning to my successor, even if I had the opportunity.' Rodney Londsdale, Rothschild's personnel director who commissioned the project, says: 'The project went far beyond expectations. Unless a new employee reads the culture here right, they are going to find it extremely difficult to be productive. It is a very efficient way of reflecting the reality of the job and the company, and a well-balanced method of crystallising all the issues that someone coming cold into this organisation needs to know. When the new appointment is made, it will give the new entrant a very good understanding of how this business ticks.'

Source: Financial Times (31 July 1996).[29]

■ Enabling technologies

There are several enabling technologies that allow organisations to share information and knowledge more easily between employees. These include:

■ local area networks (LANs) and wide area networks (WANs)

- intranets
- 'groupware' applications
- electronic mail
- voice mail.

Information is power and if it can be harnessed properly it can improve the performance of companies. Unfortunately, information is also power to the employee and a major stumbling block in the implementation of any of these enabling technologies is the reluctance of the employee to share information (and power) with colleagues (*see* Exhibit 2.14).

Exhibit 2.14

KEEPING THINGS CLOSE TO YOUR CHEST

In large organisations, the possession of information meant power, and secrecy was often justified against spurious grounds of commercial confidentiality. I am not so foolish as to believe that every organisation can work on the basis of total openness, but I am constantly amazed by how much information is held close to people's chests for reasons which have little or nothing to do with winning the competitive race. Here again, information technology is the enabler, but human nature and previous beliefs and practices are the enemy.

Source: Harvey-Jones (1993).[4]

Local area networks (LANs) and wide area networks (WANs)

A local area network is a network that links PCs within the same building or on the same floor of a building. It enables people who work in the same department to share information with each other. Typically, the information and files that are shared between employees are located on a central PC or 'server' to which all department employees have access. Different groups of employees may have different levels of access to these electronic files. For example, each person may have his or her own private 'directory' to which no other person has access. The head of the department may be the only person who is given access to certain financial information and so on. When companies want to link employees located in different buildings or different cities, a slightly different technical architecture is needed. This architecture is known as a wide area network (WAN) and is typically used to link several LANs.

Intranets

While the Internet is a global public medium for linking different businesses and individuals (see Chapter 8 for a full discussion of the topic), there are also private versions of the Internet which can only be accessed by employees of one organisation and are protected by passwords and other security features. These 'intranets' can also link to the outside world by connecting to the Internet, but they are primarily for internal use within a company or between a company and its trading partners. As Exhibit 2.15 points out, these private networks based on the same technology and software as the Internet are experiencing phenomenal growth.[30]

Exhibit 2.15

THE QUIET REVOLUTION

While the Internet has been grabbing most of the headlines over the past 18 months, a quiet revolution has been taking place inside companies. Private intranets – internal internets shielded from prying eyes by 'firewall' security software – are blossoming. 'The other side of the Internet is about to explode', said the Gartner Group in a report published late last year. The research group expects more than 50 per cent of large companies to have not just intranets, but business-critical 'enterprise-wide webs' by 1998.

Source: Financial Times (3 April 1996).[31]

Intranets are a preferred solution for many organisations with more than 100 employees and with remote locations in a wide geographical area.[32] Proponents of intranet solutions claim that they:

- are cost effective
- deliver information easily
- are relatively easy to configure, use and manage
- can be set up company wide and also by department or functional area
- are well suited for multimedia applications
- are excellent for reducing printing costs and distribution time
- are basically secure
- form a gateway to the Internet
- integrate easily with internal corporate databases
- are easy for users rather than IT staff to develop in terms of content.

In truth, many of these advantages could equally be applied to the Internet. An intranet is, by definition, more internally focused and used to support the internal sales and marketing functions of an organisation. The early adopters of intranets for marketing purposes tend to use them for the following applications:

- publishing corporate documents such as product literature, marketing literature, annual reports, newsletters, price lists, manuals and corporate policies
- providing access to searchable directories such as corporate phone books, addresses, calendars, departmental diary systems and schedules
- distributing software to a wide number of users, for example issuing updates of quotation software to life assurance and pensions sales representatives
- connecting large numbers of employees in various geographic locations by means of electronic mail.

For example, the multimedia system used by the Rover Group (*see* Chapter 8, pages 132–3) to link the company to its dealers around the UK and to a further 600 dealerships across Europe is actually being implemented as an intranet.[33] A major reason for companies going down the intranet route is cost. One provider of intranet services in the UK estimated that the cost of providing such a service is approximately £100 per year per user.[34]

Groupware

One current debate is whether intranets will displace 'groupware', the similar but more costly proprietary systems which are not based on Internet standards. Examples of groupware include Banyan's *BeyondMail*, ICL's *Teamware*, Novell's *Groupwise* and the most popular and best-selling groupware product of all, *Lotus Notes* from Lotus Corporation[35] (*see* Exhibit 2.16). Groupware tends to offer more features and better security than an intranet, but this may change. The leading developer of Internet software, Netscape, has acquired a small groupware company in the US and is likely to start offering similar features for intranet use. At the same time Lotus, which itself has been acquired by IBM, has also moved to connect to the World Wide Web[36] and the boundaries between groupware and intranets are becoming more and more blurred.[37, 38] Companies such as the pharmaceutical organisation Glaxo-Wellcome, which uses both intranet and groupware technology across 27 000 desktops, will continue to use both.[39, 40]

Exhibit 2.16

BANKING ON SPEED, QUALITY AND COST

Global investment bank SBC Warburg has adopted intranet technologies and *Lotus Notes* software to transform the way it produces research reports. Analysts in the bank's foreign exchange and economic research group produce studies and forecasts in daily, weekly, monthly and quarterly newsletters and reports. The process was paper-based three years ago when the bank set out to move to electronic methods. Alan Roberts, director of the bank's foreign exchange division in London, said the first step was defining the priorities as 'speed, quantity, and cost, in that order.' The bank also brought a coherent structure to the process. Analysts work with economic and financial market information, data from modelling and analysis, and less formal information gathered simply by being in the markets. Outputs go to the bank's traders and sales staff as well as clients. Now many customers of the research group's output can access it through Web browsers.

Source: Computer Weekly (6 June 1996).[41]

CONCLUSION

Information has always been sought by business and marketing managers to help them run their organisations more effectively. In the past, many business decisions were made using paper-based management reports and managers could rely on limited analytical support. Nowadays, a variety of computer-based systems are available for assisting managers at all levels in the organisation to carry out their jobs more effectively. The term management information systems (MIS) has been coined to cover this wide range of computer applications, while the term decision-support systems (DSS) refers to a subset of MIS used to complement the manager's own judgement in making major decisions. A further subset of DSS consists of those systems used exclusively for senior management, known as executive information systems (EIS). In reality, the boundaries between MIS, DSS and EIS have become blurred. New developments in management information include data warehouses which hold very large amounts of corporate data and which are of particular interest to the marketing manager. In addition, new analytical tools have emerged, ranging from the lowly spreadsheet to the more exotically named data mining, on-line analytical processing (OLAP) and neural network technologies. While steady advances have been made in the area of support tools available to the marketing manager, two factors have conspired to minimise their effect. First, many managers still rely on *informal* management information and 'gut feel' when making decisions. Second, as workers have become more mobile, the drain of knowledge from organisations has become a major problem. In response, companies are creating structures and information systems which allow information to be captured and disseminated more easily between employees. The enabling technologies for the creation of the 'knowledge organisation' include local and wide area networks, intranets and groupware, as well as electronic and voice mail. Creating a knowledge organisation can be particularly important in global organisations where marketing experiences in one country can be transferred to other countries.

ASSIGNMENT QUESTIONS

1 How have the nature and use of management information evolved over the past 50 years?

2 What type of information do senior business and marketing executives need?

3 Describe and discuss the issues that companies face if they decide to undertake a data warehouse or data-mining initiative.

4 What is data mining?

5 Why is corporate knowledge so important in the final years of the twentieth century?

Case study

BRITISH AIRWAYS

British Airways wants to know more about its customers and their long-term needs. In that, it is similar to banks, insurance companies, retailers, health care providers and other explorers of data warehouse technology.

However, the international nature of BA's business has led to a pragmatic 'horses for courses' approach in which several solutions, hardware and software, have to work together. Mr Bill Teather, head of corporate management, confirms that BA has been working on the data warehouse projects for the last six years, although the term has only recently penetrated beyond the technical community to managers in BA.

'To meet customers' needs and to improve our own asset utilisation, we need to be able to answer all sorts of questions. Those answers feed into decisions on how we operate in the future,' explains Mr Teather. 'The data warehouse will tell us what mix of fares will be used on what routes, who flies where, for what price, and to what extent different countries and agencies are selling different mixes of the product. We look to the warehouse for detailed information about route profitability, so we can see where our aircraft are best deployed. For that, our users need good access to warehouse statistics.'

BA's first data warehouse applications were all about customer servicing and ticketing. Ms Sandy Hulbert, head of management information services for British Airways, explains: 'The big move is to try to personalise travel: it's all about knowing your customers and treating them as individuals. We are looking at who goes where, and when, but all these factors feed into long term planning, load factors, the frequency of flights, and so on. The warehouse also records customer preferences, and the value of a customer through his or her booking history. It's all to do with trying to predict what the customer wants.'

Ms Hulbert emphasises the importance of linking applications and making data available to users regardless of barriers imposed by geography, hardware or software.

Once the data warehouse has proved its worth in strategic planning, BA plans to use the data for all sorts of different purposes, including cargo, engineering, marketing and operations, she adds. Word is already beginning to spread about the effectiveness of the data warehouse – 'luckily, the airline has taken IT to its heart, and people are very business-focused. It's wonderful when management see IT as a value-added tool, not a threat; it makes us enthusiastic about what we can do.'

Source: Adapted from 'A system for keeping air passengers happy', *Financial Times*, 1 March 1995.

Questions

1 How can BA's data warehouse lead to improved profitability and more personal customer service?

2 Where is the information to populate the data warehouse likely to come from?

3 Comment on BA adopting a 'horses for courses' approach to data warehouse projects.

4 Why is it important that data is available to users regardless of barriers imposed by geography, hardware or software?

5 Comment on BA's investment in IT and how it might enable the company to achieve its aim of becoming the 'world's favourite airline'.

Case study

VISA INTERNATIONAL

VISA International is one of the biggest of the credit card vendors. It claims the largest consumer payment system in the world, boasting more than 11 million accepted locations. Its member financial institutions have issued more than 343 million cards throughout the world. The company also holds a front runner position in the technological battle against credit card crime.

VISA International is rolling out its new neural network-based system which has already proved a major weapon in combating fraud. At present, VISA International is concentrating its efforts in neural network technology on detecting credit card fraud perpetrated by individuals. In concept, neural networks are disarmingly simple; people tend to have patterns of buying. We tend to spend within certain limits, buy certain types of goods, and acquire new baubles at a fairly predictable rate. Neural networks are designed to identify behaviours which do not fit into these patterns. Once exceptional behaviour is spotted by the system, card-issuing banks can be warned. The transaction itself is not immediately stopped, for good reason. For example, suppose you are approaching some dreaded milestone in your life such as your fortieth birthday. You need a little cheering up and decide that your spirits might be lifted by, say, a case of Dom Perignon and half a pound of best Beluga caviar. Just imagine how annoyed you would be if, mid-splurge, your credit card was seized by the merchant. It might just spoil your day.

Cathy Basch, senior vice-president for risk management and information services at VISA International, says: 'Everyone could have a pattern which, at times, appears fraudulent. And because we don't want to create any problems for customers, we send the scores to the issuing banks several times a day and the banks decide.' Those scores are established by comparing suspect transactions with a vast database of 'learned account usage patterns'. VISA International uses information gathered through its worldwide operations to create a highly complex network of interrelated data.

'We see millions and millions of transactions every day from around the world', says Basch. 'We use 30–35 different parameters made up of a variety of elements. These factors such as merchant category code, which indicate the type of merchant, the kind of locations and how often transactions are occurring. We also look at the exact type of transaction.'

An example of an established fraud pattern is as follows: a credit card is used to pay for petrol at a service station and that transaction is followed by the purchase in rapid succession of a series of large price-tag consumer electronics. The purchasing pattern would alert the neural network to possible fraud, immediately signalling the likelihood of a credit card theft by a criminal intent on using up all remaining credit as quickly as possible – the criminal knowing that he or she has only a short amount of time before the theft is detected and reported, and the card invalidated. Neural networks have been found to be extremely adept at detecting patterns in very large amounts of data, making them ideal for the credit card risk applications Visa International is developing. When risky transactions are detected they are scored (that is, evaluated in terms of the degree of risk) and reported to card-issuing banks in a list sent via electronic mail eight times each day. This enables the banks to establish their own methods of dealing with potential fraud. This is an important factor because of the sensitive nature of fraud detection. Nothing has been proven at the time the neural network flags what it has been taught to view as a high risk transaction. The banks are simply alerted and can then contact customers. By all accounts, the great majority of customers do not object to being contacted and asked whether a given purchase was legitimate. But clearly there is the potential for an invasion of privacy which could harm a bank's reputation with its customers.

Source: Adapted from 'Close to the nerve', *Banking Technology*, December 1994/January 1995.

Questions

1 Describe how the VISA neural network works to spot potentially fraudulent transactions.

2 Customer service and marketing managers are often involved in creating scripts for bank staff to follow if they have to call a customer regarding a potentially fraudulent transaction. Prepare your own script for use by a bank employee who has been asked to call a customer in connection with two potentially fraudulent transactions – the purchase of a case of Dom Perignon and half a pound of best Beluga caviar.

3 Describe some other potential applications for neural networks at VISA.

4 Comment on the role of neural networks in marketing.

References

[1] Handy, C. (1985). *Understanding Organisations*. 3rd edn, Harmondsworth: Penguin.
[2] Kuipers, B. (1992). 'Action Oriented Reporting', *Direct Marketing*, June.
[3] Dempsey, M. (1995). 'How to get the right data to the right desk', *Financial Times*, 1 March.
[4] Harvey-Jones, J. (1993). *Managing to Survive*. London: Mandarin.
[5] Gooding, C. (1995). 'Boosting sales with the information warehouse', *Financial Times*, 1 March.

[6] The Times (1996). 'Bulmer bridges the gap', *The Times* (data warehousing supplement), 5 June.

[7] Richardson, M.A. (1996). *Data Warehousing: Overview*. Datapro, April. Delvan, NJ.

[8] Radding, A. (1995). 'Support decision makers with a data warehouse', *Datamation*, 15 March.

[9] Light, M. (1995). 'Building a data warehouse: business case and budget', *Gartner Group*, 30 August.

[10] Darling, C.B. (1996). 'How to integrate your data warehouse', *Datamation*, 15 May.

[11] Gurton, A. (1996). 'Same song, different tune', *Computer Weekly*, 18 July.

[12] Varney, S.E. (1996). 'Datamarts: coming to an IT mall near you', *Datamation*, 1 June.

[13] The Times (1996). 'Churchill Insurance', *The Times* (data warehousing supplement), 5 June.

[14] The Times (1996). 'The beer and nappy revolution', *The Times* (data warehousing supplement), 5 June.

[15] Vowler, J. (1996). 'A place for everything', *Computer Weekly* (data warehousing supplement), 30 May.

[16] Darling, C.B. (1996). 'Build an app dev framework for DSS', *Datamation*, 15 April.

[17] Foss, B. and Stone, M. (1996). 'A brief guide to data mining', *Post Magazine*, 16 May.

[18] Gooding, C. (1995). 'Smart ways to reach the right market', *Financial Times*, 6 December.

[19] Block, J. (1995). 'Using data mining to gain a competitive edge, part 2', *Gartner Group*, 30 August.

[20] *Wall Street Journal* (1994). 'Companies use data mining to target customers', 16 August.

[21] Block, J. (1995). 'Using data mining to gain a competitive edge, part 1', *Gartner Group*, 23 August.

[22] Talmor, S. (1996). 'Mine for data', *The Banker*, April.

[23] Black, G. (1996). 'How to make sense of the numbers', *Financial Times*, 3 April.

[24] Gandy, T. (1995/6). 'Brainwaves in fraud busting', *Banking Technology*, Dec/Jan.

[25] Classe, A. (1996). 'The other networks', *Computer Weekly*, 30 May.

[26] Enticknap, N. (1995). 'Knowledge is the key', *Computer Weekly*, 30 November.

[27] Burton, G. (1996). 'ICL releases off-the-shelf system', *Sunday Business ComputerAge*, 12 May.

[28] The Economist (1996). 'Fire and forget?', *The Economist*, 20 April.

[29] Kransdorff, A. (1996). 'Keep know-how in the company', *Financial Times*, 31 July.

[30] Lamb, J. (1996). 'Intranet technology is key to consultancies' survival', *Sunday Business ComputerAge*, 23 June.

[31] Taylor, P. (1996). 'First the Internet: now the intranet phenomenon', *Financial Times*, 3 April.

[32] Faughan, L. (1996). 'And now the Intranet', *Business & Finance*, 26 May.

[33] Vowler, J. (1996). 'Rover contemplates intranet info system', *Computer Weekly*, 21 March.

[34] ITR (1996). 'BT MNS launches intranet service', *Insurance Technology Report*, June.

[35] Manchester, P. (1995). 'Making connections is big business', *Financial Times*, 3 May.

[36] Hewson, D. (1996). 'Lotus Notes leaps on Net', *Sunday Times*, 23 June.

[37] Mgadzah, R. (1996). 'Indoor surfing', *Computing*, 16 May.

[38] Gurton, A. (1996). 'Comparing Notes', *Computer Weekly*, 9 May.

[39] Clement, D. (1996). 'Groupware is here to stay, says dual-approach Glaxo', *Sunday Business ComputerAge*, 7 July.

[40] Oldroyd, R. (1996). 'Glaxo's intranet injection', *Sunday Business ComputerAge*, 26 May.

[41] Green-Armytage, J. (1996). 'SBC Warburg speeds up research with intranet', *Computer Weekly*, 6 June.

MARKETING INFORMATION SYSTEMS (MkIS)

- Overview of marketing information systems (MkIS)
- Users of marketing information
- The sources of marketing information
- MkIS subsystems and processes
- Marketing research

OBJECTIVES

After studying this chapter, you will be able to:

☐ Define what is meant by the term marketing information systems (MkIS)

☐ Identify the key users of marketing information and their information requirements

☐ Understand the processes carried out using MkIS

☐ Understand the main steps involved in designing and implementing an MkIS

☐ Evaluate the role of information technology in marketing research

OVERVIEW OF MARKETING INFORMATION SYSTEMS (MkIS)

■ The explosion of marketing information

Companies like AC Nielsen have been providing market research data for many years. However, as Figure 3.1 demonstrates, the sources of market research and the amount of data have increased enormously over the past 20 years. This information explosion has been instrumental in fuelling the growing interest in marketing information systems (MkIS).

■ What are marketing information systems (MkIS)?

Throughout this book we take a broad view of marketing and believe that the marketing function should be interpreted in its widest meaning. We adopt the same approach to MkIS and have a much wider interpretation of the term than do other writers. We

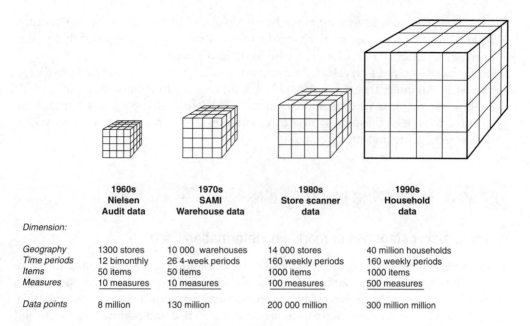

Dimension:	1960s Nielsen Audit data	1970s SAMI Warehouse data	1980s Store scanner data	1990s Household data
Geography	1300 stores	10 000 warehouses	14 000 stores	40 million households
Time periods	12 bimonthly	26 4-week periods	160 weekly periods	160 weekly periods
Items	50 items	50 items	1000 items	1000 items
Measures	10 measures	10 measures	100 measures	500 measures
Data points	8 million	130 million	200 000 million	300 million million

Fig 3.1   Growth of market research data

Source: Andersen Consulting (1994).

view MkIS as comprising all computer and non-computer systems which assist the marketing function to operate effectively. Therefore, MkIS include many systems which are not generally thought of in marketing terms, for example general ledger, accounts receivable and production-planning systems. A similar interpretation is provided by Marshall and LaMotte (1992)[1] who define MkIS as:

> 'a formal system designed with the objective of creating an organised, regular flow of relevant information for use and analysis by marketing decision makers.'

MkIS are often built up from several different systems, each with its own specific purpose which may or may not be marketing related. The design of MkIS can rely on existing systems within the organisation and are likely to end up as bespoke, compromise solutions which are unique to each company.

■ Key attributes of MkIS

Some of the key attributes of Marshall and LaMotte's definition of MkIS are as follows:

- ■ *They do not limit the definition to computer hardware or software.* Their definition places greater emphasis on the provision of relevant information rather than on the technology itself, although MkIS are typically computer based.
- ■ *The definition calls for organised, regular flows of relevant information.* MkIS should not be developed as isolated, *ad hoc* systems. They should involve many aspects of management, draw data from many different sources and organise it so that regular and useful information can be provided to marketing managers.

■ *The information must be relevant to marketing decisions.* High-level marketing decision makers must be included in planning the information requirements and these managers are an integral part of a successful MkIS implementation.

■ *Marketing managers are expected to carry out further analyses of the information provided by the system.* An integral part of any MkIS are tools which allow marketing managers to analyse and manipulate data in order to make marketing decisions. In Chapter 2 we examined some of these tools in a discussion on decision-support systems (DSS), data warehousing and data mining.

USERS OF MARKETING INFORMATION

■ Three main categories of marketing information users

To implement the marketing concept effectively, marketing managers require information on the characteristics, needs and wants of their customers. Intense competition in the marketplace and the high costs of advertising and new product development make it imperative that marketing campaigns are well researched and planned. Accurate and timely marketing information systems can prevent organisations from building campaigns on mistaken assumptions. In most organisations, marketing information is accessed by many different groups, each of which has different objectives and requires different types of information. The three main categories of people who require access to marketing information are:

■ *Senior marketing management.* Senior marketing managers will be concerned with overall strategic positioning of the brands they control and the resources allocated between brands. They will also decide which brands they will milk for cash and which they will invest in for growth.

■ *Middle marketing management.* Normally, the information needed by senior marketing managers is a summarised form of that required by middle management.

■ *Managers in other functions.* Manufacturing, product development and finance managers also rely on information supplied by the marketing function. In a manufacturing organisation, the production planners and schedulers depend heavily on sales forecasts to drive their production schedules. If the forecast is wrong, the company will end up with either too much inventory in the warehouse which ties up working capital, or a 'stock-out' situation with the resulting loss of revenue to the company. Finance managers also require sales forecasts to drive the financial-planning processes in many organisations.

The most intensive users of marketing information are those marketing managers who fall into the category of middle management. This is because they have a variety of day-to-day marketing activities which include:

■ marketing planning
■ market research
■ marketing segmentation
■ media selection
■ monitoring competitors' marketing iniatives

- product management and performance management
- above-the-line advertising
- measuring advertising effectiveness
- sales promotions
- new product development.

■ Integration of marketing and manufacturing

At this point, it is worth mentioning that different departments within the same company may have conflicting objectives which need to be managed. For example, tensions and conflicts between marketing and manufacturing will inevitably arise in most organisations[2] (*see* Table 3.1). For these reasons, it is important for marketing to create a central role for itself within the company and for its information systems within those of the company. This is a theme which we will pursue in the coming pages as we discuss the scope of marketing information systems (MkIS).

Table 3.1 Conflict areas between marketing and manufacturing

Area of Conflict	Marketing Objective	Manufacturing Objective
Managing diversity		
1. Product line length/breadth	Many and complex models	Few and simple models
2. Product customisation	Customer specifications	'Stock' products
3. Product line changes	Product changes immediately; high risk	Planned, only necessary changes; low risk
Managing conformity		
4. Product scheduling	Constant change	Inflexible
5. Capacity/facility planning	Accept all orders	Critically evaluate 'fit' of orders
Managing dependability		
6. Delivery	Immediate; large inventory	As soon as possible; no inventory
7. Quality control	High standards	Reasonable control

Source: Crittenden *et al.* (1993).[2]

The tensions mentioned above are reflected in the difficulties of implementing MkIS successfully. For every example of a successful implementation that is written up in the marketing journals, there is at least one other example of failure to achieve any significant benefit (*see* Exhibit 3.1).

Several other authors have commented on the difficulties of designing and implementing MkIS. For example:

> 'Sales force automation is one of the most high-risk, high-visibility projects that a company can undertake and, in addition, sales representatives are a particularly difficult group to include in MkIS development and daily use.'[3]

> 'Close contact between end-users, managers and designers is needed to build up an effective, functionally and technically integrated MkIS wholeness if competitive advantage is to be achieved.'[4]

THE SOURCES OF MARKETING INFORMATION

■ Overview of sources

Perhaps the biggest issue that marketers face is ensuring the ongoing sourcing and maintenance of useful marketing information. The difficulties of gathering, cleaning, collating and using marketing information can hinder the development of any marketing information system. In the next chapter, we will look specifically at the issues surrounding the capture and maintenance of customer information. For the moment, let us examine the following four key sources of marketing information (*see* Figure 3.2) as defined by Kotler (1994):[5]

- internal records
- marketing intelligence
- marketing decision-support systems
- marketing research.

■ Internal records

Often, the cheapest and best information is on the marketing manager's doorstep and a considerable amount of information can be gathered from a variety of internal sources, including:

- *Current and historic sales figures.* These can be analysed to identify patterns of sales in different areas or after promotional campaigns.
- *Price lists.* Sales of products at different prices can be analysed to determine their price sensitivities and demand curves.
- *Inventory levels.* For organisations that sell through third-party distributors and therefore have little contact with end-customer sales figures, information on stock levels and stock movements will often provide the first indication of sales levels to end-customers.

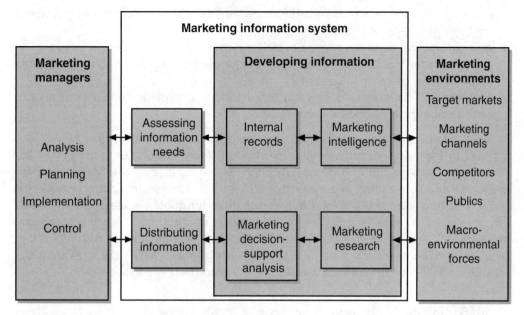

Fig 3.2   Four sources of marketing information

Source: Kotler (1994).[5] Reprinted by permission of Prentice-Hall, Inc., Upper Saddle River, NJ.

- *Receivables and payables from the internal accounting systems.* These can be used to deter-mine expected revenues and to analyse the profitability of different customer groups.
- *Customer complaints.* An underutilised source of information in many organisations is the log of customer complaints which are a valuable source of information on prod-uct/service deficiencies.

In theory, these sources of information are sensible and logical, but in practice, there are often major difficulties in gaining access to this valuable information. In many cases, the information is held on other computer systems to which the marketing department has limited or no access. A good knowledge of IT is invaluable for accessing and manip-ulating data held on other systems.

■ Marketing intelligence

To be effective, marketing managers must understand what is happening in their mar-kets and they can obtain this intelligence from a variety of sources, including:

- *Trade publications.* Most industries have specialised trade publications which are a good source of information on competitor activity and product information.
- *Books and newspapers.* These provide information on general economic trends and competitors.
- *Current advertising by competitors.* Advertising and other marketing material can be analysed to identify the competitor's target market and competitive positioning.
- *Company personnel who have worked for competitors.* A very useful source of marketing intelligence is the employee who has worked for, or has information on, competing

organisations. This can be a valuable source of information on competitors' internal business processes and strategies.

■ *Informal briefings from sales staff.* Sales staff can provide feedback on how products are accepted in the marketplace and, in many organisations, are an underutilised source of intelligence on competitor activity.

■ *Membership of trade associations.* Trade associations can provide informal information on current industry trends and initiatives.

Most of the marketing intelligence in companies tends to be informal and carried around in the heads of individuals. However, leading-edge organisations develop formal processes to capture and share information. They will regularly debrief company personnel and keep records of competitive activity. For example, marketing managers in some insurance companies phone their competitors for quotations to ensure that their own prices are competitive; retail store managers regularly shop at nearby competitors for the same reason. One of the cornerstones of any relationship marketing strategy which tries to build a much closer relationship with key customers is the software which records details of all the contacts a customer has with the organisation.

■ Marketing decision support analysis

Decision support systems and analysis provide much valuable information to the marketing manager. In a supermarket, the most valuable source of marketing information comes from the hundreds of thousands of transactions that are scanned daily at the checkouts in each store. As we have discussed in the previous chapter, data mining can provide the marketing manager of a supermarket with many insights which can determine the actions that must be taken on each of the elements in the marketing mix: product, price, place and promotion.

■ Marketing research

When organisations require specific information that is not available from any of the above three sources, they may decide to conduct marketing research. Marketing research is a major subject in itself with significant opportunities for the use of information technology. We will discuss these in greater detail later in this chapter.

MkIS SUBSYSTEMS AND PROCESSES

■ MkIS subsystems

In Figure 3.2, Kotler provides a good conceptual overview of the elements of a marketing information system. In practice, there are many different components or subsystems within the overall umbrella of MkIS which support the marketing manager. The number and type will differ from organisation to organisation but, in general, the most common subsystems tend to be:

■ *Data collection.* Data can be collected from various sources. Some sources are external, for example industry statistics, census data, market research data or advertising data. Other sources are internal, for example sales figures or telephone call centre statistics.

■ *Analysis.* A variety of DSS or OLAP applications identify opportunities for increased sales, based on buying patterns of existing customers, opportunities for additional sales from new customers or new markets, new product and service opportunities and opportunities based on competitive activity, including product launches, promotions and price changes.

■ *Forecasting.* These include statistical projections, sales modelling and other forms of financial or economic analysis.

■ *Cost and budgeting.* These systems assist in determining the costs at which products and services can be sold in order to provide a good return to the company.

■ *Marketing planning.* These include new product launches, promotional activities, sales opportunities, advertising and media activities and customer service activities.

■ *Reporting.* These include sales and promotional activities, distribution figures, sales and profit performance, customer service performance, cost and financial performance.

■ MkIS processes

Another way of viewing the components of MkIS is to think of them in terms of inputs,

Table 3.2   MkIS: inputs, processing and outputs

Inputs	Processing	Outputs
Intra-organisational inputs • Sales records • Telemarketing records • Promotion response • Accounts receivable • Pricing standards • Inventory records	*Data linkages* • Database management • Systems coordination	*Product management* • Product sales summary • Tactical product plans • Programme benchmark
	Systems controls • Access controls • Data integrity	*Communications* • Budget tracking • Media planning
Environmental inputs • Industry trends • Primary research • Economic trends • Advertising costs • Regulatory trends • Competitor trends • Supply trends	*User interfaces* • Screen design • Ergonomics	*Sales* • Territory design • Sales forecasts • Quota planning
	Analytical tools • Decision support systems • Simulation modelling • Expert systems	*Senior management* • Strategy simulation • Financial modelling • Market assessments
	Intra-organisational applications • Inventory forecasts • Financial forecasts • Customer database	
	Reporting systems • Text processing • Graphics output • Slides and viewgraphs • Electronic output	

Source: Marshall and LaMotte (1992).[6]

outputs and the processing that is done to the information. Marshall and LaMotte (1992)[6] provide such a perspective, as shown in Table 3.2.

■ Managing marketing information in international markets

As companies become more international, it becomes increasingly important for subsidiaries to share marketing information.[7] Very often, customers are becoming more international themselves and organisations have to put together multinational teams to meet their customers' needs. Benetton, for example, offers a range of 3000 products and operates a global order-entry and distribution system that allows it to manage distribution to its 5000 franchised stores across the world, from a warehouse in Italy, within days. Daniels (1993)[8] compares the Portuguese and Spaniards of the fifteenth century, who had fast ships to support speedy communications, with today's global companies which require global networks and customer databases to keep them ahead of the competition. The design and implementation of cross-border systems and databases is significantly more difficult than building a corresponding system within one set of national boundaries.

MARKETING RESEARCH

■ Categories of marketing research

There are two main categories of marketing research:

- *Primary market research.* Primary research is carried out by companies for specific purposes, such as gauging the potential for success in launching a new product, assessing customers' reactions to an existing product or service or measuring advertising effectiveness.
- *Secondary market research.* Secondary research makes use of previously conducted marketing research, for example reusing information gathered from newspapers, research publications or census surveys.

Primary market research is of critical importance when developing a new product or service and in determining if the product or service will be accepted and purchased by particular categories of consumer. Because of its importance and, quite often, its complexity, primary market research tends to be managed as a discrete project and is often outsourced to specialist research companies.

In contrast, secondary research is often carried out on an *ad hoc* basis by people within the marketing department. Depending on the complexity of the research and the resources available to the marketing department, secondary research may also be outsourced.

■ The use of IT in marketing research

There are typically five steps in any marketing research study. Figure 3.3 illustrates some applications of information technology which can be used in each of these steps.

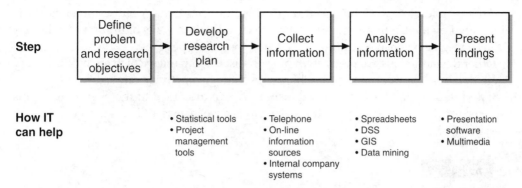

Fig 3.3 Applicability of IT during different stages of marketing research

Information technology can be used to different extents for all these activities and particularly in collecting and analysing the data. Traditionally, data has been collected using one of the following methods:

- observing how customers (or potential customers) react to a particular product, service or situation
- interviewing customers by means of face-to-face interviews or postal surveys
- interviewing groups of customers by means of buying panels or focus groups
- conducting experiments with customers (piloting or test marketing) or through simulation of expected customer responses.

Exhibit 3.2

MOVIES, MODELS AND DIRECTORS' EGOS

Film makers have long tried to predict whether the dog-eared script on their desk will make a box-office hit. As early as 1937 America's Audience Research Institute tried to gauge audience reaction by using brief, written synopses of films. Since then the industry has experimented with a string of techniques, ranging from sneak previews of films in the early stages of production to crude attempts at correlating the characteristics of a forthcoming film (e.g. violent, funny, erotic) with cinema attendance at films already on release. None has worked well. Jehoshua Eliashberg and Mohanbir Sawhney, of the University of Pennsylvania, reckon they have at least part of the answer to the film industry's problem. Films are an odd sort of consumer good, because they are 'purchases' with little or no prior knowledge of whether they will be enjoyable. Dr Eliashberg and Dr Sawhney hope to change that. They have devised a mathematical model to predict whether cinema goers will enjoy a specific film.

The model relies on established personality testing techniques to assess would-be film goers. First, it measures each against a sensation-seeking scale: do they seek adventures or new experiences, are they easily bored, and so on. Second, it assesses their emotional state (pleased or displeased, aroused or relaxed). Third, it measures the cinema goer's tendency to undergo mood changes. The model then predicts likely enjoyment levels for each individual by correlating all three factors with the film's excitement and pleasure content, as assessed scene-by-scene by a trio of independent judges.

Source: The Economist (4 July 1992).[9]

An example of how IT has been used to gather information on customer tastes is illustrated by the US film industry, which has tried to find ways of minimising the risk of investing in expensive productions (*see* Exhibit 3.2 on page 49).

Other developments are the growth of specialised companies which are building very large databases of information to which subscribing companies can access (*see* Exhibit 3.3). In line with the information explosion that we discussed at the beginning of this chapter, the number and scope of these databases have increased dramatically in the past decade.

Exhibit 3.3

DATA WARS

Forget such long-standing feuds as Coke v Pepsi or Procter & Gamble v Unilever. For the past few years, the fiercest battle in the marketing world has been fought between AC Nielsen and Information Resources Inc., two rival suppliers of market data on the sale of consumer goods, both based in Chicago. AC Nielsen and IRI have poached each other's clients and staff almost as fast as they have piled up losses. Talk to either, and it is not long before they start denigrating their fellow firm.

The main business that IRI and AC Nielsen (along with most of the other big established firms such as France's Sofres and Germany's GFK) specialise in is 'continuous' research – i.e. using data from shops and permanent panels of customers to calculate what products are sold where, and to whom. The business, which used to throng with clipboard-carrying researchers, is now dominated by point-of-sale scanners and computer databases. To keep up, both AC Nielsen and IRI have had to make huge investments in information technology, whose cost they have not always been able to pass on to their clients.

Last year alone, says Mr Cotsakos, president of AC Nielsen, they invested more than $300m in acquisitions and technology. It has equipped a panel of 40,000 households in America with self-scanning equipment to keep an electronic record of their purchases. Nielsen Media Research is now exploring ways of tracking customer use on the Internet.

Source: The Economist (22 July 1995).[10]

■ Commercial on-line services

On-line databases are rich sources of secondary market research information. These databases are dial-up information services provided by third-party information providers such as DataStar or the Financial Times. Many large companies will use at least one of these commercial on-line services for accessing general news information or research on more specialised subjects. There are at least 9000 commercial databases available worldwide, containing over six billion records and covering information on business, technical and scientific topics, company reports, broker reports, newspaper and journal articles and patent documents.[11] The advantages of commercial on-line services are as follows:

- *Variety.* Many on-line services provide a 'supermarket' service whereby different services can be accessed by subscribing to a single supplier.

- *Up-to-date information.* Many databases are updated on at least a daily basis and a large number even more frequently.
- *Cost efficiency.* Although commercial on-line services charge either an up-front or a monthly/quarterly charge, or charge on an actual usage basis, they can provide an extremely cost-efficient means of accessing a wide variety of information.
- *Accessibility of information.* Most databases can be accessed 24 hours a day, 7 days a week.

Some of the major on-line service providers which can be accessed in Europe and the services they provide are illustrated in Table 3.3.

Table 3.3 Major commercial on-line service providers

Service	Description
DataStar	Large 'supermarket' host covering a wide range of European data and information, including European news company information, country and market reports and industry-specific data. Owned by US-based Knight-Ridder.
Dialog	Large supermarket host with wide range of US and international data, including worldwide company information, US government news, patent and trademark information and industry-specific data. Owned by US-based Knight-Ridder.
Dow Jones/News Retrieval	US-based service company which provides industry information, market quotes and data, plus over 3000 news sources, including exclusive on-line access to the *Wall Street Journal*. Currently little non-US content.
FT Profile	News and business information service run by Financial Times Information (part of the Pearson Group). Offers a range of news, company, industry, market and country information.
Lexis-Nexis	Acquired by Reed-Elsevier in 1995, this US-based service provides 6200 sources of legal, news and business information. Strong US bias.
MAID (Profound)	UK-owned service with a substantial package of market research information plus a wide range of general business news and company information.
NewsEyeQ	The result of a joint venture between US-based Data Times and News International. Recently launched, provides news information, market quotes and research information from 6000 sources, many US based.
Questel-Orbit	Scientific and technical service owned by France Telecom. Specialises in patent, trademark, scientific, technical and chemical information.
Reuters Business Briefing	2000 sources of news and research information. Real-time, with 5-year archive, soon to increase to 10 years. Also offers access to Reuters' photos.
STN International	An international joint venture between Fiz Karlsruhe, US-based Chemical Abstracts Service and the Japanese Information Centre of Science and Technology. Specialises in patent, trademark, scientific, technical and chemical information. Also industry-specific data.

Source: Adapted from *Sunday Business ComputerAge* (14 July 1996).

■ The Internet

The Internet (which we will examine in detail in Chapter 8) is also becoming a growing source of marketing research information. It is a free service, other than the cost of the telephone call, and can provide researchers with some very good market information. However, for most marketing research situations, a commercial on-line service is likely to provide faster and better results. The *Wall Street Journal* and commercial on-line services such as MAID are already available over the Internet, at a cost. Eventually, the Internet is likely to become the medium of choice for accessing the many commercial on-line services that are currently available.

■ CD-ROM

CD-ROM has become a very popular medium for disseminating today's commercial market research. Many of the major market research companies that had moved into the on-line arena have now reversed this decision and are now launching their own CD-ROM-based information services. Companies such as Minitel, Euromonitor, KeyNote and Datamonitor are all seeking new audiences through this medium rather than relying on a third-party on-line service provider to act as the distribution channel for their market research.[12]

One major difference between CD-ROM and on-line versions is the pricing mechanism used to charge for access to the research. On-line services typically charge users for the time they spend connected to the service: the longer the user browses through the on-line service, the higher the charge. CD-ROM, on the other hand, has no such additional charges and is therefore likely to be more attractive to individuals and librarians where overspending a limited budget can be a major issue. Another feature that market research companies have been attempting to achieve from their CD-ROM versions of their reports is a 'look and feel' which are user friendly and more appealing to customers. Exhibit 3.4 describes how market research company KeyNote has achieved this with its latest CD-ROM offering.

Exhibit 3.4

THE CD-ROM AS A LIBRARY SHELF

Users of KeyNote's revamped market research CD-ROM may notice a fresher, slicker look. This is because it has teamed up with Microsoft to incorporate the same interface as Microsoft's 'Encarta' encyclopaedia. The result will satisfy both professional and casual users. According to General manager Joakim Arnborger, KeyNote has tried to recreate a typical manual search process for a book on a library shelf. 'You would browse through an industry section, find a title, open the book, look through the chapter contents and eventually end up at the document or a particular product. The CD-ROM's navigation process is very similar.'

The opening screen of the CD-ROM, which contains over 250 reports on UK industries, previously plunged straight into a search menu. Now it has several features including an option to explore the titles, a tour for newcomers and finally the search function.

Adapted from: Gibson (1996).[13]

■ Virtual reality

While the last 20 years have seen significant technological advances in most areas, many marketing research techniques are becoming outdated. However, one technology which offers a great deal of potential is virtual reality, which can be used to answer marketing questions[14] such as the following:

- *What is the likely customer reaction to a new retail concept?* A virtual environment can be used to compare consumers' reactions to different prices for the same product, when positioned in the same virtual store and virtual shelf as competitors' products. It can gauge the premium value of products in such situations.
- *Do we offer a sufficient variety of products?* Virtual reality can assess the demand for different types of products and investigate patterns of loyalty and substitution if, for example, one product is out of stock.
- *How should products be displayed?* A virtual store can be used to test market, in an 'almost real' environment, a wide variety of display formats. Retailers can find out if it is better to group their products by brand, by user, by ingredient or by some other combination.

CONCLUSION

The amount and complexity of marketing information have increased dramatically in the last 20 years and this fact alone is driving the need for greater computer support in its collection and analysis. Marketing information systems (MkIS) combine various computer-based and non-computer-based systems in any organisation that can be used to provide this support. These systems are often also used by managers in other functions. Production-control systems are not designed specifically for use by marketing managers, but nonetheless provide useful marketing information. There are many sub-systems under the broad heading of MkIS which allow the marketing manager to collect data, perform data analysis, conduct forecasting and budgeting, carry out market planning and generate reports.

In general, marketing information comes from four sources: internal records, marketing intelligence, marketing decision-support systems and marketing research. Marketing research is an area in which information technology has a major role to play, particularly in the collection and analysis of marketing information. In addition to the traditional sources of marketing research information such as IRI and AC Nielsen, many on-line information services are now available to the marketing manager.

ASSIGNMENT QUESTIONS

1 Who are the main users of marketing information and how do their needs differ?

2 What are the main sources of marketing information?

3 How would you go about creating an MkIS for an organisation of your choice?

4 Detail some of the ways in which IT can aid marketing research.

References

1 Marshall, K.P. and LaMotte, S.W. (1992). 'Marketing Information Systems: a marriage of systems analysis and marketing management', *Journal of Applied Business Research*, Vol. 8, No. 3, Summer.

2 Crittenden, V.L., Gardiner, L.R. and Stam, A. (1993). 'Reducing conflict between marketing and manufacturing', *Industrial Marketing Management,* Vol. 22, pp. 299–309.

3 Ferreira, J. and Treacy, M.E. (1988). 'It's more than just laptops', *Datamation*, 1 November.

4 Talvinen, J.M. and Saarinen, T. (1995). 'MkIS support for the marketing management process: perceived improvements for marketing management', *Marketing Intelligence and Planning*, Vol. 13, No. 1.

5 Kotler, P. (1994). *Marketing Management: Analysis, Planning, Implementation and Control*. 8th edn, New Jersey: Prentice-Hall.

6 Marshall, K.P. and LaMotte, S.W. (1992). Op. cit.

7 Higgins, L.F., McIntyre, S.C. and Raine, C.G. (1991). 'Design of global marketing information systems', *Journal of Business and Industrial Marketing*, Vol. 6, No. 3–4, Summer/Fall.

8 Daniels, N.C. (1993). *Information Technology: The Management Challenge.* Wokingham: Addison-Wesley.

9 The Economist (1992). 'Terminator 9', *The Economist*, 4 July.

10 The Economist (1995). 'Data wars', *The Economist*, 22 July.

11 Poynder, R. (1996). 'Searching questions', *Sunday Business ComputerAge*, 14 July.

12 IWR (1996). 'Market research firms bypass online', *Information World Review*, July/August.

13 Gibson, P. (1996). 'New-look KeyNote disc aims for broader appeal', *Information World Review*, July/August.

14 Burke, R.B. (1996). 'Virtual shopping: breakthrough in marketing research', *Harvard Business Review*, March–April.

4

CUSTOMER INFORMATION AND CUSTOMER DATABASES

- Customer segmentation
- The role of geographic information systems (GIS)
- The central role of the customer database
- Developing the customer database
- Data protection issues

OBJECTIVES

After studying this chapter, you will be able to:

- Describe the importance of different approaches to segmentation strategies
- Discuss the different categories of geographic information systems (GIS)
- Understand how customer information is gathered, managed and used
- Explain how customer databases are developed
- Discuss the impact of data-protection legislation

CUSTOMER SEGMENTATION

The importance of customer segmentation

Very few organisations have either the marketing resources or the product range to compete across all market segments. One solution is to break the markets into identifiable groups in a process known as market segmentation or customer segmentation. Segmentation involves identifying sizeable groups of customers with similar buying needs and characteristics. By identifying and understanding the major segments in any market, organisations can develop more appropriate product and service offerings targeted at particular groups. All decisions on the marketing mix are then made with the specific customer segment in mind, in contrast to a mass-marketing approach where all customers are treated in a similar fashion. A good segmentation approach should fit the four key requirements of being measurable, accessible, substantial and actionable:

- *Measurable*. Different customers have different lifestyles, attitudes and personalities.

However, until recently, there was little value in segmenting customers along these psychographic lines as there was no clear means of measuring the psychographic profiles of large numbers of customers. As we will see below, this has changed in recent years and psychographic profiles have become a popular, measurable means of segmenting customers.

■ *Accessible*. Even if the customers' attributes are measurable, the marketing manager must be capable of gaining access to the necessary customer information to enable a proper segmentation to be carried out. Without access to this information, the segmentation approach is little more than a theoretical exercise.

■ *Substantial*. A customer segment may be measurable and accessible but the segment must still contain sufficient numbers of customers to justify any major marketing expenditure. This requirement has become less of an issue in recent years as 'micromarketing' approaches, usually supported by information technology, have enabled companies to tailor marketing messages more effectively to smaller groups of consumers.

■ *Actionable*. The final characteristic of a good segmentation approach relates to the marketing manager's ability to turn the segmentation into a programme of action that yields significant business benefits. This typically means contacting specific customer groups through mail, telephone, television or other means, or using the information to reposition particular products so that they become more attractive to particular customer segments (*see* Exhibit 4.1).

Exhibit 4.1

HAVING A GO AT CUSTOMER SEGMENTATION

For many years, ICI Fertilisers (South Africa) had exhibited at a major event in the Transvaal. The exhibition was attended by farmers from all over South Africa and supported by most of the multinationals interested in the agricultural market sector. ICI felt that it had to attend as all its main competitors would be there and so, their hospitality tent was duly stocked with the necessary quantity and quality of lager for its Afrikaner clients. The utmost care was taken to ensure its tent was the last stop for its thirsty guests at the end of the day.

However, ICI questioned the return it was getting from the exhibition and eventually decided to modify its approach. The next year, it organised the erection of a rifle range and hired a number of sub-machine guns; not surprisingly, the opportunity to use these guns was irresistible to the Afrikaners who flocked to the ICI tent to 'have a go'. However, before they were allowed a turn, each farmer had to complete a detailed survey on their farm, their fertiliser usage, their spending habits, product perceptions etc. From this vital information, ICI was able to identify that a number of previously unrecognisable segments existed in what had been thought of as a price-driven commodity market. Subsequently, this information helped ICI to reposition a number of its existing products and to introduce some new ones with the result that it was able to achieve a 23% increase in market share.

Source: Customer Management Solutions (1996).[1]

■ Segmenting customers based on usage

One of the most popular traditional approaches is to segment customers based on their usage of particular products. Bradley (1995)[2] describes the selection of important customer segments through the analysis of the following product dimensions:

- usage of the product or service by particular categories of customers
- frequency of use – heavy, moderate and light users
- brand use and brand share
- product attitudes.

Bradley states that segmentation of markets based on usage is very popular and that many markets can be segmented into non-users, previous users, potential users, first-time users and regular users of a product or service. Most companies will attempt to convert potential users into users, and users into frequent users. Frequent users tend to be the most profitable category of customers and deserve to be treated accordingly. We will return to this theme in the next chapter when we discuss the concept of lifetime profitability of customers and relationship marketing.

■ Segmenting customers based on geo-demographics

Another traditional approach is to segment customers into distinct groups based on *geographic*, *demographic* and *socio-economic* information (*see* Table 4.1). The term *geo-demographic* is often used to describe the type of segmentation that is carried out using these three traditional segmentation variables.

Table 4.1 Traditional segmentation variables

Key geographic variables	Key demographic variables	Key socio-economic groupings
• Country • Region • Population density (urban, rural etc.) • Administrative area • Postal code • Climate	• Age • Education • Family • Income • Occupation • Religion • Sex	A (professional/senior managerial) B (middle managers/executives) C1 (junior managers/non-manual) C2 (skilled manual) D (semi-skilled/unskilled manual) E (unemployed/state dependent)

In the past two decades, information technology has been harnessed very effectively to provide marketers with considerable geo-demographic information about their customers. Indeed, the combination of IT and the availability of geo-demographic data based on national census information has fuelled the tremendous growth in database marketing and direct marketing. For example, the ACORN geo-demographic classification tool from the information services company CACI uses a wide range of data from the 1991 UK Census and sophisticated statistical techniques to classify all inhabitants across the UK into 54 distinct types. The 54 types aggregate up to 17 groups and six major categories (*see* Table 4.2). A separate categorisation divides Scottish consumers into 43 types which aggregate into eight different groups. These ACORN classifications provide a matrix of consumer characteristics which is comprehensive enough to define the potential for many marketing and planning operations.

Geo-demographic segmentation based on census data provides an aggregate picture of the characteristics of people living in a particular district. The smallest grouping used in such segmentation is an 'enumeration district' (ED), which contains approximately 200 households. Indeed, the term ACORN provides a good indication of how the segmentation works – it stands for 'a classification of residential neighbourhoods'. Classification systems such as ACORN are based on the premise that individuals are more similar to their neighbours than they are to people living several streets away. ACORN is not the only classification available to marketers. CCN's Mosaic system (*see* Exhibit 4.7 later in this chapter) provides a similar approach.

Table 4.2 UK ACORN categories and groups

ACORN categories		ACORN groups	Approximate socio-economic equivalent
A	Thriving	1. Wealthy achievers, suburban areas	ABC1
		2. Affluent greys, rural communities	ABC2D
		3. Prosperous pensioners, retirement areas	ABC1
B	Expanding	4. Affluent executives, family areas	ABC1
		5. Well-off workers, family areas	ABC1C2
C	Rising	6. Affluent urbanites, town and city areas	ABC1
		7. Prosperous professionals, metropolitan areas	ABC1
		8. Better-off executives, inner-city areas	ABC1
D	Settling	9. Comfortable middle-agers, mature home-owning areas	ABC1
		10. Skilled workers, home-owning areas	C1C2DE
E	Aspiring	11. New home-owners, mature communities	C2DE
		12. White-collar workers, better-off multi-ethnic areas	C1
F	Striving	13. Older people, less prosperous areas	C2DE
		14. Council estate residents, better-off homes	C2DE
		15. Council estate residents, high unemployment	C2DE
		16. Council estate residents, greatest hardship	DE
		17. People in multi-ethnic, low-income areas	DE

Source: CACI (1996). Copyright CACI Limited, 1997. All rights reserved.

Companies can also use classification systems such as ACORN and Mosaic to profile their own customers into distinct segments. From a given list of names and addresses (from the company's own customer database, for example), information services organisations like CACI and CCN can identify the major segments or profiles within the database which will enhance the company's ability to target and cross-sell to customers (*see* Exhibit 4.2).

Exhibit 4.2

SCOTTISH BLOOD

Among the non-corporate users of geographically based marketing information supplied by specialised software groups is the Scottish National Blood Transfusion Service which wanted to increase its number of doners. Using software and data supplied by CACI, it targeted groups of people living in Scotland judged to have the greatest 'propensity to give blood' – which boiled down to one fairly affluent group in professional or managerial jobs and with relatively high educational qualifications, and another less well-off groups of people who are public spirited in attitude, live close to the centres of towns and cities and who are fairly likely to live alone.

Source: Financial Times (24 May 1996).[3]

■ New approaches to customer segmentation

Even with the availability of good geo-demographic information, the marketing manager still faces the problem that two customers in the same segment (or even two people who live next door to each other) are likely to have different tastes, attitudes and purchasing behaviour. In addition, reliance on data from a national census which is carried out once every 10 years has been seen as a drawback to the traditional geo-demographic segmentation approach.[4] More importantly, geo-demographic segmentation based on census data provides an aggregate picture of the characteristics of people living in a particular district, rather than on the individual. As one industry expert points out:[5]

> 'The simple geo-demographic code is like the common currency of prediction. It is useful but to drive modelled solutions, it is individual data that provides the power.'

Traditional geo-demographic approaches can be described as macro-segmentation. The individual data described above comes from micro-segmentation approaches based on behaviour and psychographic characteristics (*see* Table 4.3).

Table 4.3   New segmentation variables

Key behavioural variables	Key psychographic variables
• Usage rate • Loyalty • Purchasing patterns	• Lifestyle • Attitude • Personality

Advances in information technology have enabled marketers to gather data on customer *behaviour* such as product usage and purchasing patterns to determine the most appropriate marketing mix for a product. The increasing use of electronic point-of-sale (EPoS) information is providing companies with detailed information by individual customer (*see* Exhibit 4.3).

Exhibit 4.3

SCANNING THE MARKET

Market research is the traditional method of collecting data on the market. While market research in the form of surveys continues to be used, factual data on purchasing behaviour is now being sourced, far more accurately, via new methods. For example, rather than asking a sample of consumers what they have bought, electronic point of sale (EPoS) data can be downloaded daily, throughout the country, to give accurate and up-to-date information on actual purchases. Furthermore, research technology has been developed to track the behaviour of individual customers, allowing them to be profiled in terms of their demographics, lifestyle and media habits. For example, consumer panel research using set meters, people meters and home barcode readers can digitally record household media and buying habits in more detail than could the old-style set meters and panel diaries. Thus, new technology has improved the accuracy and ease of collecting more personalised consumer information.

Source: Evans *et al.* (1995).[6]

Although still not as widely available as socio-economic data, the amount of *lifestyle* data being gathered and used has increased dramatically in recent years. Since lifestyle targeting took off in the mid-1980s, three companies have dominated the UK market: CMT, NDL and ICD. CMT's Behaviourbank and NDL's Facts of Living Survey were based on questionnaires which were completed by millions of consumers in return for special-offer coupons. Other organisations that have subsequently entered the lifestyle market include CSL, CCN and the Daily Telegraph. CSL only started operation in 1995 but built up a file of 3 million names in less than a year. Lifestyle segmentation often requires the amalgamation of data from a variety of different sources. For example, CCN has formed an alliance with the publishing company Emap which has 10 million customers from whom it hopes to build up a lifestyle database.

In the customer information industry, the arrival of these new methods of segmenting customers sparked a fierce 'geo-demographic versus lifestyle' debate; but as we see from Exhibit 4.4, both proponents now accept that the combination of both approaches

Exhibit 4.4

GEO-DEMOGRAPHERS VERSUS LIFESTYLERS

Geo-demographics takes a probabilistic approach to the problem of separating consumers into distinct categories and locations. It starts from the top, using Government Census information, and works down – 'birds of a feather flock together' is its premise. Lifestyle data, by contrast, starts from the bottom – questionnaires filled out by individual consumers listing their interests – and works up.

There has been much debate about the respective roles of geo-demographics and lifestyle targeting. Many proponents of lifestyle – which has only been around since the mid-80s – saw it conquering the old rival. But both groups now seem to accept that a fusion of the two techniques is the realistic way forward.

Source: Marketing (12 November 1992).[7]

offers a more complete solution than either approach on its own. For example, CACI's Lifestyle Plus targeting system is one of a number of systems that combines the individual detail of lifestyle data with the solid foundation of census information and the statistical reliability of market research to give more targeted marketing solutions.

Most of the geo-demographic and lifestyle information is gathered on a national level and multinational companies will not find it easy to collate and analyse customer data across national boundaries. We are not likely to see a coordinated approach to conducting a census across the EU in the immediate future.[8] However, some steps have been taken to adopt a more international approach to the subject of customer data. For example, CCN has divided the population of Europe into 10 generic categories, each with broadly similar lifestyle profiles: affluent apartment dwellers in Madrid and Heidelberg share the same health-conscious and adventurous characteristics, while those who live in old industrial communities, from Belgian coalfields to Spanish steelworks, prefer low-price and heavily branded products.[9]

The increased availability of detailed information on individual customers has fuelled the move towards a more targeted, direct approach to marketing. In the following pages, we will examine the use and management of customer information for marketing purposes. In Chapter 5, we will investigate how this customer information can be used to target existing and prospective customers in a process known as database marketing.

THE ROLE OF GEOGRAPHIC INFORMATION SYSTEMS (GIS)

■ What are geographic information systems?

Geographic information systems (GIS) are relatively new technology applications that enable marketing managers to access and manipulate map information in electronic format at their desk. GIS can be defined in broad terms as: 'computer systems which store, retrieve, display and manipulate geographically based information'.

The main characteristic which distinguishes GIS from other systems is the ability to point and click on a particular area and obtain a range of information which has been assembled for that particular geographic feature. GIS data consists of background

---

Exhibit 4.5

WHO SUPPLIES GIS?

Established suppliers of GIS to the public sector such as ESRI with their ARC/INFO product, Intergraph with MGE, and Tydac Technologies with SPANS all worked to develop applications for their systems in the private sector. Later entrants into the GIS market, some of which (CACI with InSite, CCN with Mosaic Systems, Pinpoint Analysis with GEOPIN) come from the marketing information industry. Others (MapInfo with the MapInfo product, Tactics with Tactician, and Geomatrix with Prospex) are adding creativity to the development of GIS applications for direct marketing.

Source: Stores (January 1993).[10]

information on roads, building outlines, branch networks and sales territories, as well as other business data of a geographic nature in which an organisation is interested. GIS enable companies to map their own customer information with other geo-demographic information down to the individual household level. Systems are available (*see* Exhibit 4.5 on page 61), each using its own combination of data sources including the electoral roll, census data, media boundaries, retail locations and market research data.

■ Marketing applications of GIS

GIS have a variety of marketing uses. Traditionally, the primary users of GIS technology were governments, which still account for more than half of the GIS market. Other industries that are showing increased interest in using GIS include the banking, insurance, publishing, utilities and retail industries.[11, 12] For example, Levi Strauss uses GIS to analyse sales and shipments by area and to make predictions on future sales, market potential and customer trends. The supermarket chain Tesco uses it for analysing changes in population, income and road and rail locations, so that it can plan the locations of its large stores more effectively; and Woolworth's also has a system for analysing local demand (*see* Exhibit 4.6).

Exhibit 4.6

GAINING LOCAL INSIGHTS

Kingfisher chain Woolworth's uses a genuine GIS for market analysis. Using CACI's InSite system, the company recently segmented its portfolio of 779 stores into 'city centre', 'heartland', and 'local' stores, each group with a different fascia. According to Chris Garthwaite, stores marketing manager for Woolworth's, the system 'is a very effective tool in understanding our local market, enabling us to respond to opportunities within key areas. It has been especially useful in understanding and responding to competitors' activity'. Since adopting the InSite system in 1987, Woolworth's has steadily built up the functions and data it uses. Local population characteristics and estimated expenditure have been aggregated to store catchment level using a shopping centre gravity model supplied by The Retail Dimension, and distance and drive-time from CACI. Counts on workers within two kilometres of each store from the 1991 census have been added to give an insight into day-time demand and the potential for lunchtime 'stepping out' products. Competitor data on 140,000 multiple retail branches is included, giving fascia name, holding company details, principal category of operation, in or out-of-town location, nearest shopping centre and distance, and whether it is an anchor store or not. In addition to evaluating new store opportunities and targeting local promotions, Garthwaite says that the chain can analyse how many Kingfisher stores face competition for music and video sales, for example.

Source: Marketing Week (17 May 1996).[13]

In conjunction with geo-demographic and psychographic information, GIS can help companies target their marketing efforts more effectively. For example, they can graphically illustrate that, on average, people in Merseyside spend one-fifth more on toys, prams and other children's products than do those elsewhere in the UK. Similarly, they can show that people in Surrey are 20 per cent less likely to visit pubs regularly and only half as likely to visit wine bars as the average British citizen.[14] Another example of the use of GIS for direct marketing is shown in Exhibit 4.7.

Exhibit 4.7

DOOR-TO-DOOR DISTRIBUTORS

One big user of geographically based software is Circular Distributors, a privately-owned UK company that claims to be the leader in Britain in delivering advertising leaflets and free samples door to door. The company, based in Maidenhead, Berkshire, delivers 1 billion items of this sort each year, a fifth of the UK total. It claims to deliver, using an army of mainly part-time workers, to 19.5 million out of the UK's 22 million households. It works on behalf of a range of customers including big store chains such as Boots, Wickes and Ikea, as well as small enterprises which think leafleting will improve their custom among people living close by.

'We would not be able to operate as we do without software that enables us to target particular consumer groups according to where they live and the kind of lifestyles they have,' says Charles Nielson, the company's planning director. In Circular Distributors' case, it uses software supplied by CCN called Mosaic that splits UK residents into a number of consumer types, categorised by income levels, addresses (grouped into post-code areas) and tastes as indicated by use of certain products and services. The data on these people have been built up by CCN using a range of sources including census details and marketing information supplied by other consumer companies with which it has business contacts.

Using this type of data from CCN, and split up into much smaller areas, Circular Distributors can decide on which areas of Britain, comprising around 700 or so households, are most likely to be receptive to specific promotional offers or adverts that one of its own customers wants pushed through people's letterboxes on a targeted basis.

Source: Financial Times (24 May 1996).[14]

The main marketing uses of GIS include:[15, 16]

- determining the catchment areas for branch or store locations
- coordinating with other advertising media such as regional television or newspaper coverage
- determining the dynamics of a direct marketing campaign within a catchment area
- planning distribution routes
- tracking competitor activity
- managing salesforce performance and utilisation.

The research company Gartner Group believes that this last category, salesforce management and effective utilisation of the sales team, is one area where GIS have considerable potential but where the technology is being underutilised.[17] In Exhibit 4.8, Gartner Group describes three types of situation where GIS are particularly useful.

Exhibit 4.8

Exhibit 4.8

BALANCING THE WORKLOAD

Clients who are likely to find benefits in geographic information systems (GIS) for territory balancing tend to fall into one or more of the following groupings:

1. *fast growth industries, geographic in orientation*. These sorts of firms find that they are more than just salespeople, and they have the freedom to enter or exit territories as needed (e.g. this would not apply to a deregulated public utility). The ability to rapidly analyse sales potential and re-deploy salespeople to the highest potential sales, levelling the load across them, enables these firms to be more successful.

2. *high turnover of sales staff*. Territory balancing is critical when the composition of the sales staff is dynamic and often changing. GIS is effective because it enables more rapid re-deployment of remaining and new staff. This re-deployment is based on historic sales prospecting data as well as actual performance.

3. *personal relationships are not critical*. Sales is a lot about personal relationships, but GIS and territory balancing is more effective when the personal side of the deal is not such a large component.

Source: Gartner Group (May 1996).

■ Different categories of GIS

There are three major categories of GIS:[18]

- *True GIS*. These are sophisticated databases that aggregate, analyse and interpret data based on geography rather than traditional database metrics. They are used for solving complex planning and management problems. Major providers of true GIS include ESRI and Intergraph. Tactician is another vendor which provides a GIS aimed specifically at marketing applications.

- *Mapping systems*. Mapping systems are less sophisticated but still display information graphically, usually with standardised maps. Major providers of mapping systems include MapInfo and Strategic Mapping.

- *Presentation graphics systems*. These systems display data geographically but are relatively unsophisticated in comparison to the other two categories of GIS.

■ Availability of geographic information

The availability of good-quality geographically-based data is a pre-requisite for a good GIS. The quality and availability of such data differ from country to country and Table 4.4 provides a snapshot by country and region.

Table 4.4   Quality of GIS data by world region

Quality of GIS data	World region
Excellent	• US • Canada • England • France • Holland • Germany
Good	• Rest of Western Europe • Japan
Average	• Mexico • Isolated major cities in South America, Asia, Africa and Australia
Poor	• Most of South America, Africa and Asia • Rural Australia

Source: Gartner Group (1995).

THE CENTRAL ROLE OF THE CUSTOMER DATABASE

■ Customer databases

The most valuable information in a truly customer-focused organisation is its intimate knowledge of the customer base. As Peters (1987)[19] states:

> 'A market has never bought things. Customers buy things. That's why database marketing's ability to target the individual customer in the crowded marketplace is so valuable.'

There are typically two generic uses of customer information: *operational* uses and *analytical* uses (a distinction mentioned in Chapter 2). By *operational*, we mean the day-to-day support of the business. Examples include:

■ a customer service representative of an electricity company requires speedy access to a customer's account details in order to answer telephone queries

■ a bank teller needs to access a customer's current balance in order to decide whether or not to make a cash advance

■ a hotel receptionist needs to key in a customer's name to find out which room the customer has been booked into.

By *analytical*, we mean the analysis of historic and transaction data in order to create or adjust a particular product offering or promotion. For example:

■ the selection by an electricity company of the most appropriate customers for a mailshot in order to promote and sell home heating appliances

■ the profitability analysis of a bank's customers

■ the analysis by a hotel manager of the home addresses of customers to measure the effectiveness of a particular advertising campaign.

The distinction is an important one, as we will see in the following pages when we discuss the design and development of customer databases. It is not that long ago that the majority of information on customers was stored on paper files. In some companies this is still the case, but the days of filing cabinets crammed with customer records are fast disappearing. Typically, the modern company now has its customer data stored in one or more databases which are used for a variety of purposes. Figure 4.1 illustrates the central role of the customer database.

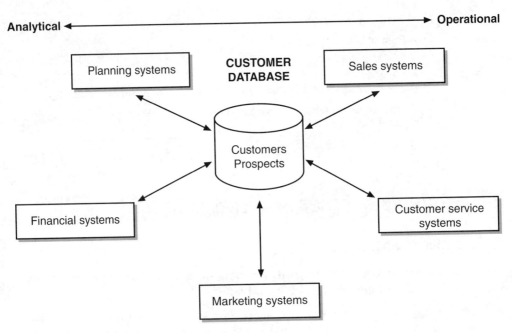

Fig 4.1   The central role of the customer database

There are a few points to note about Figure 4.1. First, a single customer database is depicted as supporting a variety of operational and analytical systems. The information in the customer database is often downloaded into separate information systems which are designed specifically for analytic purposes such as data mining (*see* Chapter 2). Note also that the customer database may contain information on potential, as well as existing, customers. The benefits that can be gained from investing in building a database of existing customers is illustrated by the example of Samsonite (*see* Exhibit 4.9).

A CONVINCING CASE FOR A CUSTOMER DATABASE

Samsonite Corp. is looking to expand its use of database marketing next year after improving its sales and return-on-investment through its use. In 1994, Samsonite sales grew 10 to 15 percent. The company began building its customer database to better understand why customers bought Samsonite luggage, which is frequently more expensive than other luggage. The company has used the database primarily to build customer profiles which include information such as age, income, gender, colour preferences, education, credit card usage, occupation, hobbies, favourite features of a particular product, and likelihood of purchasing another Samsonite product in the next year. Using these profiles, Samsonite convinces retailers that there are enough prospects living in the neighbourhood to justify carrying certain Samsonite products.

Samsonite has about 1.5 million customers on its database, which it began building in early 1991. The company's goal is to expand the database by 300,000 names a year through its retail sales. The programme is based on the product-registration cards customers return after they purchase a piece of Samsonite luggage.

Source: DM News (16 October 1995).

Customer databases also provide a means to capture, analyse and use information to determine customer profitability. By analysing the characteristics of long-term profitable customers, new sources of profitable business can be identified and unprofitable segments can be avoided (*see* Exhibit 4.10). Even the ability to identify the top 10 per cent of customers in terms of profitability can be a major benefit to organisations.[20]

Exhibit 4.10

WHISKY DRINKERS

Contrast the person who buys a bottle of whisky – no matter the brand – once a year, with a brand-loyal regular drinker. Both names might appear on the same database and may be sent the same direct mail. Eventually the cost of communicating with the first customer will outweigh the revenue they contribute to the company. The money it is costing you to maintain a fruitless relationship with that person would be better spent generating more revenue from the loyal one. Most companies faced with this situation would have the sense to cease communicating with the non-profitable customer. For some it is not that simple – profitable or not, they remain stuck in the relationship.

Source: Precision Marketing (5 February 1996).

The issue of which customer names to include on the database is an interesting one. The drinks company Seagram, for example, has a worldwide database policy which restricts customer information on the database to that which is both recent and relevant. Names will not get onto the database in the first place unless they pass certain criteria. Similarly, if customers stay on the database for too long without responding to any offers, they are removed.[21]

■ Sources of customer information

Customer information can be sourced from within the company or purchased from external sources (*see* Table 4.5).

Table 4.5 Internal and external sources of customer data

Internal sources of data	External sources of data
Accounts/general ledger	Census data
Customer application forms	External lists of particular types of customers
Customer complaints	Market research (specially commissioned)
Customer enquiries	Records from sister companies
Customer information files	
Market research (existing)	
Merchandising statistics	
Promotional campaigns	
Service reports	
Warranty cards	

The most useful sources of customer information are often the internal systems within an organisation. Additional external information and lists can be sourced from list operators such as those in Table 4.6.

Table 4.6 Top 10 UK-based database marketing list operators

	Company	Volume of names traded	Number of lists owned or exclusively managed	Date of establishment
1	Mardev/Ibis	103 million	200 +	1971
2	Dudley Jenkins List Broking	100 million	140	1970
3	NDL International	87 million	3	1985
4	HLB	85 million	38	1986
5	Cheryl Nathan List Broking	75 million	43	1985
6	CDMS Marketing Services	50 million+	3	1985
7	CCN Marketing	40 million	4	1980
8	Independent Direct Marketing	30 million	39	1990
9	DunsMarketing	24 million	3	1974
10	The Mail Marketing Group	17 million	37	circa 1950

Note: Data not available from CACI, one of the largest and longest established companies in the business.

Source: Precision Marketing (10 April 1995).[22]

DEVELOPING THE CUSTOMER DATABASE

■ Steps in developing a customer database

There are seven steps that should be followed in designing a customer database. As Figure 4.2 shows, the first six steps need to occur only once while the final step, maintaining the database, is an ongoing activity.

Step 1. Define the database functions

The first question that any company must ask when deciding to design or build a customer database is: 'What functions do I want this database to perform?' This may seem

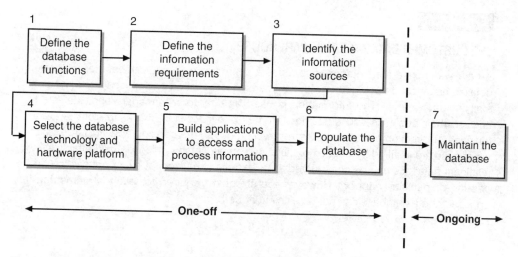

Fig 4.2   Seven steps in developing a customer database

obvious, but it is fundamental to the success of any customer database initiative. The design of the customer database, and the ways in which data is held on it, will differ depending on whether the database is to be used primarily for operational or analytical purposes.[23]

Operational applications have different demands on the customer database, such as quick response time and easy access to transactional or account data. If an electricity company is to provide good customer service, the customer service representative (CSR) who takes the call from the customer needs to be able to access that customer's latest account details within a matter of seconds, just by keying in the customer's name or address.

There are some technical reasons for this not being as easy as it sounds. Many operational systems are still indexed on the customer's account number, rather than name or address. This means that if the customer does not know the account number when calling, the CSR may not be able to access the correct customer record on the system.

The same customer information system that is needed for such a customer service function is probably also used to send out the monthly or quarterly bills, but it may be of limited (or no) use when it comes to analysing trends, selecting particular groups of business customers for a mailshot or for analysing electricity consumption across different geographic areas. For marketing analysis, a much wider set of data will be required and that data needs to be organised in a different fashion. Speed of access to individual items of information is probably less important to the marketer, but significant processing power to crunch through millions of calculations per second may be critical (see Exhibit 4.11).

Many organisations fail to appreciate that the design and organisation of a customer database are critically dependent on the use to which the database is put. The IT people in many organisations tend to focus on the operational aspects of systems, which can, unfortunately, lead to the design and development of marketing systems which fail to meet the expectations of the marketing and sales staff.

Exhibit 4.11

THE CUSTOMER DATABASE IS A WAREHOUSE

A data warehouse architecture consists of a separate relational database of integrated detailed historical data, together with summarised information customised into a series of smaller 'data-marts'. The information is used by directors, managers and analysts to analyse their business and customers to make key decisions, ranging from strategic changes of direction to micro-marketing to customers. The considerable costs of a data warehouse are justified by the competitive advantage which it brings if used effectively. A relational database can be constructed to be extremely efficient at either transaction processing or decision support. However, the structure required for each is diametrically opposed and a database can not be efficient at both.

Source: Financial Times (3 April 1996).[24]

Step 2. Define the information requirements

There are two approaches that can be taken to defining the information required. The first is to recognise that only a small amount of the customer information captured will actually be used to make marketing decisions and focus effort on identifying and capturing this key information. The second approach is to capture as much information as possible and then start looking for trends within the data. This is the data-mining approach, where an organisation creates a large data warehouse which marketing analysts use to identify meaningful trends. In trying to determine which approach to take, the following questions should be asked:

■ *Have we prioritised the information required?* Regardless of which approach is taken, there will be key pieces of information which the marketing manager must have. At a minimum, a bank must have data on customer address, age, profession and income. Other information on nationality, language spoken and personal hobbies may be useful, but will be of secondary importance to the core information.

■ *Is the information consistent with our marketing segmentation strategy?* As organisations become more sophisticated in targeting specific market segments, it becomes more important to capture data to support these segmentation strategies. Airlines broadly segment their customers into business travellers or leisure travellers. Business travellers are less price sensitive and value the flexibility to change flight times at very short notice, whereas leisure travellers are usually more price conscious and do not require the same flexibility. It is important that an airline's reservation system can capture the reason people are travelling in order further to refine the segmentation strategies and the marketing mix used to target segments.

■ *How easily can the information be updated?* If data changes regularly and cannot be easily updated, it may not be worth the cost of obtaining it.

■ *What are the costs and benefits associated with gathering information?* For organisations such as supermarkets, the initial investment in setting up and implementing an electronic point of sale (EPoS) system is usually very high but, once it is in place, it can provide large amounts of information at relatively low incremental cost.

■ *Should the database include prospective customers?* As we discussed earlier, marketing managers must decide whether to limit the number of customers on the database to all (or a subset of) existing customers or whether to extend the database to include information on prospective and target customers.

Step 3. Identify the information sources

Having defined the information required, the next step is to identify how the information will be acquired and updated on an ongoing basis. Customer information can be sourced from within the organisation or from third parties. While the purchase of mailing lists is still a popular method of finding potential new customers, the effectiveness of using such lists for direct marketing can be poor. Unless carefully targeted, response rates can be low and the cost of generating a sale can be higher than traditional methods of advertising. Therefore, the most commonly used sources of customer data are normally internal.

Step 4. Select the database technology and hardware platform

There are several different ways in which data can be held in a database. The choice of database technology and database management system depends on the uses that are intended for the database. We will not explore the technical issues in detail in this book, other than to mention that a relational database is likely to be the preferred solution for the vast majority of applications.[25] The main advantages of relational databases are faster processing speeds and the flexibility to create more complex queries to determine relationships between data. The selection of a hardware platform will depend on a number of factors, including the existing hardware, the size of the database and the number and location of potential users.

Step 5. Build applications to access and process information

Once the technology has been selected, the applications to utilise the information held on the customer database can be built. We will examine database marketing applications in more detail in the next chapter.

Step 6. Populate the database

The task of populating a customer database is a major exercise and poor-quality customer data is the primary reason for most database marketing failures. Much of the required information on existing customers is already held in paper or electronic format within the organisation. However, a major problem is the number of different locations where such customer information can be found.

In many organisations, such as banks and insurance companies, the computer systems that hold the data are organised on a product, rather than a customer, basis. In other words, if Joe Bloggs has a current account, a savings account, a credit card and a pension with the same financial institution, it is entirely feasible that his details are held on four different databases. When data is centralised onto one database, it is likely that four separate entries will be made for Joe Bloggs. When a mailshot is planned, it is also entirely possible for Joe Bloggs to receive four separate pieces of direct mail. Apart from the cost of unnecessary paper and postage, Joe Bloggs will not be left with a very favourable impression of the company.

Software can be purchased to assist in the 'de-duplication' or 'auto-merging' of customer records so that there is only one record for each customer on the database. However, such software is not foolproof. In some instances there is no alternative to contacting large numbers of customers to obtain or confirm their details. Several creative techniques can be employed to persuade the customer to divulge such personal information. One such technique is to enrol them in a free prize draw or to provide them with a discount when they next purchase the company's products. Whichever approach is used, the exercise of populating the database will take time, require considerable resources and will not always achieve 100 per cent of the desired information.

Step 7. Maintain the database

Once marketing managers are satisfied with the quality of the information in the database, an ongoing maintenance activity is required to keep it up to date, otherwise its effectiveness as a marketing tool diminishes quickly. As Curtis (1996)[21] states:

> 'the database is a living breathing thing that requires constant attention – you can't just build it and say "that's it".'

This maintenance activity is a major task. Births, deaths, marriages and changes of address can alter between 8 and 12 per cent of the information in a database in any one year. In the UK, Royal Mail has been changing an average of 5 per cent of its post codes annually.[26] It only takes a few years for the integrity of customer information in any database to degrade to a level where its usefulness becomes questionable. Incorrect or out-of-date information can drive customers away rather than enhancing the relationship (*see* Exhibit 4.12).

Exhibit 4.12

DRIVING THE CUSTOMER AWAY

Nurturing customers correctly can lead to a long-term commitment between two parties. Information systems designed to build and uphold this relationship can, however, lead to the demise of the relationship. Some sellers fail to recognise when a customer has moved into a new phase. For example a mother whose youngest child is 10 may still be labelled a 'new mom' on a direct marketer's database and still receive catalogues on baby supplies. Others do not change procedures or train employees after implementing a new technology.

To use information systems effectively and prevent loss of customers, identify perishable descriptors ('new parent', 'student', etc.) and find ways to identify when specific customers' characteristics change. Pay as much attention to systems that help listen to customers as to systems that tell customers about products.

Source: Information Week (12 June 1995).[27]

Ideally, companies should regard all contacts with a customer as an opportunity to update the customer's details on the database. For example, if a customer walks into a bank branch to open up a new account, all the relevant details should be entered onto the database at the point of contact with the customer, and any existing information that the bank may have on the customer should also be verified at the same time. In reality, few organisations can claim to have up-to-date information on their customers. Consider the following case of a European bank[28] which carried out an analysis of the quality of its customer information:

- 10 per cent of accounts in the customer database did not have a valid name
- 13 per cent did not have a full address
- 47 per cent did not have a title/sex for the customer
- 55 per cent did not have a marital status
- 72 per cent did not have a home phone number
- 75 per cent did not have a date of birth
- 77 per cent did not have a occupation
- 85 per cent did not have a record of the number of dependent children.

The percentage of customer records where all eight fields were completed was extremely low and, with complete information on only a few per cent of all customers, the effectiveness of the bank's customer database was seriously compromised.

A mindset and attitude change is required in most companies before employees treat every contact with the customer as a means of improving the level of information held on that customer. Often, there is no incentive to log a customer telephone call or ask all those questions when a new customer walks in the door. More often than not, major process and procedural changes are required to ensure that each customer contact can be captured without hindering or slowing down the transaction. For example, many airlines have loyalty schemes. However, when a customer arrives at the check-in counter, there may be another half a dozen people in the queue and the last thing that the check-in clerk (or the person in the queue who is already late for a flight) needs is the additional delay of accepting the loyalty card and typing the details into the system. One answer is to have a self-swipe mechanism for customers to record their own flights, or to implement a system for recording the flight when the ticket is purchased rather than when the boarding card is issued.

DATA PROTECTION ISSUES

■ Customer concerns

The rapid growth in the number of organisations that collect large amounts of data on all aspects of consumer behaviour and the value of this information have led to consumers becoming increasingly concerned about the amount of information that is being gathered on them and how this information is used. Research in the US indicates that the four most sensitive areas of customer information are financial, health, family issues and sex. As one marketer puts it:[29]

> 'Using a customer's birthdate in an offer is fine – if the customer gave you that information. But if you don't have a relationship with a customer, and you approach her with an offer using that birthdate, that's fairly offensive.'

Most companies understand these customer sensitivities and try to address them. Some have even made their own attempts to restrict the transfer of customer information outside their own organisations. Organisations such as the Red Cross, AT&T and Readers Digest refuse to market their customer lists to other firms and others, such as the retailer Land's End, will retain all customer information and rent out only the names. One large credit reporting agency, with 120 million names in its file, has also decided to stop providing mailing lists to direct marketers. While such efforts at self-regulation are a step in the right direction, they are unlikely to be sufficient.[30]

■ Data protection legislation

In response to consumers' concern about the unauthorised use of personal information, the Data Protection Act was passed in the UK in 1984. The Act was designed to limit the ways in which organisations could acquire and use personal data on customers, but is already regarded by many as out of date. Other countries have also introduced legislation to protect consumers and to place limits on what companies can legally do with data on individual customers.

More importantly, a 1995 EU directive on data protection requires all member states to update their data protection legislation. This directive will have a major impact on the way customer data is used across the EU. Under such legislation, companies will be allowed to 'process' personal data on individuals only where the people concerned have given their unambiguous consent or where, for legal or contractual reasons, this 'processing' is deemed to be necessary (for example, consumer credit legislation requires financial institutions to ask certain questions of any individual applying for a loan). Personal data 'processing' is given a much wider definition in the directive than in most existing data protection legislation in operation around Europe. Individuals will also have the right to object to being targeted by direct-marketing activities. Furthermore, the directive will extend the scope of the legislation to include manually held, as well as electronically held, data on individuals.[31] As EU member countries enact their own laws in accordance with the 1995 directive, the protection afforded to the individual will be increased, as will customers' understanding of their rights to privacy. These changes will pose particular issues for the holders and users of customer information, particularly where direct-marketing activities are concerned. As the marketing potential of the Internet and other electronic services is realised, these areas are also likely to become the subject of increased legislation (*see* Exhibit 4.13).

A final area of concern about the protection of customer data relates to the way in which credit information is held and used. Already, the credit history of most UK adults is held on a database operated by one of the two large credit reference agencies, CCN and Equifax (*see* Exhibit 4.14). The Office of the Data Protection Registrar, the body that regulates computer files containing personal information in the UK, has already warned both of these companies to tighten up their safeguards on how such sensitive personal information is used.[32]

Exhibit 4.13

DEALING WITH JUNK E-MAIL

It was bound to happen. The direct marketing industry's first large list of e-mail addresses was introduced at the Direct Marketing Association (DMA) convention in October 1995. The list contains 250,000 e-mail addresses of individuals who use the Internet to obtain and transfer information. The addresses were gathered from users of Internet newsgroups, chat groups, and Web sites. The identity of the list owner has not been revealed.

The list appears to violate DMA guidelines for mailing list practices, which state that each party must be identified in all list transactions. In addition, consumers who provide data that is rented, sold or exchanged for marketing purposes should be informed periodically. The Internet users on the file probably did not realise that their e-mail addresses were being captured. The list is broken down by interest: adult, computer, sports, science, education, news, investor, etc.

Privacy and information policy consultants pointed out that the Internet community does not take kindly to unsolicited e-mail, but wonder whether the collection of e-mail addresses is anything different from how physical mail names and addresses have been bought and sold for years without the individual's knowledge.

Source: DM News (16 October 1995).

Exhibit 4.14

THE ELECTRONIC POLICE

Two of the world's most comprehensive personal databases swing into action virtually every time someone in the UK attempts to persuade a credit agency to lend him or her some money. Roughly once every three seconds a company lending money – most likely a bank, building society finance house or retailer – electronically interrogates one of two private databases to check on the financial status of the individual seeking credit. The operation of the two databases is a big business for the two companies involved – CCN, a subsidiary of the UK's Great Universal Stores (GUS), and Equifax, a US company based in Atlanta, Georgia. Each of the two databases contains credit files on about 44m citizens in the UK.

Source: Financial Times (25 October 1995).[32]

CONCLUSION

Customer segmentation involves identifying and understanding a subset of the market with similar buying needs and characteristics so that the most appropriate marketing mix can be developed for that subset. Recent advances in information technology are allowing organisations to segment the market in newer and more sophisticated ways, particularly on lifestyle and behavioural dimensions. Geographic information systems

(GIS) provide an additional perspective on customer information by presenting it in graphical format and allowing marketing managers to visualise store catchment areas, salesforce territories, trends in customer behaviour and a variety of other applications which lend themselves to geographic representation on a computer screen. Customer information can both be sourced internally from existing company systems and purchased from external sources. Typically, this customer information will be stored in a customer database and used for a variety of operational and analytical uses.

There are seven generic steps in developing a customer database but one of the most critical steps is the ongoing exercise of keeping the database up-to-date. Finally, the increasing use of customer information and customer databases for marketing purposes has led to concerns about how such information is used. Data protection legislation has become more rigorous and will continue to be a major issue for marketing managers in the future.

ASSIGNMENT QUESTIONS

1 What new approaches to segmentation are being facilitated by information technology?

2 Describe the different categories of geographic information systems (GIS).

3 Where does customer information come from?

4 Discuss the steps in developing a customer database.

5 What impact will data protection legislation have on the marketing function?

Case study

BARCLAYS BANK

Barclays Bank recently introduced a new customer database which has dramatically improved its ability to effectively target its different customer groups. With over 2,000 branches throughout the UK and over 14 million customers, Barclays is one of the largest UK banks. Specialising as it does in three major activities – personal banking, credit cards and financial services – its customer records were, until recently, held on three separate databases. This system presented obvious difficulties, as it was impossible to tell if, for example, a Barclaycard credit card customer also held a personal account with the bank. This made cross-selling to existing customers a somewhat 'hit and miss' activity, and meant that Barclays did not have a full picture of who its customers were.

Barclays decided in 1989 that it was essential to integrate the three databases into one, creating a company-wide database which would support the sales effort both at branch level and within central marketing. The bank could then implement a centralised marketing approach which could be both coordinated and targeted. What was needed was a new database which would hold a complete profile of each customer's relationship with Barclays and which would be accessible throughout the whole organisation. 'Since we used to have account-based databases, we knew how many accounts were held – more than 25 million, in fact – but we had no idea how many customers we had', said Ken Pilbeam, head of operational systems management at the bank. 'Therefore, as part of our new database, we wanted to build a profile of each person, with information on every Barclays product he or she held.'

The new Customer Information System (CIS) was piloted in 1991 and later implemented nationwide, greatly enhancing how the bank holds and accesses its information, according to Pilbeam. Barclays can now look at its direct marketing activity from the customer's perspective, he said, and implement properly targeted cross-selling campaigns. 'It is now an easy task to monitor the perceptions and attitudes of our customers against the frequency and type of direct mail and telephone contact.'

Equipped now with a better understanding of the customer, Barclays claims it finds that not only are the direct marketing campaigns more cost effective through improved targeting, but they are receiving a better response. Using the new system, customers' names are now associated with the accounts they hold, allowing Barclays to sort by name for the first time. The Barclays marketing team can now be confident that when they select, for example, a Barclays loan campaign for branch customers, that they are not including any existing Barclays loan customers – a phenomenon which has always caused much irritation to customers. Prior to the new database, name and address de-duplication was all outsourced to computer bureaux, and direct marketing was done by a product group, rather than on a company-wide basis. With the new integrated database, customers no longer risk being the target of marketing efforts by two different departments at the same time that marketing is now more 'customer friendly'. Although data is held centrally, each of nearly 3,000 staff in the branches can have on-line access to the database via workstations, and can see all the bank's relationships with each of its 14 million customers. The customer database maintains customer details, displays product information, creates sales leads, records customer contacts, captures credit and insurance applications and even prints application forms.

Another benefit that the marketing department has discovered is the speed of the new system, Pilbeam said. 'Before, branch counter staff could only look up records by account number. If an account customer wanted to enquire about the status of his Barclaycard account, this would involve phonecalls which were both time-consuming and irritating. Now, Barclays has the database at the counter and if a customer from Aberdeen walks into a branch in the Isle of Wight, his details will be available on screen.' Another useful feature of the new system at Barclays is the phonetic name and address matching. When staff deal with customers over the phone, they can match by the sound of the name rather than by the exact spelling. The customer's address verifies the match. On a database of this kind, it is essential that customer data is kept accurate and up-to-date, so the database is updated every day at Barclays Computer Operations in Gloucester. Details in a new account opened today, will be on the screen nationwide by 9 a.m. the following day. Pilbeam said the system has allowed him and his team to become customer focused rather than product focused. 'As a result, we have improved our customer service and reduced our costs.'

Source: Adapted from *FSI* (October 1995).[33] Reproduced by kind permission of The Lafferty Group, IDA Tower, Pearse Street, Dublin, Ireland.

Questions

1 Why did Barclays build a CIS?

2 What benefits has CIS brought to the bank?

3 'We had no idea how many customers we had.' Discuss.

4 How can Barclays use the customer database to improve its relationship with customers?

5 Did Barclays follow the seven steps for developing a customer database?

References

[1] Haughton, D. (1996). 'Measuring marketing effectiveness – a true short story', a marketing pamphlet from Customer Management Solutions, Dublin.

[2] Bradley, F. (1995). *Marketing Management: Providing, Communicating and Delivering Value*. Hemel Hempstead: Prentice Hall.

[3] Marsh, P. (1996). 'Picked out by programs', *Financial Times*, 24 May.

[4] Mazur, L. (1994). 'Taking lifestyle into their hands', *Marketing*, 12 May.

[5] Reed, D. (1996). 'The data game', *Marketing Week*, 3 May.

[6] Evans, M., O'Malley, L. and Patterson, M. (1995). 'Direct marketing: rise and rise or rise and fall?', *Marketing Intelligence & Planning*, Vol. 3, No. 6.

[7] Dwek, R. (1992). 'The meeting of two different minds', *Marketing*, 12 November.

[8] Cobb, R. (1991). 'Counting the national census', *Marketing*, 11 April.

[9] Dempsey, M. (1995). 'Customers compartmentalised', *Financial Times*, 1 March.

[10] Stores (1993). 'Retail GIS use growing', *Stores*, January.

[11] McGinn, J. (1996). 'Geographical information systems', *Computing*, 11 July.

[12] MapInfo (1995). 'MapInfo drives Daewoo Cars marketing strategy', *MapInfo*.

[13] Reed, D. (1996). 'Streets ahead', *Marketing Week*, 17 May.

[14] Marsh, P. (1996). Op. cit.

[15] Fischer, C. (1992). 'GIS – a role to play in direct marketing?', *Direct Response (UK)*, August.

[16] Reed, D. (1996). 'Streets ahead', *Marketing Week*, 17 May.

[17] Nelson, S. (1996). 'GIS: the sales force and territory balancing link', *Gartner Group*, May.

[18] Nelson, S. (1995). 'Geographic information systems: questions and answers', *Gartner Group*, 27 October.

[19] Peters, T. (1987). *Thriving on Chaos*. New York: Knopf.

[20] Cohen, H. (1992). 'Shooting gnats with an elephant gun?', *Bank Marketing*, February.

[21] Curtis, J. (1996). 'Sorting out the wheat from the chaff', *Precision Marketing*, 5 February.

[22] Barry, K. (1995). 'Top lists hit 100m mark', *Precision Marketing*, 10 April.

[23] Gendelev, B. (1992). 'MIS and marketing: secrets of strategic information mining', *CIO Journal*, Summer.

[24] Newing, R. (1996). 'Data warehousing explained', *Financial Times*, 3 April.

[25] O'Connor, J. and Brennan, R. (1993). *Help! I've Just Been Told to Design a Customer Database*. Dublin: Andersen Consulting.

[26] Reed, D. (1996). 'Power merge', *Marketing Week*, 12 July.

[27] Information Week (1995). 'Systems designed to support customers can actually drive them away', *Information Week*, 12 June.

[28] O'Connor, J. (1990). Unpublished research.

[29] Dowling, M. (1993). 'When you know too much', *Catalog Age*, October.

[30] Morris, L. and Parr, S. (1992). 'Invasion of privacy: a dilemma for marketing research and database technology', *Journal of Systems Management*, October.

[31] Dresner, S. (1995). *Privacy Laws & Business Newsletter*, April.

[32] Marsh, P. (1995). 'The electronic police', *Financial Times*, 25 October.

[33] FSI (1995) 'A sophisticated marketing tool', *FSI*, published by Lafferty Publications.

5

DATABASE MARKETING

- The evolution of database marketing
- The uses of databases in marketing
- Direct marketing
- Relationship marketing

OBJECTIVES

After studying this chapter, you will be able to:

☐ Understand what is meant by database marketing

☐ Describe the evolution of database marketing and the importance of databases in marketing

☐ Understand what is meant by direct marketing

☐ Explain the concept of relationship marketing

THE EVOLUTION OF DATABASE MARKETING

■ What is database marketing?

Database marketing can be defined in a number of different ways. The phrase *direct marketing* is often used instead of database marketing and, more recently, the use of such phrases as *relationship marketing* or *customer relationship marketing*[1] has become commonplace. However, database marketing is much more than this, and we agree with Shaw and Stone's (1988)[2] broad definition of database marketing as:

> 'an interactive approach to marketing, which uses individually addressable marketing media and channels (such as mail, telephone, and the sales force) to:
>
> - extend help to a company's target audience
> - stimulate their demand
> - stay close to them by recording and keeping an electronic database memory of customer, prospect and all communication and commercial contacts, to help them improve all future contacts and to ensure more realistic planning of all marketing.'

Exhibit 5.1 provides an example of how one company uses database marketing for designing mailshots, but a closer examination shows how the database marketing system is also used to reduce marketing costs, improve the quality of communication and generally manage the interaction between the company and each individual customer.

Exhibit 5.1

HAVE I GOT A CAR LOAN FOR YOU!

First Direct's database marketing system builds customer profiles and allows the bank to identify the next products the customer is most likely to buy. 'We can predict that a particular 30-year-old family man with a mortgage is most likely to purchase a new car, so we'll target car loan information at that customer,' says Peter Simpson, First Direct's commercial director. The bank claims it has cut marketing costs by 40% as a result of lower cost promotions yielding higher returns. The system allows First Direct to mark on the database appropriate and inappropriate customers for particular products and then target those customers in mailshots accordingly.

Source: Precision Marketing (5 February 1996).[3]

■ The evolution of database marketing

Database marketing has evolved from the use of unsophisticated direct-mail or telemarketing lists where the marketing process was relatively straightforward. All that was required for a direct-mail or telemarketing campaign was a list of addresses or telephone numbers. However, the large amounts of junk mail arriving at people's homes caused many consumers to switch off and ignore further mailshots. The route to more effective direct-marketing campaigns was through better customer information to increase the relevance of the offer and better management of the communication between the company and the customer. Shaw and Stone's definition describes such a complex and ongoing two-way communication process, yet few organisations have achieved this level of sophistication and there are clear differences between the theory and practice of database marketing (*see* Exhibit 5.2).

Exhibit 5.2

FINE IN THEORY BUT ...

Marketing once had a personal touch. Customers shopped in small stores where their tastes and preferences were known, and shopkeepers would do what they could to suit them. But by the time the multiple chains took hold in the 1960s and 1970s, shops had relinquished their individual relationships with customers in favour of mass marketing techniques.

Cheaper and more sophisticated database technologies are now encouraging marketers to try to get the best of both worlds. As well as benefiting from economies of scale that allow them to offer variety and low prices, they are developing a detailed picture of their customers' needs that allows them to deliver a better service. This insight into customer behaviour has been made possible by more sophisticated methods of storing and analysing information. Increasingly, marketing experts can sift, slice and manipulate data in ways that give them new insights into their customers and new marketing options. The perceived importance of this application is immense, according to a recent survey of 100 UK companies by the Manchester School of Management. Nearly all the respondents plan to use IT-driven direct marketing within the next five years; over half of them expect it to become their most common promotional method. Findings like this support the Henley Centre's assertion that 'database marketing is one of the hottest topics in the marketing community'. Yet enthusiasm is often tempered by scepticism. A third of the respondents to a Henley Centre survey agreed that 'database marketing is fine in theory but less good in practice'. Some companies are put off by the speed at which technology is moving. They have had bad experiences of investing in technology that proved obsolete. Many organisations own outdated database systems left over from the 1980s.

Source: Financial Times (28 November 1995).[4]

Despite the practical difficulties of achieving such a sophisticated database marketing operation, the subject has become a major growth area. Indeed, it can be argued that the database is the greatest single application of information technology within marketing. The rapidly declining costs of computer hardware and software have increased the attractiveness of database marketing, resulting in a massive shift in the last decade towards its importance and use. By some accounts,[5] the cost of storing and accessing a single customer name on a database has dropped from over $7 in the US in 1974 to less than one cent today. Nowadays, companies are becoming much more precise about the type of potential customer they will mail to and the size of mailshots is reducing correspondingly. At the same time the effectiveness, or response rate, from these mailings is increasing.[6]

THE USES OF DATABASES IN MARKETING

■ Improving performance through marketing databases

Linton (1995)[7] states that database techniques allow marketing managers to improve performance in at least seven different ways:

- understanding customers
- managing customer service
- understanding the market
- understanding competitors
- managing sales operations
- managing marketing campaigns
- communicating with customers.

It is worth taking each area on Linton's list for further discussion.

■ Understanding customers

In Chapter 4, we have already examined the use of customer information and the role of customer databases. Yet it is surprising how few companies examine and analyse their customer databases for answers to questions such as:

- How many customers do I have?
- What products are they buying?
- Which segments do those customers fit into?
- Which delivery channels do they prefer?
- Which customers can I not afford to lose?

A marketing database which allows marketing managers to understand their customers is the first step towards building long-term relationships with them. We will examine the subject of relationship marketing in more detail later in this chapter.

■ Managing customer service

One of the most commonly used applications of database marketing is in the area of customer service. Database marketing, in the narrow definition of the term, is associated with direct-mail campaigns, but the broader definition encompasses a wide variety of operational functions such as the following:

- *Helpdesk facilities.* Helpdesks allow customers to phone a central telephone number for answers to commonly asked questions and solutions to commonly encountered problems (*see* Exhibit 5.3).
- *Enquiries.* Enquiries can be supported through marketing databases which allow access to a variety of customer, product, price and transaction information.
- *Complaints.* Complaints handling is typically supported through the use of databases which categorise, monitor and track customer problems.

In most cases, these customer service applications are provided both in face-to-face situations and via a telephone service. The use of marketing databases in supporting telephone-based customer service activities is examined in more detail in Chapter 13.

■ Understanding the market

In Chapter 3, we examined the use of information technology in marketing research. The integration of marketing research data with other information on the marketing database will allow companies to answer strategic questions such as:

- What direction should we take with new product development?
- Which new delivery channels should we be experimenting with?
- Which new markets should we be expanding into?

■ Understanding competitors

According to Linton, competitor assessment is easily overlooked and very often is not captured in a formalised way. The integration of competitor information into a

---

Exhibit 5.3

HANDY HELP FOR PETROL PROBLEMS

BP Oil, part of the UK's largest company British Petroleum, is introducing a helpdesk across Europe. The scheme has started in Germany where it will support point-of-sale and back office systems being installed at 1,300 petrol stations. Until recently, many of BP's retail systems problems were tackled with fairly cumbersome paper procedures. BP's helpdesk in Hamburg, which is staffed by 12 operators, has access to data on all earlier calls from a particular petrol station which may throw light on a problem. If they cannot resolve the matter on the spot, they can send a fax from their PC to call in expert support. The helpdesk is logging calls at a rate of 1,800 per month and, on average, a query takes two days to resolve. BP is hoping to integrate its helpdesk systems between countries so that experience of handling calls can be aggregated in an international database and solutions shared.

Source: Financial Times (6 March 1996).[8]

---

marketing database, rather than in the heads of individual marketing managers, will allow the following questions to be answered with greater speed and accuracy:

- Who are our main competitors by product or market segment?
- How have their market shares changed in recent weeks/months/years?
- What is their pricing structure and what impact have price changes had on market share?
- How much are our competitors spending on promoting their products and services?

The formal analysis of competitor activity and the impact of marketing decisions taken by competitors will enable the marketing manager to make better-informed decisions and have a clearer understanding of the likely impact of those decisions.

■ Managing sales operations

Another major area of operational support which is enabled by database technology is in the management of sales operations. We will provide a more extensive examination of the use of marketing databases within sales in Chapter 13, but a sample of sales activities that are supported through marketing databases includes:

- managing the performance of different sales representatives
- managing customer contacts and client portfolios
- demonstrating product features and providing quotations
- capturing and fulfilling customer orders.

■ Managing marketing campaigns

The management of marketing campaigns using database technology can be examined under the following headings:

- analysis
- planning
- contact
- response
- follow-up
- monitoring.

Figure 5.1 provides a pictorial representation of the different technologies which can be used to support campaign management under each heading.

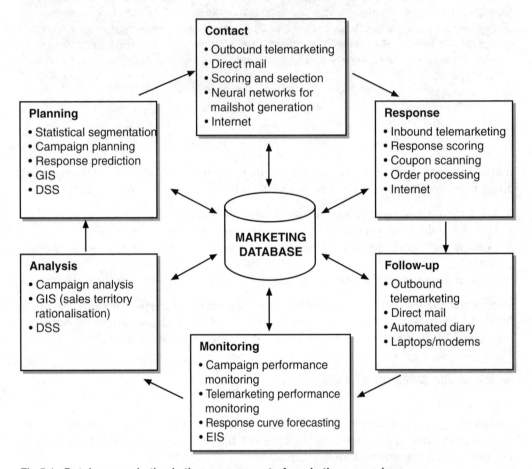

Contact
- Outbound telemarketing
- Direct mail
- Scoring and selection
- Neural networks for mailshot generation
- Internet

Planning
- Statistical segmentation
- Campaign planning
- Response prediction
- GIS
- DSS

Response
- Inbound telemarketing
- Response scoring
- Coupon scanning
- Order processing
- Internet

MARKETING DATABASE

Analysis
- Campaign analysis
- GIS (sales territory rationalisation)
- DSS

Follow-up
- Outbound telemarketing
- Direct mail
- Automated diary
- Laptops/modems

Monitoring
- Campaign performance monitoring
- Telemarketing performance monitoring
- Response curve forecasting
- EIS

Fig 5.1   Database marketing in the management of marketing campaigns

■ Communicating with customers

It is sometimes forgotten that communication is a two-way process. All too often, marketing managers substitute the periodic mailing of promotional material for a meaningful and relevant dialogue with customers. Marketing databases should be used for issuing customer communications at appropriate times, such as in the case of the 'Flora-minder card' in Exhibit 5.4. Marketing databases should also be capable of reminding customer service staff of all previous customer contacts, whether that contact was by mail, telephone or in person.

Exhibit 5.4

SAYING IT WITH FLOWERS

Telemarketing firm 800-FLOWERS has grown significantly over the past several years and is the leader in the floral arrangements business. One of the key elements to their success is telemarketing software that prompts customer service representatives (CSRs) to ask customers a full range of sales questions and make suggestions. The most important aspect, perhaps, has been asking the customer for the occasion which is initiating the flowers. Every time an order is placed, the CSR encodes the reason (e.g., birthday, anniversary, sympathy) so that follow-up marketing can be performed. If the occasion warrants (sympathy, for example, would not), the customer who placed the order is sent a Flora-minder card a year later. 800-FLOWERS says the programme has been very successful.

Source: Chain Store Age Executive (March 1994).

DIRECT MARKETING

■ What is direct marketing?

The concept of direct marketing is simple. Instead of broadcasting a mass marketing message through television or print to a wide number of people, a customised message is instead sent on an individual, and direct, basis to a much smaller number of people who are more pre-disposed to listening to the message and buying the product or service. National television advertising is very expensive and many organisations are questioning its effectiveness. Where a direct salesforce is used, it can cost £100–£200 for a face-to-face sales call and it may take several calls to close a sale. Direct marketing can be a more cost-effective alternative for generating a sale.

The most commonly understood form of direct marketing is *direct-mail advertising*. Two other types are *direct-response advertising* and the telephone-based version of direct marketing known as *telemarketing*. We will examine each of these types of direct marketing in more detail in Chapter 11.

■ The decline and revival of direct marketing

Direct marketing had its first golden age in the 1950s as the post-war boom drove consumer spending but, as Exhibit 5.5 (overleaf) points out, this golden age was coming to an end in the 1960s and 1970s as competition from television intensified.

In recent years, direct marketing has seen a major resurgence. The forces behind the re-emergence of direct marketing in the 1990s are:

■ *Fragmentation of media.* The arrival of commercial television may have heralded the decline of direct marketing in the 1960s, but commercial television itself has come

Exhibit 5.5

BUYING 'ON TICK'

In 1833, Antonio Fattorini, a refugee to Britain from Lake Como, established his first watch club in Bradford. This provided credit to poor factory workers enabling them to buy watches 'on tick'. Fattorini's watch club eventually grew into the first mail order catalogue giant, Empire Stores. Others followed such as Littlewoods, Freeman's, GUS, Grattan. Mail order became an important industry in Britain, although because its roots lay in the provision of credit to the industrial poor, it acquired class connotations, traces of which still remain.

All this came under threat 40 years ago with the launch of commercial television. By the 1960s the tide was running away from direct marketing towards this glamorous impactful, ultra-modern mass medium. A prime spot on 'Coronation Street', Britain's top soap opera, could reach half the homes in Britain instantaneously. At the same time society became obsessed with novelty, change, technology and image – or, in the case of marketing, brand image. Television was perfectly in tune with these trends. Traditional direct marketing was suddenly very old hat.

Source: Business Strategy Review (1995).[9]

under fire in the 1990s from a variety of different cable and satellite channels. Advertisers began to understand what Livingston and Schober (1995)[9] refer to as the 'dishwasher powder effect' – why advertise dishwasher powder on television if 85 per cent of households do not have a dishwasher and if direct marketing can help you identify the 15 per cent who do?

■ *Increasing retailer power.* Manufacturers are now facing an increasingly tough battle for 'mindspace and shelfspace'.[10] The increasing power of retailers and the success of own brands have made it more and more difficult for manufacturers to gather information and develop relationships with their customers. An increasingly effective means of bypassing the manufacturer and gaining the 'mindspace' of the end-customer is via direct marketing.

■ *Declining brand loyalty.* The product proliferation that we discussed in Chapter 1 has done nothing for brand loyalty. Direct marketing can help win back that brand loyalty by keeping a particular product or service in the consumer's mind on a regular basis.

■ *Search for long-term customer relationships.* Not all customers are profitable. And those customers that are profitable often only become profitable after the company has recouped the costs of recruiting them in the first place. Companies are beginning to understand the desirability of retaining customers and maintaining their loyalty. Regular communication, via direct marketing, can help.

The recent resurgence in the popularity of direct marketing is largely due to the increases in productivity and processing power of information technology. As the technology continues to develop and marketers became more skilled in using it to its maximum advantage to target key customers, it will continue to grow in importance.

RELATIONSHIP MARKETING

■ The value of customer relationships

Direct marketing and database marketing also help companies to become more targeted in their approach to customers. However, the ultimate database marketing is the creation of a series of one-to-one, long-term, profitable relationships with individual customers. This is known as relationship marketing. As mentioned in Chapter 1, a considerable amount of analysis has been done on the lifetime value of customers. The longer a customer can be retained, the more profitable that customer becomes. The use of information technology to help build such long-term profitable relationships is currently a hot topic in the marketing community (*see* Exhibit 5.6).

Exhibit 5.6

BUILD THE DATABASE, CREATE THE RELATIONSHIP

Insurance giant Prudential is to implement a massive reorganisation of its 10 million computerised customer records in order to identify its best and worst customers. The group hopes to be able to sell more products to profitable customers and possibly to weed out those who are not providing adequate returns. The reorganisation involves bringing together customers' records in one database, principally to identify which of Prudential's products they do not currently hold, in the hope of increasing sales. Prudential describes the moves as 'an initiative that will help us create total relationships with our customers'. It is joining the likes of American Express, Abbey National and other financial services companies already exploiting the power of database marketing. This is based on computer analyses of customer records to identify groups of people sharing particular characteristics, such as age, wealth, occupation and other such lifestyle factors.

Source: Sunday Business (26 May 1996).[11]

In any business, it is inevitable that an organisation will lose customers. Part of the concept of relationship marketing is to identify which customers are worth losing and which are worth keeping. The better companies will have procedures in place to win back those worth regaining and rebuilding the relationship. Customer exit interviews, or telephone calls, are an effective means of finding out what went wrong and potentially winning the customer back.

Relationship marketing can only happen as part of a wider, all-encompassing programme which puts the customer at the heart of the organisation and where processes are designed, or redesigned, around pleasing and delighting the customer. The approach that some retailers have taken to implement relationship marketing is illustrated in Exhibit 5.7.

LISTENING TO THE DATABASE

In the next decade, retailers will only grow revenues and prosper to the extent that they meet the needs and wants of an increasingly demanding customer. Customer Relationship Marketing (CRM) is currently the most touted solution. By capturing, measuring, and monitoring existing (especially best customers) and new customer activity, retailers can build close relationships with their customers. Retailers must actively 'listen' to the customer database.

The first rung of customer relationship marketing includes all frequent shopper programmes, ranging from 'buy 20, get one free' to membership club programmes (Zeller's Club Z and Sears' Bonus Club Programme). Most retailers are on this rung and essentially created add-on programmes to reward repeat visits. There is little integration into the overall marketing strategy.

The second rung involves not just having a database, but analysing the database to identify and track best customers, recognise and reward, target specific customer segments, and create customer communications. Retailers such as Neiman Marcus, Bloomingdale's, Saks, and Sears, which have a customer-driven strategy or catalogue heritage are on this rung. Retailers planning programmes include Dayton Hudson, Federated, and The Limited.

The third level is the realm of sophisticated catalogue retailers such as Fingerhut and Spiegel, but is currently devoid of store-based retailers. These companies have a fully integrated CRM programme, which impacts all business processes. Buying decisions are based on what the best customers are buying, or better still, on what they say they want, rather than overall product movement.

Source: Chain Store Age Executive (August 1995).[12]

Fletcher (1995)[13] proposes a slightly different variation of the ladder analogy, with five levels of loyalty in building a relationship with customers. At the bottom of the ladder are *suspects* who might fit your market profile but who know neither you nor your product. Next level up are the *prospects* who have contacted you at some time or other and are probably a better fit with your target market. *Customers*, who actually buy your product, are the next step on the ladder, although this is no guarantee of future loyalty. Then come *clients* who are customers who have made some commitment to you, possibly through a customer loyalty programme. At the top of the ladder are *advocates* where the commitment has an emotional or psychological element to it and where the customer is likely to promote you or your product to friends and colleagues. Advocates are likely to be the most profitable, with a high lifetime value, and are the types of relationships that companies must strive to build with their customers.

■ 'Crowning the customer'

The only way to make sure that you are satisfying and delighting your customers is to have a very clear understanding of what they want. One of the ways to achieve this is to invite them to become part of your organisation and to help you design and refine your product offerings. Customer-focused companies have traditionally been able to do this without recourse to information technology. Market research and focus groups have provided the means of achieving this and some organisations have developed customer contact to a fine art. Feargal Quinn, who runs an upmarket supermarket chain in Ireland, refers to this as 'crowning the customer'.[14] Quinn sits in on all his company's focus groups and has an enviable knowledge of what his customers want. Because he is the managing director, he can also make sure his customers' views are acted on. Superquinn customers can cut the stalks off the broccoli they purchase, because some customers thought that they should not have to pay for the part of the product that they would throw away in any case. Similarly, when they weigh their fruit and vegetables, they find a magnifying glass at the weighing scales because some elderly customers complained that the scales and labels were difficult to read. And when they pass through the check-out, they find their receipts identify the amount of Irish-produced goods that make up their total bill, again because customers asked for this information. Superquinn was also the first Irish supermarket retailer to implement a card-based loyalty scheme which has been very successful and is now linked to petrol retailers and DIY stores. When customers join the programme, they receive a keyring with a small plastic card with a unique customer number bar-coded onto it. When their purchases are scanned at the checkout, the operator scans the card and the system automatically gives loyalty points based on the value of goods purchased. By allocating double points for purchases made during off-peak days at the beginning of the week, Superquinn is also attempting to avoid large checkout queues. Superquinn's loyalty scheme does more than provide customers with loyalty points for shopping at the supermarket or affiliated retailing outlets. It provides a wealth of marketing information that could not have been accessed using his traditional focus groups. It is not a question of replacing the focus groups and the direct contact with customers by using IT, but of complementing the older techniques.

Information technology can help to crown the customer. It can also help in inviting customers to talk to you and tell you what they really want. McKenna (1995)[15] refers to this as 'real-time marketing' (see Exhibit 5.8). Regardless of which term one prefers, the uses of database technology in crowning the customer, engaging in real-time marketing and satisfying and delighting the consumer provide illustrations of the true meaning of the phrase 'database marketing'.

Exhibit 5.8

IT'S GOOD TO TALK (TO YOUR CUSTOMERS)

Today marketing sits at the end of the production chain. Companies strive to reduce time to market – the time it takes to design and manufacture new products and push them out the door. They expect marketing professionals to make the product succeed once it's in the marketplace. But time to acceptance is what determines success in a crowded market-place, not time to market. A product that cannot win customers quickly will not compete well against a product that has a ready base of customers. Improving time to acceptance means integrating marketing with design and manufacturing. That's done by involving potential customers as early as possible in the development process.

Information technology can help companies with time to acceptance and more. To build customer loyalty – to build brand – companies need to keep their customers engaged in a continuous dialogue. The conversation between customers and the organization should not be limited to the development cycle. How the product works, the customer's experiences

▶

with the product, and how the company supported the product after the sale also contribute to customer loyalty. Companies must keep the dialogue flowing and also maintain conversations with suppliers, distributors and others in the marketplace. To do so effectively, the technology linking these groups to the company must be integrated with internal systems managing production and design schedules, field sales information, and even competitive intelligence. Combined, these systems allow companies to interact with their customers and the marketplace in real time and to incorporate into their products the service experiences that will keep their customers loyal. Dialogue will be the way companies build brand.

Marketing must take responsibility for managing these systems. Although real-time marketing has a growing number of supporters, few people recognize how dramatically organizations must change in order to engage the customer in an effective conversation. Real-time marketing requires:

■ replacing the broadcast mentality that has long dominated marketing with a willingness to give customers the access to the company and to view their actions and feedback as integral to developing or improving products
■ focusing on real-time customer satisfaction, providing the support, help, guidance and information necessary to win customers' loyalty
■ being willing to learn how information technology is changing both customer behaviour and marketing, and to think in new ways about the role of marketing within the organization.

Source: Harvard Business Review (1995).[15]

CONCLUSION

Database marketing may have evolved from the use of unsophisticated direct-mail lists, but the term now encompasses a complex process of ongoing, two-way communication with the customer. Database marketing is used to describe the use of database techniques to understand customers, manage customer service, understand the market, understand competitors, manage sales operations, manage marketing campaigns and communicate with customers.

Database marketing is much broader than direct marketing which involves sending a customised message to a target group of people who are likely to buy a product or service. Direct marketing contrasts with mass marketing where a message is broadcast to a large number of people.

Customers are not all equally profitable and a major focus of marketing in recent years has been to create an ongoing relationship with the more valuable customers and customer segments. Relationship marketing has spawned the wide variety of customer-loyalty programmes that are in evidence today. However, loyalty programmes on their own are no substitute for what Feargal Quinn, of the Irish supermarket chain Superquinn, terms 'crowning the customer'. Crowning the customer and real-time marketing, to use the phrase coined by Regis McKenna, are true examples of the complex two-way communication process better known as database marketing.

ASSIGNMENT QUESTIONS

1 What do you understand by the term database marketing?

2 Describe how databases are used to manage marketing campaigns.

3 What do you understand by the term direct marketing?

4 What is relationship marketing?

5 Loyalty programmes on their own are no substitute for what Feargal Quinn terms 'crowning the customer'. Discuss.

Case study

RSPCA

The Royal Society for the Prevention of Cruelty to Animals (RSPCA) is one of Britain's most famous charities and has been working to protect animals since 1824. Today, direct mailing is its lifeline: its activities are funded entirely through donations from the public, which last year reached £30m, a remarkable £10m increase on the previous year.

The aim of its marketing database project is to increase revenue by producing focused mailings. Like any charity, the RSPCA is concerned with getting good value for money. Its new marketing database is dedicated to producing market statistics and tailored membership lists, so that direct mailing becomes more efficient and cost-effective, the main aim being to release funds for animal welfare work. From the RSPCA headquarters in Horsham, where its fund-raising and membership activities are based, project manager David Stechler explains the problems that faced him. 'We had 40 different databases, which we wanted to consolidate into one source of information for in-house control and reduced cost.' It was not just a matter of co-ordinating the various sources for the 450,000 names on the RSPCA lists, but also of bringing together three separate services, the Axciom bureau which produced the lists, Brann Direct which performed direct marketing and Mail Marketing, which would analyse and deliver response information back to Axciom.

Costs were considerable, as the RSPCA was mailing at least one campaign monthly, and a major mailing every three months, and paying each time for the use of the Axciom data. Mr Stechler sent his 'wish list' of features to 26 suppliers of packaged solutions. These whittled down to a shortlist of six who were able to offer systems for charities. The plan was to integrate all the older payroll, library and membership systems, currently on different hardware platforms. Now all the core systems, donations, accounts, contacts and membership, are in one integrated system. 'Our objective was to create a system where any authorised user could access any application from any terminal. This system is cheaper to run, and it is more effective at getting donations because we can identify the hierarchy: people who are just interested, those who have given, members, and active members. If we know who all our contacts are, it's easier to convert a one-off contact into an active member.' The RSPCA's own data includes details of donations, legacies, covenants, responses to mailshots and information from mail order trading operations. In addition, it buys in 'cold lists' from third parties such as list broker Dudley Jenkins. The system draws on Royal Mail address files for postcodes and is linked with CCN's Mosaic system for socio-demographic analysis of postcode addresses.

The next step, now that the system is in place, is to sample the database, an exercise which will allow the RSPCA to target its mailings more closely, and achieve its aim of bringing in more funds, spending less on information technology – and more on rescuing animals in distress.

Source: Adapted from 'A better way to raise funds', *Financial Times*, 2 October 1992.

Questions

1 How would you describe the marketing database that the RSPCA now operates?

2 What were the reasons for moving to the new database marketing system?

3 Where does the RSPCA draw its information from to create a mailshot?

4 Discuss how different categories of customers should be targeted by marketing campaigns.

5 How can the RSPCA use information technology to 'crown the customer'?

References

[1] Agri Marketing (1994). 'Evolution of database marketing', *Agri Marketing*, June.
[2] Shaw, R. and Stone, M. (1988). *Database Marketing*. Aldershot: Gower.
[3] Curtis, J. (1996). 'Sorting out the wheat from the chaff', *Precision Marketing*, 5 February.
[4] Holder, V. (1995). 'Database mining', *Financial Times*, 28 November.
[5] Welch, M. (1993). 'Database marketing begins to register', *Business Marketing*, March.
[6] Barry, K. (1995). 'Top lists hit 100m mark', *Precision Marketing*, 10 April.
[7] Linton, I. (1995). *Database Marketing: Know What Your Customer Wants*. London: Pitman.
[8] Black, G. (1996). 'A helpdesk for Europe', *Financial Times*, 6 March.
[9] Livingston, A. and Schober, U. (1995). 'Ready . . . aim . . . fire', *Business Strategy Review*, Winter.
[10] Corstjens, J. and Corstjens, M. (1995). *Store Wars: The Battle for Mindspace and Shelfspace*. Chichester: John Wiley.
[11] Baird, R. (1996). 'Prudential may use database to weed out low-value clients', *Sunday Business*, 26 May.
[12] Chain Store Age Executive (1995). 'Customer relationship marketing – one of the hottest topics in retailing', *Chain Store Age Executive*, August.
[13] Fletcher, K. (1995). *Marketing Management and Information Technology*. 2nd edn, London: Prentice Hall.
[14] Quinn, F. (1990). *Crowning the Customer*. Dublin: O'Brien Press.
[15] McKenna, R. (1995). 'Real-time marketing', *Harvard Business Review*, July–August.

Part II

THE INFORMATION REVOLUTION

Part II of this book provides the background and context for understanding the use of modern computers and IT in marketing and contains three chapters:

6   The information revolution and its impact on marketing

7   The drivers of the information revolution

8   The marketing potential of multimedia and the Internet

6

THE INFORMATION REVOLUTION AND ITS IMPACT ON MARKETING

- The information society and the information revolution
- The impact on business
- The growth of electronic commerce
- The impact on marketing

OBJECTIVES

After studying this chapter, you will be able to:

☐ Describe how information is transforming society

☐ Describe the impact of information technology on business

☐ Understand the differences in thinking between the business community and the IT community

☐ Describe the key features of electronic commerce

☐ Identify the implications of information technology on marketing

THE INFORMATION SOCIETY AND THE INFORMATION REVOLUTION

The birth of the 'information society'

In early 1995, the members of the Group of Seven (G7) leading industrial countries met in Brussels in an attempt to respond to the growth of the information society and the information superhighway on which it would depend.[1] The UK government has already allocated £35 million to support various initiatives primarily aimed at encouraging the use of information technology among small and medium-sized companies[2] and has also taken steps towards utilising technology itself (*see* Exhibit 6.1 overleaf).

Other EU countries have established their own initiatives to promote awareness and encourage the development of information technology skills, with Germany, in particular, investing heavily in creating the environment which will help the information revolution thrive. Deutsche Telecom has already laid 100 000 kms of fibre optic cable in Germany alone and over 24 million German households are wired up to access multimedia via their TV screens. Asian countries have moved even faster to support the

---

Exhibit 6.1

MOTHER GIVES BIRTH

A moment in history: the Mother of Parliaments is inching on to the slip road of the information superhighway. Today for the first time, a report from a parliamentary committee will be published on the Internet (http://www.hmsoinfo.gov.uk/hmso/document/inforsoc.htm).

So it should be, given the subject of the report. *Information Society: Agenda for Action in the UK* follows an enquiry, chaired by Lord Phillips of Ellesmere, by the Lords science and technology committee. Its remit was the digital revolution and its consequences from the 'convergence' of broadcasting and telecommunications industries to the birth of a full-blown information society.

Source: Financial Times (31 July 1996).[3]

---

creation of an information society. Singapore, which launched a National IT Plan as far back as 1985, has enjoyed consistently high GDP (gross domestic product) growth and is now the South East Asian country with the highest standard of living behind Japan.

The objective of these initiatives is to stay abreast of the information technology revolution that is sweeping the world. To this end, 1996 was designated the 'Year of Lifelong Learning' by the EU as the starting point for equipping its 300 million people with the skills necessary to operate in the information technology age. In another initiative, 10 EU members are issuing European computer driving licence (ECDL) qualifications to candidates who pass a series of seven training modules on their knowledge of computer applications such as spreadsheets, wordprocessing, databases, graphical software, electronic mail and the use of networks.[4]

While it may take some time for the information society to mature fully, with some commentators maintaining it will be 2030 before a true all-embracing information society emerges,[5] it clearly has arrived. Take, for example, the emergence of the Internet as a means of communication between individuals and businesses. Despite its relative immaturity, the Internet offers tremendous potential as a technology to support marketing and we will examine this potential in some detail in Chapter 8. Already, governments have latched onto the Internet as a medium with great educational and commercial possibilities (*see* Exhibit 6.2).

Exhibit 6.2

THE INFORMATION SOCIETY: THE FINNS LEAD THE WAY

This is the scenario: The Internet is growing by gigantic leaps and bounds. Today's PCs are powerful multimedia machines. A broadband network can simultaneously deliver multimedia data to several thousand PCs. Compression technology squeezes audio and video data down narrow pipes. So why not deliver video, live radio and music over the Internet? That's the thinking behind the world's first nationwide digital media pilot, and Telecom Finland is doing it. The communications firm is providing business information, educational material, and news programmes, including audio and video, to 400,000 Finnish Internet users. Finland has always had an unregulated telecommunications market. It has the most advanced telecom infrastructure in the world and the lowest telecoms charges in Europe.

Source: Byte (March 1996).[6]

■ PC ownership

One measure of the speed at which the information society is growing is the growth rate of PCs. The ownership of home PCs is increasing every year and the number of PCs that are equipped with a modem, allowing facilities such as home banking to be used, is also increasing. The US market is currently the most advanced in terms of home PC usage and will probably provide a good model for European countries to follow (*see* Table 6.1). Eventually, the home PC market is expected to be split approximately 50 per cent for home business applications, 30 per cent for education and 20 per cent for entertainment.[7] Examining the PC usage of an organisation's own customer base can also identify potential opportunities. In the US, the largest mutual fund group Fidelity Investments surveyed its 3 million customers in 1994 and found that two-thirds of them had computers in their homes and 1.1 million of these had modems. With over one million potential Internet users, and nearly 400 000 current users of on-line services such as Prodigy, CompuServe and America Online, Fidelity decided to launch an Internet site.[8] Other organisations have moved into the Internet age without carrying out the same level of research. They sense that if they do not move to test the waters with an Internet service of their own, they will be left behind. They are right.

Table 6.1 PCs and Internet penetration

Country	Estimated number of PCs (per 1000 people, 1994)	Number of Internet users (per 1000 people, 1994)	% of PCs with an Internet connection
US	298	67	22
Switzerland	288	40	14
Australia	217	50	23
Denmark	193	28	15
Canada	175	35	20
Sweden	172	49	28
Netherlands	156	32	21
UK	152	23	15
Germany	144	14	10
France	140	9	6
Belgium	129	10	8
Japan	120	4	3
Austria	107	21	20
Italy	72	3	4
Spain	70	4	6

Source: ITU.

THE IMPACT ON BUSINESS

■ The changing nature of work

Information technology has transformed how companies do business. Banks simply could not exist today without information technology. Manufacturing companies rely on automated processes to manage and control the production environment. Newspapers are composed, edited and printed electronically. Even the most basic industries would find it difficult to operate without information technology.

All of this is in sharp contrast to the predictions of Gerdon[9] in 1983 that the use of the computer would not change the job of top managers. Gerdon claimed that, while the PC might be of interest to top managers, it would not alter the way in which they would do their job. In fairness to Gerdon, many others also failed to see the impact that PCs would have on business and many of today's older managers are still uncomfortable with the use of a PC to send e-mail messages or memos, check financial results on-line and so on. Akio Morita, the founder of Sony Corporation, makes this point clearly in Exhibit 6.3.

Exhibit 6.3

PROBLEMS WITH THE GENERATION GAP

I am sometimes amazed that as technologically progressive as we think we are in top management, young people coming through the lower ranks today often scold us for being slow to pick up on the new technologies. I guess we did the same thing in our day. A couple of decades ago, the senior people in this company passed down their know-how to the younger ones. The older managers knew the analogue technology inside and out, and they were idolised, and rightly so. But today some of our newer graduated people know more about digital technology, more than their seniors, and they pass their know-how up; it is a completely new development.

The precise direction in which all this will head by the end of the century is hard to guess. Obviously at the end of the century the information systems we are starting on now, combining television, computers and communications, will become common-place in the home. We are in the midst of a cultural and social revolution. And it may be more and more difficult to impress people as time goes on, because even today, although the fact that we can pick up the phone and dial directly all the way around the world is a wonder to people of my generation, younger people whose memories do not go back very far don't seem to give it a second thought.

Source: Morita (1994).[10]

Like it or not, information technology is pervading all aspects of business today, including the marketing department. Using the simple example of e-mail, 60 per cent of large companies and 47 per cent of medium-sized businesses in the UK now use this facility.[11]

■ Evolution of organisation structures

IT has not only transformed the ways in which we work; it has transformed the ways in which companies organise themselves. One of the foremost writers on management and organisation, Peter Drucker,[12] viewed the business world in the late 1980s as being on the verge of an era where companies would move from traditional 'command and control' structures to flatter information-based organisations full of knowledge special-ists (*see* Exhibit 6.4). Today, while most companies are still organised into divisions and departments, newer structures have begun to appear alongside the traditional ones.

Knowledge specialists or 'knowledge workers' may not yet be the norm, but there are more of them around today and, as we have seen in Chapter 2, the tools are now available to create and support the 'knowledge organisation'. In companies such as General Motors and Skandia in Sweden, a new breed of executive, called a Chief Knowledge Officer or equivalent title, is being created.[13]

Exhibit 6.4

THE HOSPITAL, THE UNIVERSITY AND THE SYMPHONY ORCHESTRA

The typical large business 20 years hence will have fewer than half the levels of management of its counterpart today, and no more than a third of the managers. In its structure, and in its management problems and concerns, it will bear little resemblance to the typical manufacturing company, circa 1950, which our textbooks still consider the norm. Instead it is far more likely to resemble organisations that neither the practising manager nor the management scholar pays much attention to today: the hospital, the university, the symphony orchestra. For like them, the typical business will be knowledge-based, an organisation composed largely of specialists who direct and discipline their own performance through organised feedback from colleagues, customers, and headquarters. For this reason, it will be what I call an information-based organisation.

Source: Drucker (1988).[12]

■ The impact on business

Various organisations have put forward their own views on the impact that the information society will have on business. Hewitt (1995)[14] provides a succinct commentary on the impact it will have on business:

■ *Business will drive the information society.* The convergence of computing, communications and content is driving the information society and creating a new world of commercial opportunity. Businesses, not the consumer, will be the first to exploit these opportunities and are already using new multimedia technologies to find new ways of adding value to customers.

■ *No single, predictable information society will emerge.* Nearly eight out of ten US business leaders expect interactive, multimedia markets to emerge unevenly and unexpectedly.

■ *'Old' businesses and business supply chains will be destroyed.* Traditionally businesses have been organised into industries and industries into 'supply chains', a division of labour between different organisations which turns raw materials into products. As technologies enable organisations and individuals to connect with each other in new ways, old supply-chain relationships will be destroyed.

■ *New, knowledge-based connections with customers will be created.* One example is a sophisticated, networked multimedia kiosk used by the Nationwide Building Society. The kiosk acts as a 'virtual' branch giving customers interactive access to Nationwide services. Customers are guided through the system by a Nationwide 'receptionist' on video, while personal advice is available immediately through a videoconference link to the organisation's call centre. Public access systems of this type will enable suppliers to reach customers without intermediaries.

- *New, knowledge-based goods and services will be created.* Firms will supplement physical outputs with new electronic 'knowledge products'. For pharmaceutical companies, this means offering on-line medical advice as well as drugs. They are evaluating how to deliver the right information effectively from their vast knowledge of drugs to medical staff when a treatment is being made.
- *Businesses will transform the workplace.* Convergence will allow businesses to strip out routine work and connect employees in real time from a variety of different locations.
- *Some organisations will die.* Some businesses who fail to access and use available information will die from information thirst, while others without effective information management will drown in an information flood. Successful organisations will develop approaches to filtering, storing and disseminating knowledge both between and within organisations.
- *New global networks will be created.* Global networks will be created of people and organisations who can communicate but who do not know each other. In this environment, buyers will look to brand names they can trust and having a strong brand which consumers know will be increasingly important in a crowded advertising marketplace.
- *Competition will intensify.* Global information networks will make price and quality information more readily available to buyers and sellers, leading to intensified competition. The more information consumers have the easier it will be for consumers, service users and citizens to demand the best service at the lowest price.
- *Businesses must grasp the opportunity.* The greatest risk for businesses is not confronting the threats and opportunities created by the convergence of computing, communications and content (*see* Exhibit 6.5).

Exhibit 6.5

CARS AND WASHING MACHINES

Most businesses have been remarkably slow to understand the power which the Internet offers to their customers. Very few have taken up the opportunity of participating in the thousands of noticeboards operated by consumers of products as diverse as Volkswagen cars and Zanussi. Microsoft is one of the few companies to participate regularly in the Internet newsgroups devoted to its products.

Source: Hewitt (1995).[14]

■ The business/IT gap

Even if only half of the above propositions are true, the implications for business and marketing are still profound. Yet there continues to be a major gap in communications and understanding between business managers, who often fail to understand the power of information technology, and IT managers, who often fail to explain its power. This is an important issue, as information technology costs can account for anything between 2 and 10 per cent of a company's annual operating costs. The benefits from investing in IT can be enormous if the technology is utilised correctly yet, unfortunately, this is not always the case. Many business and marketing executives today do not understand, or feel comfortable with, information technology. The information society may be upon us, but there are many people who are not equipped with the skills, knowledge or understanding to make the best use of IT. In addition, technology staff have also failed to grasp the opportunity to help lead the business community through this revolution. A common frustration in business today is this lack of understanding between these two communities (*see* Exhibit 6.6), a situation which can lead to poorly designed IT systems, delays and large 'white elephant' projects.

Exhibit 6.6

WATCH THOSE EYES GLAZE OVER

During the seventies and eighties, information technology was used almost exclusively to automate operations which had hitherto been done manually, or by the application of people power. Surprisingly the expected explosion of productivity did not occur. It did not occur for two reasons. Firstly, people were slow to adapt to new methods and secondly, these new models tended to produce a barrage of information, which in turn took even more people to analyse and use it. Nothing is more useless or infuriating than asking a simple management question and getting a response delivered to your desk in the form of several hundred yards of computer print-out.

The boards of most companies pursued a sort of 'dialogue of the deaf' with their Information Technology Management during the seventies and eighties. Neither side was able to appreciate the totality of the picture and this was not helped by the almost impenetrable jargon used by most IT people. The trouble is that they love their skill and are absorbed by the technological possibilities, as well as the ever-increasing scale of what is possible. One only has to pass a simple management request to an I.T. man to see his eyes glaze over and watch him disappear into a totally different world of bytes and mega-bytes. Frankly, most managers could not care less. Above everything, they do not want to be told that yet another new system will have to be built. They also do not want to be told that, in any event, the system will be incompatible with everything they already have and that the entire investment (which has been put in at enormous expense, and a marked effect on their profits) has been invalidated by this new and totally unreasonable request.

Source: Harvey-Jones (1993).[15]

We often tend to think of IT as a key part of any operational infrastructure in a company, yet we think of it less often as a key component of the marketing infrastructure. Even if we take a very narrow definition of marketing, IT is important. Marketing support staff must be computer and network literate; in one company, one-sixth of the IT department was dedicated to marketing support.[16] Drucker describes information as 'data endowed with relevance and purpose'.[17] He also echoes the views of John Harvey-Jones, the former chairman of ICI, who feared that all this new information technology might simply result in managers drowning in a sea of data.

THE GROWTH OF ELECTRONIC COMMERCE

■ Electronic payment systems

Electronic commerce is a term used for a variety of different methods of conducting business electronically. The term covers a wide variety of different concepts and payment mechanisms. In this section, we will examine the main categories of electronic payment systems as well as the different types of plastic card which enable electronic payments to be made. The three broad categories of electronic payment systems are:

- electronic funds transfer (EFT) and electronic funds transfer at point of sale (EFTPoS)
- electronic data interchange (EDI)
- electronic money.

■ Electronic funds transfer (EFT)

EFT can be used for both commercial and personal payments. In the commercial arena, SWIFT stands out as the international standard for the transfer of high-value financial transactions. It was established in Brussels in 1973 to automate the function previously carried out by telex and is used by more than 4000 financial institutions worldwide to process approximately 500 million transactions a year.[18] In the UK, CHAPS is the standard for same-day high-value payments (processing 12.5 million transactions worth £27 trillion in 1995[19]), while BACS is the standard for salary payments and other relatively low-value financial transactions. Individual banks have also set up their own electronic commerce systems for their customers. One of the first banks to employ technology in this way was the Bank of Scotland, with its Home and Office Banking Service (HOBS)[20] for commercial customers. Another development by a Scottish bank is IBOS (InterBank Online System) which was developed by the Royal Bank of Scotland in conjunction with French, Spanish and Portuguese banks in 1991 as an alternative to using SWIFT for international funds transfers.[21]

When credit or debit cards are used to purchase goods or services in a shop, supermarket or retailing outlet, the transaction is referred to as *electronic funds transfer at point of sale* (EFTPoS), and usually refers to personal rather than commercial payments.

■ Electronic data interchange (EDI)

EDI is an electronic data-transfer mechanism used in a wide range of business transactions. It is usually associated with the automation of the 'billing cycle', where invoices and purchase orders are generated and sent automatically from one company to another. There are different standards for different industries, although convergence and rationalisation are inevitable. The primary benefit for organisations that implement EDI is reduced transaction costs. US sources claim that EDI can cut the average cost of processing a purchase order from $150 to $25.[22] However, the applications for EDI are much broader than the transfer of invoices and purchase orders (*see* Exhibit 6.7). One clothing retailer, working with the jeans manufacturer Levi Strauss, has automated the entire ordering and billing process for producing custom-made jeans.[23] Custom Clothing of Massachusetts has set up a system where customers' measurements are sent electronically to the fabric cutter every evening. By the following afternoon, the jeans are made up and sent to the store, or directly to the customer. Invoicing, billing and the entire distribution process have been simplified and automated. Given that three-quarters of the total cost of producing a pair of jeans relates to these activities, the system has clear benefits. Similarly, Campbell Soup Company has seen fit to spend $30 million on redesigning its order-processing system around EDI.[24]

Exhibit 6.7

FOR RICHER OR POORER

The true value of Electronic Data Interchange does not lie in the saving of cost on invoices, even though no one in the their right mind would turn down the reduction in countless pieces of paper. It does not even lie in direct debiting, desirable and helpful though this is to both parties. The real advantage of Electronic Data Interchange is that it enables supplier and customer to be in each other's minds, each looking after their own part of the business. With luck, and with a good relationship, they can help each other to achieve the ultimate advantage in the marketplace. This involves massive philosophical and attitudinal changes. The customer is no longer your enemy, but indeed your best hope. The relationship between you is no longer one of conflict but of collaboration. The end result is that both of you grow richer together because, if you persist in the bad old ways, you will inevitably grow poorer together.

Source: Harvey-Jones (1993).[15]

The European market for EDI is growing at a rate of 20 per cent annually[25] and the UK is the region's leading user. However, this rate of growth is much slower than forecasters have predicted in the past.[26] There are 30–40 000 organisations in the US who use EDI and another 15–20 000 outside of the US. This represents a very small percentage of commercial organisations, as EDI is only being employed by larger companies such as Glaxo, Marks & Spencer, Courtaulds, ICI and Cowie (*see* Exhibit 6.8). For smaller companies, the benefits of implementing EDI are often outweighed by the costs of implementation.

Exhibit 6.8

ELECTRONIC TAX DISKS

Car-fleet operators like Cowie Interleasing expect to make substantial cost and staff savings from an electronic data interchange (EDI) system for issuing tax disks by the government's Driver and Vehicle Licensing Agency (DVLA). The scheme will replace the cumbersome paper-based system and could cover eventually more than 500,000 cars. The electronic system dispenses with the present costly and time-consuming process which involves the DVLA sending out a postal reminder that the tax disk is due for renewal on each car – even where fleets of up to 50,000 cars are run by one operator, as is the case with the biggest leasing companies. Instead, each month the DVLA will send a reminder to each fleet operator by EDI with the operator responding also by EDI with a list of the vehicles it wishes to re-license. The total tax bill is paid electronically by direct debit and the DVLA prints out the tax disks as a batch and sends them to either the operator or to a collection point.

Source: Griffiths.[27]

The implementation of EDI is not easy as it requires considerable resources, in terms of manpower and time, to implement it.[28] The main obstacle is obtaining agreement between several parties on the message and business standards. These parties may be in direct competition with each other or have an antagonistic customer/supplier relationship. Worse, where agreement is required between competitors, proceedings will only take place at the speed at which the least committed partner is willing to move. The most successful implementations of EDI have been in industries such as retailing where the customer is the dominant party and is in a position to force through standards on suppliers. In such cases, the blunt message to suppliers is: 'If you want to do business with us, you need to conform to our way of doing business.' While this may not seem the most democratic method of doing business, there are considerable advantages to be gained by the supplier.

The implementation of EDI often locks in the supplier with the customer, making it more difficult to break the relationship (*see* Exhibit 6.9). It also increases the likelihood that suppliers will gain a greater share of the customer's business.

Exhibit 6.9

CARROT OR STICK?

Only when a critical mass of trading partners are using EDI will the real financial and operating benefits be seen. The greater the percentage of partners using EDI, the more possible it will be to scale down the paper-based operation (an important point to remember when assessing the cost/benefits of the project). There are basically two approaches to enlarging the EDI fraternity – persuasion or coercion. The latter is only available to organisations who have some leverage over their trading partners. This approach carries the risk of losing a valued trading partner who may not want to move towards EDI at the present time.

Persuasion is perhaps the most favoured method. It involves educating partners of the advantages – for both partners – of using EDI. The mutual benefits have to be explained and illustrated. Pilot project partners can be very valuable here in helping sell the message. Nothing convinces as effectively as someone who has first-hand experience.

Source: Jackson (1988).[29]

■ Electronic money

The benefits that are claimed for electronic money include greater efficiency, as hard currency and cheques are not required, and greater security, as no cash is handled. Given that cash accounts for 80 per cent of all payments made in the UK,[30] its displacement by electronic means is likely to be a slow process. It is already beginning to happen, but there are still many issues to be overcome before the use of electronic cash becomes commonplace. Flohr (1996)[31] cites four main issues:

- *Security:* to ensure that on-line transactions, transferring funds and creating, or minting, electronic money are secure.
- *Authentication:* so that buyers and sellers can verify that the electronic currency is real.

- *Anonymity:* to assure consumers and merchants that the transactions remain confidential.
- *Divisibility:* so that electronic money comes in small (cent, penny or smaller) denominations that can make high-volume, small-value transactions practical.

Despite these issues, several electronic money initiatives have been started. In the UK, a number of organisations have come together to develop the Mondex card (*see* Exhibit 6.10), while in France, VISA cards have carried microchips since the 1980s. Europay, MasterCard and VISA have created the EMV standard for electronic payments involving smart cards. In Sweden, the two banks that control 70 per cent of the retail banking market, Sparbanken Sverige and Nordbanken, have also launched an electronic purse scheme based on the EMV standards[32] and in Japan, Toshiba and VISA have collaborated on a project to promote electronic commerce and smart cards which can be used in PCs to purchase goods over the Internet.[33] Other electronic payment systems in operation around the world include Danmønt, a smart card scheme that was launched in 1991 by all the Danish telephone companies and banks, Proton, the electronic purse system in Brussels,[34] Avant in Finland and FISC in Taiwan.

Exhibit 6.10

MONDEX MANIA?

The trial of the Mondex card shows there is still some way to go before magnetic stripe is replaced with chip card technology. The Mondex card, an electronic purse, has been on trial for a year in Swindon, Wiltshire. Investors include Midland, NatWest, BT, Hitachi and Panasonic. But while Mondex professes itself pleased with the results so far, the fact remains that out of a population of 170,000, a mere 10,000 residents – or 24% of NatWest and Midland customer card holders – have so far taken up Mondex. The number of retailers taking it is 700, or 70% of the town's retailing population, which is the same number as a year ago.

A spokesman for Mondex says: 'The number of Mondex holders is more than we hoped for. A 100% take-up by retailers would not be realistic because there are many shops where items are too expensive to be purchased by Mondex. The average amount loaded onto the card is between £20 and £30 and it is going well in newsagents, fast food outlets, petrol stations and supermarkets. Mondex is far more radical than credit and debit cards because it's replacing a cash-based system that has been around for a long time. Getting people to move across to an electronic form of exchange is something of a challenge but each time people are faced with a new piece of technology, take-up becomes progressively quicker.'

Source: Computer Weekly (11 July 1996).[35]

Transactions can be carried out at the point of sale using a variety of different payment mechanisms, some of which are electronic or information based and some which are not. The electronic mechanisms include plastic cards, of which there are several different types, the most common of which are described in Table 6.2.

The magnetic stripe card is the most widely used of the four. If you examine the back of a credit or debit card, you will see a black magnetic stripe running the full length of

Table 6.2 Main categories of plastic card

Card category	Technology	Uses	Advantages	Cost
Bar-code	• Simple technology • Data storage of 10–12 characters	• Identification (library, cheque cashing) • Inventory and product tracking • Supermarket scanning	• Universally accepted • Implemented on a worldwide basis • Very cost effective • Easy to use	• Inexpensive to produce – less than $0.10 per card
Magnetic stripe (or mag. stripe)	• Most widely used card in the world • No computational ability on the card • Data storage of 75 characters	• Bank numbers • Serial numbers • Secure door access • Identification • Credit/debit transactions	• Accepted worldwide • Implemented worldwide • Cost effective • Easy to use	• Inexpensive to produce – about $0.25–0.50 per card
Memory card (uses 'chip' technology but does not contain a microprocessor and is not generally regarded as a true smart card)	• No computational capability – intelligence lies outside the card • Capacity from 1024 to 65 000 bits • No security in basic form of card	• Telephone prepaid cards • Car warranty programmes • Supermarket loyalty programmes	• Stores value on the card • Low cost • More memory than mag. stripe card • Portable data file	• Medium price – about $1–3 per card
Smart card	• Contains a microprocessor built into card	• All applications supported by other types of plastic card	• Very secure • Multiple uses • Very high capacity	• Expensive – about $5–10 per card

Source: Based on Kaplan (1996).[36] Copyright International Thomson Computer Press, 1996. Reprinted with permission.

the card onto which is encoded a small amount of information. This information enables the cardholder to perform a variety of different functions, including:

- withdrawing money from an automated teller machine (ATM card)
- paying for goods in a store or supermarket (credit or debit card)
- providing identification for gaining entry into secure buildings (identity card)
- accumulating points on a loyalty scheme (loyalty card).

The newest variant of the plastic card is the smart card, which is one of the latest applications of chip miniaturisation. A microprocessor is embedded onto a piece of plastic which gives it an astonishing increase in functionality over the capabilities of credit and debit cards. A variation of the smart card is already used in many countries in the form of public telephone cards. Shell UK has had a smart card initiative in operation for a number of years. Customers use their Shell SMART card to collect electronic points when they purchase petrol. For every £6 spent on petrol (or oil or car washes), the customer receives one SMART point. The points are stored in the smart card's memory and can be redeemed for free cinema tickets, air miles, tapes and CDs. Alternatively, the points can be donated to charity. Shell agreed to double the first 333 000 points donated by its customers to the British Heart Foundation and the first 500 000 points to the Save the Children Fund.[36] Other more creative applications of smart card technology are illustrated in Exhibit 6.11.

Exhibit 6.11

'HE-MAN WEEKLY'

You are buying a newspaper at your local newsagent. 'That's 65p, please,' says the cashier clerk. You whip out your bank card and the terminal purrs quietly. Suddenly, the clerk, who is studying the terminal screen, lights up and says: 'Why Ms Jones! I see it's your husband's birthday next week! Can I interest you in a subscription to *He-Man Weekly*?' Sound far-fetched? Developments are afoot to make such a scenario reality. With the growth of 'smart' cards – plastic cards which store information on a microchip – retailers will be able to access far more customer data than they can with the debit and credit cards which are already so familiar to the modern consumer.

Source: Financial Times (5 July 1995).[37]

■ The future of electronic commerce

The reality of electronic commerce today is that it is more or less confined to EDI and EFT (including EFTPoS).[38] Electronic money is still very much in the trial stages and is unlikely to become a common form of electronic commerce until the twenty-first century. The full colonisation of cyberspace that is referred to in Exhibit 6.12 will have to wait until the use of electronic money becomes commonplace.

Exhibit 6.12

THE COMMERCIAL COLONISATION OF CYBERSPACE

The commercial colonisation of cyberspace began in earnest in 1994 when First Virtual Holdings opened for business on the Internet. FVH operates as a financial middleman between buyers and sellers of low-cost goods.

A more ambitious system is E-cash, pioneered by Dutch software house DigiCash. The company has invented a form of digital money which people can use to pay for products and services on the Internet. Almost 4,000 volunteers from 45 countries have so far participated in the trials of the service. Participants in the trials have been able to spend their money in diverse ways: a Dutch university is inviting punters to try their luck in an on-line casino; a South African newspaper, technology magazine *Wired*, and the *Encyclopaedia Britannica* are downloading pages to users' screens for a small fee; and a Canadian mail order company has dispatched postcards of Canada to shoppers as part of a programme to demonstrate the efficacy of on-line catalogue shopping.

Source: Banking Technology (March 1995).[39]

THE IMPACT ON MARKETING

■ Technology-enabled marketing

The impact of information technology on marketing is dramatic. Customer segmentation is moving into a new information-rich era based on behaviour rather than the traditional demographic methods. Sales promotions are becoming more targeted as a result of more, and better, information. Distribution channels are multiplying and intermediaries are coming under increasing threat as manufacturers market their products directly to the customer. The changes that are taking place within marketing as a result of the technology revolution are summarised in Table 6.3.

Table 6.3 Traditional versus technology-enabled marketing methods

Marketing area	Traditional	Technology-enabled marketing	Implication marketing
Segmentation	Demographics	Behavioural	Database
Advertising	Push	Pull	Interactive
Promotions	Mass	Tailored	Re-emergence
Pricing	Set by firm	Set by customer	Tailored pricing
Sales management	Data with sales	Data shared	Marketing and sales are partners
Distribution channels	Intermediaries	Direct	Multi-channel
New products	Constrained	Customer driven	Marketing expansion
Monitoring	Share, profit	Retention, value	New metrics

Source: Gartner Group (1996), based on a framework developed by John Deighton, Harvard Business School, and Robert Blattberg, Northwestern University's Kellogg School of Management.[40]

These changes are examined throughout this book. For example, we have already seen in Chapter 4 how the nature of customer segmentation has been changed by IT and the importance of the database in marketing. In Chapter 8, we will discuss interactive advertising using multimedia, the Internet and interactive television. The essence of marketing on the Internet is that customers must choose to visit your site. Multimedia is interactive and marketers must learn the art of advertising interactively (*see* Exhibit 6.13).

Exhibit 6.13

DEALING WITH FLASH HARRY

On the Internet, as a colleague is fond of observing, nobody knows if you are a monkey. In cyberspace, in other words, there is no way of determining the integrity of an individual or an organisation from an electronic image. Harry's Half Price Corner can seem as respectable as Harrods, especially if Flash Harry has the gall to name his Website 'The Harold Hardman Partnership, Purveyors of Fine Goods since 1884' or some such label indicating irreproachable integrity.

Source: Financial Times (10 June 1996).[41]

CONCLUSION

The information revolution is in full swing. To a great extent it is being driven by the increasing penetration of PCs in the home and the astonishing growth rate of the Internet. Governments are supporting IT-driven initiatives to ensure that their citizens are not left behind by this revolution and countries such as Finland and Singapore are to the fore with these initiatives. The information revolution has not just had impacts on society; it has also changed the way people go about their day-to-day jobs. In the workplace, IT has automated many formerly manual processes and brings information quickly to the fingertips of managers. Voicemail and e-mail have begun to replace hastily scribbled messages. Some organisations have even created senior executive positions with titles such as Chief Knowledge Officer. However, as IT continues its relentless advance, some workers are feeling disenfranchised by its progress. Indeed, some organisations are unlikely to survive in the information age as new supply-chain relationships are created and old ones broken. The clear message for organisations is to adapt to the new ways of working or go out of business.

Electronic commerce has already become a reality, with considerable growth being experienced in the areas of EFT, EFTPoS and EDI. Ultimately, electronic money will transform the ways in which products are marketed and sold, but this is unlikely to happen for some years.

The clear message to be taken from these trends is that marketing needs to embrace the information revolution and drive the technology agenda in organisations today.

ASSIGNMENT QUESTIONS

1 What is meant by the information society?

2 How has information technology changed the way in which businesses are run today?

3 To what extent has the business community embraced the information revolution?

4 What are the key benefits and risks of using electronic commerce?

5 Select three areas of marketing from Table 6.3 and discuss the implications which the information revolution has for them.

References

[1] Black, G. (1996). 'Complications delay birth', *Financial Times*, 3 July.

[2] Oldroyd, R. (1996). 'Minister puts his back into post', *Sunday Business ComputerAge*, 26 May.

[3] Hogg, S. (1996). 'Relaxed hand on the wheel', *Financial Times*, 31 July.

[4] Sheridan, C. (1996). 'What's happening – Ireland', *IT's Monday*, Vol. 211, 8 July.

[5] Cane, A. (1995). 'Era of the "information society"', *Financial Times*, 3 October.

[6] Emmerson, B. (1996). 'Finns watch Internet TV', *Byte*, March.

[7] Manchester, P. (1995). 'Home consumer market is leading the way', *Financial Times*, 7 June.

[8] Kehoe, L. (1995). 'Surge of Internet business', *Financial Times*, 1 March.

[9] Gerdon, J. (1983). 'Will the computer change the job of top management?', *Sloan Management Review*, Vol. 25, No. 1.

[10] Morita, A. (1994). *Made in Japan: Akio Morita and Sony*. London: HarperCollins.

[11] Burton, G. (1996). 'Fax holds its own in face of e-mail onslaught', *Sunday Business ComputerAge*, 2 June.

[12] Drucker, P. (1988). 'The coming of the new organisation', *Harvard Business Review*, January–February.

[13] Shillingford, J. (1996). 'Computer managers put in the shade by know-alls', *Sunday Business ComputerAge*, 2 June.

[14] Hewitt, P. (1995). 'The information society: ten propositions for business', *Andersen Consulting*, December.

[15] Harvey-Jones, J. (1993). *Managing to Survive*. London: Mandarin.

[16] Weixel, S. (1992). 'Rewards, challenges in marketing support', *Computerworld*, 29 June.

[17] Drucker, P. (1988). Op. cit.

[18] Black, G. (1994). 'Challenges for Swift', *Financial Times*, 15 November.

[19] Power, C. (1996). 'APACS opts to upgrade thriving BACS', *Electronic Payments International*, April.

[20] Shillingford, J. (1996). 'The net effect: banking', *Sunday Business ComputerAge*, 26 May.

[21] Dempsey, M. (1994). 'Still room for enhancement', *Financial Times*, 15 November.

[22] Verity, J.W. (1996). 'Invoice? What's an invoice?', *Business Week*, 10 June.

[23] McLeod, M. (1996). 'Wired for business', *Sunday Business ComputerAge*, 26 May.

[24] Verity, J.W. (1996). Op. cit.

[25] Computer Weekly (1996). 'EDI market enjoys 20% growth', *Computer Weekly*, 28 March.

[26] Black, G. (1995). 'UK still leads the field', *Financial Times*, 15 June.

[27] Griffiths, J. (1996). 'DVLA tries out online renewals', *Financial Times*, 25 September.

[28] Palmer, D. (1988). 'The enabling factors for EDI'. In Gifkins, M. and Hitchcock, D. (eds) *The EDI Handbook*. London: Blenheim Online.

[29] Jackson, D. (1988). 'Preparing the organisation for EDI'. In Gifkins, M. and Hitchcock, D. (eds) *The EDI Handbook*. London: Blenheim Online.

[30] Rich, M. (1995). 'The dash to replace cash', *Financial Times*, 5 July.

[31] Flohr, U. (1996). 'Electric money', *Byte*, June.

[32] Daniel, E. (1996). 'Two banks plan purse launch in Sweden', *Electronic Payments International*, April.

[33] Van der Velde, H. (1996). 'Banks take charge', *The Banker*, March.

[34] Smart Card Bulletin (1995). 'Proton roll-out in Belgium', *Smart Card Bulletin*, March.

[35] Smith, S. (1996). 'Mondex mania', *Computer Weekly*, 11 July.

[36] Kaplan, J.M. (1996). *Smart Cards: The Global Information Passport*. Boston: International Thomson Computer Press.

[37] Rich, M. (1995). Op. cit.

38 Reilly, B. (1995). 'Approaches to electronic commerce', *Gartner Group*, 27 October.
39 Penrose, P. (1995). 'The next generation', *Banking Technology*, March.
40 Nelson, S. (1996). 'Will technology help reinvent marketing?', *Gartner Group*, 17 April.
41 Cane, A. (1996). 'Dealing with Flash Harry', *Financial Times*, 10 June.

7

THE DRIVERS OF THE INFORMATION REVOLUTION

- What is information technology?
- Hardware trends
- Software trends
- Telecommunications trends
- The information superhighway

OBJECTIVES

After studying this chapter, you will be able to:

- ☐ Understand what is meant by information technology and what are its main components
- ☐ Appreciate the different types of computer and the trends in computer processing power and storage capacity
- ☐ Describe the three different eras of computing
- ☐ Describe the changes that have taken place in software development in recent decades
- ☐ Understand how the telecommunications industry is being radically restructured and how businesses and individuals will be affected by these changes
- ☐ Define what is meant by the information superhighway

WHAT IS INFORMATION TECHNOLOGY?

■ Definition

It is surprisingly difficult to get a consistent definition of information technology (IT). *The Penguin Dictionary of Computers*[1] refers to it as:

> *'a portmanteau phrase to cover all aspects of the art or science of processing data to produce information'.*

The *Oxford English Reference Dictionary*[2] describes it as:

> *'the technology involved in the recording, storage and dissemination of information, esp. using computers, telecommunications, etc.'*

Perhaps a more useful way to understand IT is to break it into its constituent components and examine each separately. We can describe IT as having the following three components:

- hardware
- software
- telecommunications.

Although we will keep the technical jargon to a minimum, we will delve into the 'bits and bytes' of information technology in this chapter. It is worth taking the time to understand some of the more important technical elements of information technology without getting overly concerned about all the details. Rather, get a feel for the trends that are happening and regard this chapter as a reference section to come back to as you read the other chapters. If in doubt, refer to the glossary at the end of the book.

HARDWARE TRENDS

■ The evolution of computers

The first modern computing machine for adding and subtracting (if we choose to ignore the abacus) dates from 1642 and was designed by the French mathematician and philosopher, Blaise Pascal. The first modern computer is a much more recent invention, dating from 1948, and the early computing machines were dinosaurs compared to the computers we use today. In terms of the evolution of computer hardware, there have been three major species, as depicted in Table 7.1 and Exhibit 7.1. Almost half a century after their first introduction, mainframes are still used to provide much of the processing power required by today's big businesses. Mainframes support hundreds or even thousands of users who are attached to the mainframe through terminals or PCs. In 1960, Digital Equipment Corporation developed the first mini-computer[3] and by the 1970s the mini-computer had become very popular because it could automate the smaller tasks which proved too expensive to automate using the mainframe. The first PC was not invented until 1981 but has since spawned its own subspecies of workstations (high-powered PCs), laptops (truly portable PCs) and palmtops (even smaller versions).

Table 7.1 Three major species of computer

Species of computer	Number of users	Era
Mainframe	Hundreds	1950s (but still very much alive today)
Mini-computer	Tens	1960s (and still very much alive today)
Microcomputer or personal computer (PC)	Single user	1980s and 1990s

SURVIVAL OF THE FITTEST

Down through the ages, life has tended to evolve in sudden great leaps, separated by long periods of slow change. The same is true for technology. In the past half-century, computer technology has evolved in three large jumps, each one followed by an explosion of new computers, a period of rapid change, and then the gradual emergence of a few dominant species that rule until the next digital disturbance. Jose Ortega y Gasset, a Spanish philosopher, once said that 'a revolution lasts only 15 years, a period that coincides with the effectiveness of a generation'. As it happens, computer revolutions have taken place at roughly the same intervals.

Start around 1950, with the IBM mainframe, when the term 'data processing' entered the language. The next big upheaval came in the mid-1960s, when the mini-computer arrived to open the computing market to a host of upstarts such as Digital Equipment, and programmers – the spiritual fathers of today's code geeks – started to abandon their ties. Then in 1981, IBM introduced the personal computer, causing a market explosion from which emerged some of today's strongest competitors: Intel, Microsoft, Compaq.

Source: The Economist (25 May 1996).[4]

■ Increases in processing power

The innovation that really transformed the computer and heralded the birth of the mini-computer and the PC was the invention in 1958 of the silicon microchip. The microchip, otherwise known as the 'chip' or 'integrated circuit' because it contains numerous transistors in a tiny sliver of silicon, was the start of the miniaturisation which has powered the computer industry over the past 40 years. In that time, the power of the microchip has grown exponentially. Even since 1970, the so-called price/performance ratio of the microchip has increased one million-fold.[5] A task that would have taken a computer one year to complete in 1970 can be done on today's computers in about 30 seconds – for the same cost. The world's largest supplier of microchips for PCs is a company called Intel. The Intel 386 chip powered the generation of personal computers sold in the early 1990s. Since then, the Intel 486 range of chips has come and gone, while the latest industry standard, the Intel Pentium chip, will soon be replaced by the next, even more powerful generation of microchips.

The application of microchip technology is not confined to computers. Microchips can also be built into a wide variety of everyday products such as washing machines, dishwashers, cars, stereos and televisions to increase the functions which they can perform. As Exhibit 7.2 shows, this trend is set to continue for some time to come.

■ Increases in computer storage capacity

In addition to the exponential increase in the price/performance ratio of the microchip, the amount of data that can be retained on computer storage devices has also increased dramatically. These computer storage devices come in many forms, including 'hard disks' on PCs, floppy disks and optical storage devices called CD-ROMs (more about those in Chapter 8).

THAT ASTONISHING MICROCHIP

It may be hard to believe, but it is less than 20 years since this newspaper was introducing readers to the existence of the integrated circuit, then still exotic, and predicting that it would change the world. It did, and in pretty short order. The world's appetite for chips has so far been almost as abundant as the silicon from which they are made.

Throughout this period, chip technology has evolved rapidly, more or less in conformity with the exponential growth in power predicted by Gordon Moore, a founder of Intel, America's leading chip-maker. Every time engineers seem close to bumping against the technology's limits, they find some new way to make circuits smaller, faster and cheaper. As a result, the chips that were exotic yesterday are now the commonplace components not just of the computer but also of the car, the camera and the cash card. By common consent it has been the most productivity-enhancing, life-changing technological revolution since the harnessing of steam power in the 18th century or, in the 19th, of electricity itself. And by common consent, this revolution also has much further to go.

Source: The Economist (23 March 1996).[6]

In computer terms, the smallest unit of measurement is a byte which corresponds to one unit of electronic information. In 1970, the typical *Fortune* 500 company possessed about 8 billion characters of electronic data. By 1990, this figure had increased to nearly 28 000 billion and, by the year 2000, the amount of data amassed by the same company will reach an astounding 400 000 billion pieces of information.[7] Such numbers are impossible to comprehend and, as the amount of information held by companies has grown, new terms have come into common usage to describe the ever-increasing capacity (*see* Table 7.2).

Table 7.2 Units of computer storage capacity

1 000 bytes	= 1 kilobyte (Kb)			
1 000 000 bytes	= 1 000 Kb	= 1 megabyte (Mb)		
1 000 000 000 bytes	= 1 000 000 Kb	= 1 000 Mb	= 1 gigabyte (Gb)	
1 000 000 000 000 bytes	= 1 000 000 000 Kb	= 1 000 000 Mb	= 1 000 Gb	= 1 terabyte

In the early 1990s, PCs could read information from devices known as floppy disks which had a storage capacity of 1.44Kb. By the mid-1990s, many PCs had CD-ROM drives which have over 400 times the capacity of a floppy disk. In the near future, a new storage device known as a digital video disk (DVD),[8] which is the same size as a CD-ROM but with eight times its capacity,[9] will be commonplace. This rapid growth in storage capacity is illustrated graphically in Figure 7.1.

The result of the increases in processing power and storage capacity is that organisations can store and process information at a customer level. The trends discussed earlier, such as database marketing, relationship marketing, data mining and data warehousing, are all made feasible by these technology changes.

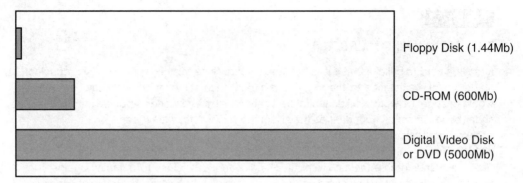

Fig 7.1   Storage capacities of different storage media

SOFTWARE TRENDS

■ Definition

Computers on their own can do nothing for business or marketing without the software that breathes life into the machine. When people talk about a 'computer system', they are typically referring to the software – the set of instructions contained in a computer program – rather than to the hardware on which the software runs. Browning (1995)[10] light-heartedly describes software as

> *'those information technologies that you cannot drop on your foot, particularly computer programs.'*

The performance of software has improved in tandem with the exponential increases in the power of the microchip and, while computers have become smaller and more powerful, software has also evolved in stages.

■ Three waves of computing

Since the introduction of the first modern computer, there have been three distinct waves of computing which closely parallel the three species of hardware discussed at the beginning of this chapter:

■ *Wave 1 – the data-processing era*. In the 1950s and 1960s, computer software and computer operations ran in batch mode where all the transactions from a particular day were processed together overnight. The computer – a mainframe – was little more than a big number-crunching machine which was not designed to give instant answers to queries. If sales managers wanted a report on the latest sales figures, they would send the request to the IT or data-processing department and the report would be generated whenever the next batch of computer reports was run, probably that night. If a manager then decided additional information on sales per customer was required, it might take another day for the additional report to be generated.

■ *Wave 2 – the on-line era.* In the 1970s the first on-line systems became available. Throughout the 1980s, computers became more and more user friendly and allowed users to conduct transactions and queries in 'real time', while the users waited for the answer and perhaps created additional queries. Sales managers could access information directly from the mainframe whenever they wanted and computers still used batch programs for standard, time-consuming tasks.

■ *Wave 3 – the client/server era.* Today, there is enough power available on a personal computer to run many applications that could previously only be carried out on mainframes. The processing is often distributed between a PC or workstation (a high-powered PC) and the larger mainframe or mini-computer. This process, known as client/server and sometimes referred to as distributed computing, requires complex programming and operations to ensure that data is synchronised between the various components of the computer system. The sales manager could now access a block of data from the central computer and perform his or her own analysis either on a desktop PC or by sharing the processing with the larger, more powerful mainframe.

■ Operating systems

When a computer is turned on, the first piece of software that is loaded into the computer's memory is the operating system which runs other applications or computer programs. In the mainframe era, computers had their own operating systems which were owned by the manufacturer. An IBM mainframe could not run programs developed on a Digital computer and vice versa. When the first PCs came off the production line in the early 1980s, they all ran on an operating system known as DOS (disk operating system), a product that has earned a considerable fortune for Bill Gates, CEO of Microsoft. DOS became the dominant operating system for PCs and the standard for the industry.

In the 1990s, a new PC operating system from Microsoft, known as Windows, became commonplace. It supported what is known as a graphical user interface (GUI – pronounced 'gooey') which replaced the somewhat boring white text on a black or green background with a colourful, graphical set of icons, text and a strange pointing device known as a mouse. From the user's perspective, it was a major change in the way a computer was used. The PC became easier to use and graphically presented figures and results became easier to create and interpret. However, Microsoft did not invent the GUI or the mouse. Years earlier, an American company called Apple Computer had developed a GUI for its Macintosh range of computers. Apple Mac users claim that the Apple interface is still far superior to that of Windows. Yet, like the Betamax technology that lost out to VHS in the war for VCR standards in the early 1980s, Bill Gates's business instinct has ensured that Windows dominates the PC operating system market in the late 1990s.

In the mini-computer market, the two main operating systems are UNIX and the 'industrial strength' version of Windows known as Windows NT. UNIX comes in many different flavours which reflect its difficult history as an 'open' (i.e. non-proprietary) operating system which the major computing companies were not really interested in promoting. UNIX is a popular operating system in continental Europe but less so in the UK. There are also many other operating systems, such as IBM's OS/2 and the many mainframe operating systems in use today.

■ Trends in software development

The past decade or two have seen a number of trends in software and software development which include the following:

- *Greater use of packaged systems.* In the early days of computing, all computer programs were custom developed for a particular purpose, which made them expensive and time consuming to create. In the past decade, many software programs have been packaged as generic solutions. In marketing, a wide variety of software packages are available for functions such as customer service, preparing mailshots, forecasting and statistical analysis. The most widely used software packages of all are the so-called 'office automation' products such as wordprocessing software, spreadsheets such as Microsoft *Excel* and *Lotus 1-2-3*, database products and graphics products, all of which are used by the marketing department.
- *Greater use of productivity tools.* The use of such tools as third- and fourth-generation languages (3GL or 4GL) increase a programmer's productivity. The latest development is object-oriented programming, where entire blocks of code, known as objects, can be reused again and again by programmers (see Exhibit 7.3).

Exhibit 7.3

SOFTWARE BOTTLENECK

The production of software is likely to become one of the main bottlenecks in the development of advanced information handling systems. While the performance of hardware has increased by several orders of magnitude over the last 30 years, the productivity of programmers has probably not even doubled. An important reason for this is that virtually every program is written afresh – there is very little re-usability of existing design and program segments.

Source: Zorkoczy and Heap (1995).[11]

- *Greater openness between different systems.* Major computer companies such as IBM have a vested interest in promoting their own proprietary systems which generated higher margins. However, the use of open systems based on operating systems such as UNIX, and the *de facto* standards of PC systems based on DOS, Windows and Windows NT, have increased the ability of companies to choose software from a variety of different vendors and provide a high degree of confidence that they can be integrated in a relatively seamless fashion.
- *Systems integrators.* Major IT projects undertaken today typically involve a number of different hardware platforms, different software programming languages and the issue of building 'interfaces' between these different systems. Complexity has also been increased as new systems encompass multimedia, telephone technology and television. The additional complexity of building computer systems is now likely to involve professional 'systems integrators' who have the skills to cope with this increased complexity.

TELECOMMUNICATIONS TRENDS

■ Advances in telecommunications

While tremendous advances have been made in all three areas of information technology, the telecommunications component is the one which is likely to undergo the greatest change in the next 10 years. The main driver of this change will be an insatiable demand for telecommunications capacity reinforced by the requirements of the Internet and such new technologies as interactive television and multimedia. In addition, the traditional PTT (post, telegraph and telephone) companies across Europe are already under pressure as the EU begins to liberalise and deregulate markets. The main technology developments that have underpinned these changes in telecommunications are:

- the digitisation of communications
- advances in cable technology
- improvements in compression technologies
- the development of 'broadband' communications
- the proliferation of mobile telephony
- developments in wireless telecommunications.

■ The digitisation of communications

Traditionally, homes and companies were connected by analogue telecommunications systems. The word analogue describes a signal that varies smoothly and continuously over time, as opposed to digital which is encoded as a sequence of 'on or off', 'one or zero' bits. Analogue signals reproduce voice and music more faithfully than digital signals and, since the first telecommunications networks were designed only to handle voice, the concept of a digital network made little sense. However, computers only operate on digital signals and if they want to talk to each other they have to use digital signals. When an analogue telephone network is the only thing that is available, here's how a computer might think:

> 'First, I'll have to convert my digital signal to analogue so that I can send it across this telephone network to my friend at the other end. That means I'll need a device called a modem to do the conversion. Next, my friend will have to convert it back to a digital signal at the other end which requires another modem and as the telephone lines are very slow, I could end up talking to my friend for a very long time.'

Although analogue systems work well for carrying voice messages from home to home, or from business to business, their limitations are severe when businesses want to transmit large quantities of data at high speed. The increasing convergence of telecommunications and computer technology has helped to speed up the transition from analogue to digital technology and most western countries have now installed advanced digital telephone exchanges.

■ Advances in cable technology

As most analogue and digital signals are still transmitted using a cable, the characteristics and bandwidths of the three main types of cable have a major impact on the amount of data and speed at which data can be transmitted (see Table 7.3). Bandwidth is a term used to describe the capacity of a cable and can be likened to the number of lanes on a motor highway.

Table 7.3 Three generic cable types

Cable type	Characteristics	Capacity (bandwidth)
Twisted pair	This is the standard telephone cable that can be found in any home or office and is primarily used for carrying telephone calls but can also carry data.	0.01 million bps (bits per second)
Coaxial	This is a thicker copper cable that carries the signal into most people's televisions at home.	100 million bps
Fibre optic	This is a cable made from a very pure glass which has an extremely high capacity to carry data.	2500 million bps

The capacity, or bandwidth, of twisted pair cables is limited, particularly when one starts to examine the opportunities and requirements of the information superhighway and the Internet. Fibre-optic cables offer the greatest opportunity for data transmission and the creation of the information superhighways that many people talk about today (*see* Exhibit 7.4). Many telecommunications companies are only now beginning to upgrade their existing networks.

Exhibit 7.4

THE DEATH OF DISTANCE

The technological changes that have swept across the telecommunications industry have two distinct effects. One is to create glut instead of the capacity shortages in the past. The other is to reduce barriers to entry and make possible new sorts of competition. Together, they will transform the industry – although the pace at which they take effect will be partly set by regulation.

The increase in capacity is essentially due to two changes. The first is the increasing use of fibre-optic cables. These now cost much the same as copper wire to lay down and much less to maintain, but carry vastly more traffic. A single fibre thinner than a hair can carry 30,000 simultaneous telephone conversations. Second, switches – telephone exchanges – have moved on from eavesdropping operators and clunky electro-mechanical devices to become increasingly like computers, their costs falling and their capacity expanding inexorably.

Source: The Economist (30 September 1995).[12]

■ Improvements in compression technologies

Digital communication consists of sending signals as a series of '1s' and '0s' across a wire. When these signals get to the other end, they are converted into something meaningful, such as the sound of a voice, a picture or a series of words. Alternatively, they can be left in digital form, for use in computers. Part of the digital message that is transmitted across the wire might look something like:

1,0,1,1,1,1,0,0,1,0,0,0,0,0,1,1.

The fact that there are four '1s' or five '0s' in a row gives rise to the possibility of compressing this message down to a smaller number of digits that can be sent much more quickly using one of several compression techniques that are available. High compression ratios can be achieved when transmitting video using some of the standard compression techniques such as MPEG (*see* Exhibit 7.5). These techniques include the reduction in the number of 'lines' of video transmitted, or the use of an algorithm which transmits only those changes from one frame to the next. However, there is a price to be paid in a reduction in quality of the picture that is transmitted.

Exhibit 7.5

CRAMMING MORE IN

In contrast with text, files in sound and graphics media are considerably larger. The average number of characters in a word is between 5.5 and 6.0 and a medium-sized book of around 100,000 words therefore occupies not much more than half a megabyte (Mb). A single high-resolution image takes up nearly as much space in memory and on disk. A second of full motion video uses 25–30 frames per second and at this rate a minute of uncompressed video would occupy over 1,300Mb. Sound files also take up large amounts of space, although not on the same scale as video. The higher the quality of the sound is, the larger a digitised sound file will be. A minute of CD quality sound in mono rather than stereo requires about 5Mb of disk space.

Without data compression, digital video would not be feasible. MPEG 1 is the leading digital video compression standard adopted by the Moving Picture Experts Group (MPEG). MPEG 1 can reach compression ratios of 200:1 although the average ratio is approximately 100:1. The MPEG 2 standard for higher resolution video takes more space. Other compression techniques are being considered for the MPEG standards 3 and 4, which are intended for video conferencing and high definition television (HDTV).

Source: Datapro (1994).[13]

■ The development of 'broadband' communications

The traditional telephone network is limited by the speed at which data can be sent and in other ways. For example, only one conversation can take place between two telephones. If a modem is used, the process of establishing the connection can take as long as 20–25 seconds. As new technologies such as the Internet, multimedia and interactive television expand (*see* Chapter 8), the limitations of the plain old telephone system (POTS) mean that it is simply not able to support these technologies effectively. However, several initiatives will alleviate this problem. The most important are:

- *Integrated services digital network (ISDN)*. ISDN is a relatively new, but proven technology. It is common in Germany, which now accounts for more than 50 per cent of the world ISDN market.[14] France, Switzerland and the UK are not too far behind with this technology, but the rest of Europe is still relatively underdeveloped. ISDN is 'narrowband' as the amount of data that can be transmitted using ISDN technology is still regarded as limited.

■ *Asynchronous transfer mode (ATM).* ATM technology – not to be confused with the automated teller machines operated by banks – is a broadband technology. ATM is still in its infancy but several large European companies have already committed to using it and it is being tipped by many as the key data communications method of the twenty-first century.[15] For example, the Post Office in the UK is installing an ATM network to link 180 sorting offices and 22 regional communication centres.[16] In Finland, Finland Telecom is installing a private ATM network for the Finnish Social Insurance Institution. The potential of ATM, which is 400 times faster than the best ISDN technology, is illustrated in Table 7.4.

■ *Asymmetric digital subscriber line (ADSL).* While ISDN and ATM require fibre-optic cable, ADSL makes use of the existing copper wire telephone system using devices which plug into a regular phone line like a modem. These special devices, called transceivers, must be installed both in the home or office and at the telephone company.[17] ADSL appears to offer great potential but, as Exhibit 7.6 points out, this is no guarantee of future success.

■ *Cable modems.* Cable modems are being hailed by the cable television companies as the means of bringing the Internet to the home using the same coaxial cable that brings a multitude of channels to the television set. There are, however, many technical difficulties to be overcome before this technology becomes commercially viable.[18]

Table 7.4 Bandwidth and quality of different technologies

Technology	Bandwidth	Quality
Modem	14.4 Kbps	• AM-quality sound • Small, jerky video
Modem (high sped)	28.8 Kbps	• FM mono-quality sound, or • AM-quality sound with embedded stills
ISDN (basic rate)	144 Kbps	• FM stereo sound • Low-end videoconferencing
ISDN (primary rate)	1544 Kbps	• CD sound • MPEG-quality video
ATM	Up to 622 000 Kbps	• CD sound • Broadcast-quality video • Virtual reality applications

Source: Datamation (February 1996).[19]

■ The proliferation of mobile telephony

Traditional telephone systems have a fixed cable link to the telephone company, compared to mobile, or cellular, telephones which rely on a wireless connection to a local base station. These base stations are dotted across the countryside in an overlapping fashion resembling the cells of a honeycomb; hence the term 'cellular'. The world leaders in cellular telecommunications are the Nordic countries where a combination of low

---

Exhibit 7.6

THE TROUBLE WITH COPPER

Telephone companies have long envied the profits cable television firms make by delivering television programmes into homes. But this was a business that seemed impossible for them to enter. Most telephone networks run on twisted copper wires. Even with the fastest modems, signals on the wires were interrupted by too much noise to carry much more than pictures and text. In 1987, however, along came a technology that solved the problem. Asymmetric digital subscriber line (ADSL) technology works by exploiting unused capacity in copper wire. Voice calls barely use one half of one per cent of the capacity of ordinary telephone lines. ADSL modems make use of the remaining 99.5% or so. So while the top of the range analogue modems struggle to reach 33,200 bits per second (bps), ADSL can race to 300 times that. For ADSL to become the favoured Internet-access technology, the telephone companies may have to change their ways. Their decades-old monopoly of voice telephony has endowed them not only with lots of money but also with slothful habits. They have done almost nothing, for example, to market a slower digital technology called ISDN, despite having spent billions to upgrade their networks to support it.

Source: The Economist (13 July 1996).[20]

---

population density and aggressive pricing has led to more than 10 per cent of the population having their own mobile phones[21] (*see* Table 7.5). In many other countries, the mobile telephone market is also growing rapidly.

Table 7.5 Top 10 cellular telecommunications markets by market penetration

Country	Number of cellular telephone subscribers per 1000 inhabitants (1 January 1995)	Annual % growth (1994/5)
1 Sweden	159	64
2 Norway	138	12
3 Finland	129	36
4 Denmark	99	61
5 Australia	97	88
6 US	94	51
7 Singapore	84	62
8 Bermuda	84	65
9 Iceland	84	25
10 Hong Kong	77	53

Source: Mobile Communications (quoted in *Financial Times*, 3 October 1995).

Global system for mobile (GSM) is a European standard for digital mobile telecommunications and is one of the fastest-growing developments in mobile telephony in recent years. The standard was established in 1982 and the first GSM service was launched in 1992. Today more than 40 countries have adopted it, although Japan and the US have yet to do so. Apart from its very high sound quality and security, a major benefit of the GSM service is its 'roaming' capabilities which allow the mobile phone to be used in different countries, as long as an agreement has been signed by the service providers. For example, Swedish GSM users can use the handset across Europe, Australia or South Africa.

As the GSM system relies on a series of base stations to pick up the signal from the handset, the greatest problem is the lack of coverage in many rural areas. In the UK some of the GSM networks are concentrated in the main urban areas and motorway connections between these centres, leaving large gaps in coverage; this has also been a problem in the Nordic countries. As GSM operators have been building up their coverage and adding more base stations in particular geographic areas, this problem is decreasing. Other issues have included poor levels of customer service as subscriber numbers have increased rapidly, health scares from the use of the handsets and the associated media coverage from all the above.

Despite these problems, mobile digital communications will continue to expand rapidly.[22] Perhaps more important than the predictions for the increasing usage of GSM are the predictions for its use as a means of transferring data as well as voice. By the turn of the century, some experts believe that half the traffic on GSM could be data rather than voice.[23] Even if this is only partially true, the impact on areas of business such as mobile salesforces and customer service will be enormous.

■ Developments in wireless telecommunications

Wireless telephony using radio signals is another technology which offers interesting opportunities, although its providers are unlikely to achieve a high penetration in the telephone market.[24] There are several commercial uses for wireless technology which are relevant to the marketing manager. Consider, for instance, the following example of customer service from Hertz. When customers return their Hertz cars at any major European airport, they are met by a Hertz representative who records the details of the vehicle registration number, rental agreement, mileage and fuel level on a handheld wireless data terminal. The information is immediately relayed via a base station to the Hertz headquarters in the US and within 60 seconds the customer receives an itemised receipt from a printer attached to the handheld terminal.[25]

■ The impact of telecommunications trends

The effect of all these communication technologies is relatively easy to predict: telecommunications costs will continue to go down while capacity and variety increase. Exhibit 7.7 provides a taste of the possible future increases in telecommunications capacity. The net impact will be to make more and more high-technology options available to the marketing manager.

Exhibit 7.7

CRAMMING EVEN MORE IN

In separate experiments, researchers from Fujitsu, Nippon Telegraph and Telephone (NTT), and AT&T achieved transmission rates of one trillion bits per second over a fibre optic cable. That rate is 2.5 times higher than the previous record achieved last year by NTT Laboratories and 400 times higher than the highest-capacity commercial systems deployed today.

Source: New York Times (1 March 1996).[26]

THE INFORMATION SUPERHIGHWAY

■ Information superhighways and infobahns

The information superhighway is the name given to the hardware, software and telecommunications infrastructure that allows universities, businesses, government, communities and individuals to share information across a global network. Sometimes referred to as 'infobahns', the exact nature of their development is difficult to predict and the following quotations from several well-respected sources represent a wide range of opinions:[27]

'We are committed to the goal of connecting every classroom, every library, every hospital, and every clinic to the national and global infrastructures by the end of this decade.'
(Al Gore, US Vice-President)

'We will socialise in digital neighbourhoods in which physical space will be irrelevant.'
(Nicholas Negroponte, Director of MIT Media Laboratory)

'A global and highly competitive tele-economy will be born within a generation.'
(The World Bank)

'The full information superhighway is 15 to 20 years away in the United States and in Europe – 50 years in the rest of the world.'
(Rupert Murdoch, Chairman of News Corporation)

While there is no agreed view on where the information superhighway will lead, its development has already started, although as Exhibit 7.8 points out it may still take some years to complete the journey.

Exhibit 7.8

THE FUTURE LOOKS ROCKY

National broadband networks are already at the early planning stage. US West, which provides telephone services to the Rocky Mountain region, aims to have a fibre and coaxial network in place by 2003. And in Japan the government has said that it wants a broadband network built by 2010. But whether these and other projects come to fruition depends on public demand. If enough people want the services that a broadband network can bring, and are prepared to pay enough for them, it will make economic sense to build a network.
Source: Whitehorn (1996).[27]

■ Teleworking

A trend in recent years, fuelled by the emergence of the information superhighway, has been towards teleworking, or working from home using computer and telephone technology. Newcastle University (1995)[28] defines five broad categories of teleworking:

1 *Electronic home working.* This is the most common form of teleworking and consists of

the teleworker using a PC and modem to connect between home and the workplace.

2 *Telecottages and neighbourhood centres.* These are shared multimedia facilities located close to houses to reduce costs and are favoured by development agencies.

3 *Mobile or nomadic working.* This group includes people who work both at home and on the road using mobile computers and telephones.

4 *Group or team telework.* This group includes any group of workers who are not located together but who are connected through the use of information technology.

5 *Call centres and remote offices.* These are companies which have begun to separate production functions to handle 'back office' functions or to provide customer service or sales functions (*see* Chapter 13).

Currently, about 5 per cent of European organisations are involved in teleworking. However, teleworking has failed to take off as quickly as many people optimistically forecast. In the UK, less than 250 000 people – less than 1 per cent of the workforce – can be classified as a teleworker and the UK figures are the highest in Europe.[29] Only a little over one million workers fit into any of the above five categories of teleworking and predictions that this number will eventually rise to 11 million are unlikely to be realised for many years to come.

CONCLUSION

The future of information technology will be one of further continuous change. Hardware will continue to become more powerful, more miniaturised and more affordable. Developments in software and computer programming will continue, although probably not at the same rate. The area of telecommunications is likely to undergo the greatest change in the next decade as broadband technologies such as ISDN, ATM and ADSL mature, as newer technologies such as satellite and wireless find a niche of their own, and as telecommunications markets in Europe – and elsewhere around the world – continue to open up to competition. GSM will rapidly become the telecommunications standard for mobile data transmission across national borders and the Internet will continue to make such boundaries less relevant as more and more goods and services are traded electronically. The so-called information superhighway, although still in its infancy, will open up new opportunities for doing business.

ASSIGNMENT QUESTIONS

1 Which of the three strands of information technology – hardware, software and telecommunications – is likely to change the most in the next decade, and what are those changes likely to be?

2 Describe the evolution of the computer.

3 Describe the three waves of computer programming.

4 Give examples of broadband telecommunications technology and discuss their importance.

5 What is meant by the information superhighway and what are its implications for marketing?

SCOTTISHPOWER

Utility company ScottishPower is investing in a new customer service centre at its Glasgow headquarters, merging all its Scottish regional service centres. An advanced computer telephony integration (CTI) system is enabling customer service staff to respond quickly to the needs of its 1.7 million Scottish customers. Although updating the communications infrastructure will cost £20m, and the IT and telephony elements of the customer service system alone will cost £4m, David Jones, ScottishPower's managing director of information systems, expects the investment to pay off quickly by saving the company £50m over four years. 'But we're not doing it to save money,' he says. 'We want to ensure our IT systems can deal with the challenges of the business.'

The first phase of the project, giving the 500 staff in ScottishPower's main Glasgow customer service centre access to the new system, went live in June 1996. In phase two, staff from the company's nine regional service centres were moved to the Glasgow site and onto the network. The old mainframe-based customer service system, which all ScottishPower's customer service staff used until this year, did not support the kind of service levels the company wanted to offer its customers. Its new system will give staff the information they need to solve a wide variety of problems. 'Before, when a customer called in, the best we could do was to take note of the problem and promise to get back to him,' says Jones. 'Now, 95% of problems can be resolved in a single phone call.' Instead of their old green-on-black terminals, staff are being issued with new terminals that will give them a graphical user interface to access a range of information systems. Through this interface, they can connect to new and 'legacy' (old) systems to answer customers' questions on issues such as billing and scheduling of meter readings, and give instant feedback to queries such as 'when will the engineer be calling to fix this fault?'.

Enhancing the customer service system by adding graphical applications will make operators' jobs easier. For example, it plans to enable staff to call up images of a customer's meter, with accompanying instructions enabling them to talk the customer through the process of reading the meter. When customers phone in to report problems with their electricity supply, operators will be able to call up a graphical map of the supply system, in order to get an instant picture of which sub-stations are involved. Plans are also underway for a document image processing system to store documents and customer correspondence electronically.

To support these kinds of bandwidth-intensive applications, the company decided it had to move to asynchronous transfer mode (ATM) technology. 'To support multimedia, we had to deliver 10m bps to operators' desktops, and ATM was the best way to provide that,' says Jones. As well as supporting call centre staff, the ATM network will provide a full range of office automation applications, including word processing and electronic mail, and support new client/server-based business applications such as work management, geographic information systems and asset management. The deadline for completion of the customer service system and network was tight. It had to be coordinated with completion of the new customer service building in Glasgow, and the arrival of staff from the regions. The application itself was built in nine months, by a team of 16 developers. Careful planning and the use of expert partners, says Jones, were the secret of the project's success. ScottishPower recognised that implementing distributed systems would involve a lot of skills it did not have in-house – and which it did not want to acquire. 'Part of our strategy was to work with key outside suppliers, who understand the infrastructure requirements of distributed systems,' says Jones. 'If you have a good team and you plan the project well, then it delivers – it's as simple as that.'

Source: 'The big switch', *Computer Weekly*, 20 June 1996.

Questions

1 Which elements of the technology revolution will combine to save ScottishPower £50 million over four years?

2 Discuss the pros and cons of ScottishPower's implementing an ATM network infrastructure to improve customer service.

3 How will the new system improve the level of service which ScottishPower can give to its customers?

4 As a marketing manager for ScottishPower, what messages would you want to communicate to your customers about the new system and how would you go about communicating them?

5 Why did ScottishPower need to use external specialists to implement the systems, rather than relying on its own in-house IT staff?

References

[1] Chandor, A., Graham, J. and Williamson, R. (1985). *The Penguin Dictionary of Computers*. 3rd edn, London: Penguin.

[2] Pearsall, J. and Trumble, B. (eds) (1995). *Oxford English Reference Dictionary*. Oxford: Oxford University Press.

[3] Browning, J. (1995). *The Economist Books: Pocket Information Technology*. London: Penguin Books.

[4] The Economist (1995). 'A survey of the software industry', *The Economist*, 25 May.

[5] Microsoft (1995). *Creating the Information Society in Europe – A Look Ahead*. Microsoft, Dublin.

[6] The Economist (1996). 'That astonishing microchip', *The Economist*, 23 March.

[7] Taylor, P. (1995). 'Hidden sales prospects revealed', *Financial Times*, 5 July.

[8] The Economist (1996). 'Carving out a new future', *The Economist*, 1 June.

[9] Patton, R. (1996). 'Write on target', *Banking Technology*, June.

[10] Browning, J. (1995). *Op. cit.*

[11] Zorkoczy, P. and Heap, N. (1995). *Information Technology, An Introduction*. 4th edn, London: Pitman.

[12] The Economist (1995). 'A survey of telecommunications', *The Economist*, 30 September.

[13] Goleniewski, L., Horak, R. and Ellis, P. (1994). *Multimedia Technology: Overview*. Datapro, Delran, NJ.

[14] Ewing, J. (1996). 'Herr Professor Schindler heads out west', *Sunday Business*, 23 June.

[15] Taylor, P. (1995). 'Link between two worlds', *Financial Times*, 3 October.

[16] Raymond, M. (1996). *Wide Area Communications in Europe: A Strategic Analysis*. Datapro Information Services, January.

[17] Salamone, S. (1996). 'Higher data speeds coming for plain phone lines', *Byte*, January.

[18] The Economist (1996). 'From couch potato to cybersurfer', *The Economist*, 6 July.

[19] DeJesus, E. (1996). 'How the Internet will replace broadcasting', *Byte*, February.

[20] The Economist (1996). 'The telephone's second chance', *The Economist*, 13 July.

[21] Grubman, J. (1995). 'International telecommunications map', *Financial Times* in association with Salomon Brothers, 3 October.

[22] Shillingford, J. (1995). 'Next big market will be in data', *Financial Times*, 15 June.

[23] Emmerson, B. and Greetham, D. (1996). 'GSM's extraordinary growth', *Byte*, March.

[24] The Economist (1996). 'Built on thin air', *The Economist*, 18 May.

[25] Baxter, A. (1996). 'Wonders of wireless', *Financial Times*, 15 August.

26 Pollack, A. (1996). 'Researchers transmit one trillion bits per second', *New York Times*, 1 March.
27 Whitehorn, A. (ed.) (1996). *Multimedia: The Complete Guide*. London: Dorling Kindersley.
28 Newcastle University (1995). *Review of Telework in Britain: Implications for Public Policy*. Newcastle: University of Newcastle.
29 Price, C. (1995). 'Numbers stay limited', *Financial Times*, 15 June.

THE MARKETING POTENTIAL OF MULTIMEDIA AND THE INTERNET

- Marketing in cyberspace
- Multimedia
- The Internet and the World Wide Web
- Internet commerce
- Interactive television
- Animation and virtual reality
- CD-ROM

OBJECTIVES

After studying this chapter, you will be able to:

- ☐ Understand the marketing potential of multimedia technology
- ☐ Explain what the Internet and the World Wide Web are and how they can be used for marketing products and services
- ☐ Understand the potential of Internet commerce
- ☐ Describe the marketing potential of interactive television, animation and virtual reality
- ☐ Understand the different marketing applications for CD-ROM technology

MARKETING IN CYBERSPACE

■ Cybermarketing

The term 'cybermarketing' has been coined to describe the type of marketing that is beginning to be carried out through the use of computers and telecommunications.[1] The methods employed by so-called cybermarketers include:

- multimedia
- the Internet and the World Wide Web

- interactive television
- animation and virtual reality
- CD-ROM.

We will explore each of these methods in this chapter. First, let us examine the benefits that are claimed for these new and emerging technologies. Keeler (1995)[1] claims that cybermarketing can:

- save money and help stretch the marketing budget
- save time and cut steps in the marketing process
- give customers another way to buy while enabling them to take control of the purchasing process
- be information rich and interactive
- offer instant international reach
- lower barriers to entry and offer equal opportunity access
- be continuously available.

In the remainder of this chapter we will examine these claims. First, a couple of words of caution about cybermarketing. There is a tendency to overstate the benefits of these new multimedia technologies. History teaches us that the reality often fails to match the initial hype surrounding such claims. The area of multimedia, and its applications for marketing, is also one which is moving incredibly fast. Keeler's book, published in 1995, is already out of date in certain areas.

MULTIMEDIA

■ What is multimedia?

Of the many new and exciting technologies which have great potential for marketing, multimedia has created the most interest among both marketing and business managers. Multimedia can be defined as the combination of different formats, including text, pictures, animation, narrative, video and music, into a single medium. It is also interactive, allowing customers to do things, to control where they want to go and to skip backwards and forwards. The earliest multimedia applications have been in the areas of education and learning. Students learning a foreign language could click on a word and hear the correct pronunciation; a mathematics student could click on an equation and see the numeric values move on the screen; or a young child could click on an elephant and retrieve text information on the animal, a picture or perhaps even a video clip. Consumers are attracted to using multimedia because it is not a passive medium like watching TV or reading a book, and they can move at their own pace and receive immediate feedback on their progress.

Research at Northwestern University, Chicago,[2] shows that people tend to remember 70 per cent of what they see, hear and do, compared to 40 per cent of what they see and hear or 20 per cent of what they see. Because multimedia combines seeing, hearing and doing, it is a very powerful tool for both learning and marketing, where the retention of information is so important.

■ The use of multimedia technologies in marketing

In recent years, multimedia has moved out of education and training into the commercial arena. Many of the initial commercial uses of multimedia have been in the financial services industry, where banks such as Barclays, NatWest and Lloyds, as well as building societies like the Nationwide, have all started to experiment with it.[3, 4] NatWest was the first bank to move into multimedia when it launched a videoconference link for its customers in July 1994.

Multimedia is a powerful tool for communicating information in an exciting format and is only limited by the imagination of the marketing executive as to the most effective way to utilise it. The following are just some of the ways in which multimedia can be used in marketing:

- *Staff training.* Multimedia provides a very effective way of training staff at their own pace. Once developed, it is cheaper than bringing staff to a central training location and providing instructors as they can learn at their own offices. Staff can also select the modules that are relevant for them and the software can provide feedback on their progress by giving them self-evaluation questions and scoring their answers.
- *On-line help.* A bank employee might be faced with a request from a customer to process an unusual foreign-currency transaction about which the employee has little knowledge. By accessing a multimedia knowledge database the employee could find information on how to process the transaction.
- *Internal communications.* An organisation which is about to undertake a major organisational change might decide that it is appropriate to develop a multimedia presentation for all employees which would be communicated via their PCs. The presentation could include a small video clip of the CEO explaining why the organisation change is necessary and different icons which employees could click to find out more information about different aspects of the change.
- *On-line help to external customers.* A multimedia application can be used to explain to customers how to use a software product or a complex piece of machinery and is usually much more effective than a traditional paper manual.
- *Customer interaction.* Multimedia can be used by customers to design or select the product/service option they require. Rover has a very sophisticated system which allows customers to design their own car (*see* Exhibit 8.1).
- *Promotional material.* A multimedia application can communicate information on a company or present a more exciting version of its annual report. It could also be used, for example, to demonstrate how a company's food products can be used in different recipes.

Exhibit 8.1

DESIGN YOUR OWN CARS

The increasingly competitive motor car industry is always looking for new ways to sell its products. It is no surprise, therefore, that manufacturers should turn to advanced technology as a means to gain an edge over their competitors. Multimedia point-of-sale kiosks are an obvious choice. The glamorous nature of the product lends itself to multimedia presentations and interactive features can let prospective customers 'configure' their own model.

The Rover Group claims to have the most advanced system of its type. Under the name Discus, the system is being rolled out to the manufacturer's 500-strong UK dealer network this year and there are plans to extend it across Europe in 1996. What makes Discus different to most multimedia 'kiosk' applications is its connection to other information technology systems. Not only does it link through to Rover's manufacturing systems – so orders can be processed quickly – it also links into the dealer's own systems.

'As far as I am aware Rover is the only manufacturer that is integrating with the dealer's own systems. Modern cars are so complex that customers can easily be bombarded with facts. You could give them a telephone directory and tell them to study the options. But with Discus they don't have to drink from a firehose – they can sip from a glass,' says Mr Stubbs, Rover's product manager for Discus. 'It also helps the sales staff. It is so hard to keep up with the changes. This system makes sure they give the right answers to customers,' he adds.

Source: Financial Times (7 June 1995).[5]

One of the main advantages of multimedia, apart from its presentational qualities, is that it allows the customer to take charge of the process. This is one of the specific aims[6] of the share-dealing service called BarclayZone that was launched by the UK bank in early 1996 (*see* Exhibit 8.2). Customers can watch videos which provide general information on the stock market and, when they feel they have enough information to make a purchase, they can make the deal or begin a videoconference with the stockbroker.

In understanding multimedia, it is important to differentiate between the content of a multimedia application and the way in which it is delivered. Once an application has been developed it can be delivered to the end-user in a number of ways including CD-ROMS, multimedia kiosks and the Internet. The choice of delivery mechanism depends on both the volume of information to be communicated and the target audience. CD-ROM is appropriate for applications which use video images because it can store large volumes of information.

Exhibit 8.2

STAR TREK STOCK DEALING

Barclays Bank unveiled an electronic approach to customer service in the age of interactive multimedia and the Internet. The interactive stock dealing and information service – called BarclayZone – features a two-way live video link between the customer and Barclays Stockbrokers' head office in Glasgow and leans heavily on imagery from *Star Trek*, the cult television and film space adventure. BarclayZone was developed by Barclays Multimedia, an in-house unit established by Mr Joseph de Feo, Barclays' head of technology, to pioneer new developments in electronic banking.

Source: Financial Times (4 January 1996).[7]

THE INTERNET AND THE WORLD WIDE WEB

■ The Internet

The Internet is a computer network or, more accurately, a collection of interrelated networks which span the globe and which allow users with a PC and the appropriate software to communicate with each other. It was conceived as a US government research project in 1969, primarily to allow computer scientists, engineers and military researchers to communicate with each other. It remained within the domain of government, government agencies, universities and libraries until 1991 when a ban on its use for commercial purposes in the US was lifted.[8] However, it was not until 1993 that public interest in the Internet really took off, mainly because a newer multimedia version of the Internet, called the World Wide Web, was invented. When people talk about the Internet nowadays, they are invariably referring to the facilities available through the World Wide Web.

The current interest in the Internet, from individuals and organisations, is phenomenal. If you wander into any bookshop today, you will find as many books on the Internet as you will on marketing. As a marketing tool, the Internet, and in particular the World Wide Web, offers tremendous possibilities to organisations and some forward-thinking companies have already moved to seize them (*see* Exhibit 8.3). Many other organisations are still trying to come to grips with this new technology and understand the marketing opportunities.

Exhibit 8.3

VIRTUAL BOOKS

Huge consumer-goods companies such as Sony, Virgin Records and Reebok are now turning to the Internet for marketing. Newspapers, magazines, music and book publishers see the on-line world as a combination of threat and opportunity. As a new medium with almost no distribution costs, the Internet has the potential to reshape the media world, letting new competitors in and forcing established giants to evolve or die. Already sales of the *Encyclopaedia Britannica* have collapsed in the face of competition from CD-ROMs; the next battlefield will be on-line.

Source: The Economist (1 July 1995).[9]

■ How the Internet is constructed

All the information that can be accessed on the Internet is held on computers known as 'servers' which are attached to this gigantic network at points called 'nodes'. These servers are owned either by companies that want to distribute information on the network or by organisations that charge people for access to the network and for supporting services. A recent count puts the number of servers attached to the Internet at approximately 80 000.[10] The actual number of people across the world who use the Internet on a regular basis is probably several million, although the total number of people who have some form of access to it may be as high as 50 million. From a marketing perspective, this is a significant opportunity for companies to extend their reach and their marketing message.

■ Connecting to the Internet

There are five pre-requisites for 'surfing' the Internet:[11, 12]

- ■ a PC
- ■ a communications link (usually a phone and a modem)
- ■ an Internet service provider (ISP)
- ■ an Internet address
- ■ access software.

Most individuals and small businesses will access the Internet via a PC and a standard telephone connection to an internet service provider or ISP. The ISP's computer is attached to, and part of, the Internet. The ISP can provide a range of services from an account or address on its computer and the access software which allows access to the Internet, through to the provision of Web sites, dedicated high-speed telephone lines and other services (*see* Exhibit 8.4).

Exhibit 8.4

SUFFERING FROM NET FEVER

Talk about turnarounds. It wasn't that long ago that corporate America was taking a wait-and-see approach to the Internet. Now the same folks seem to have come down with 'Net fever'. Corporate officers all across the country are seeing that on-line resources are a great way to boost employee productivity. And more than a few of them see the Web as the perfect way to advertise their products and services to some 40 million registered cyber-consumers. So what happens when the top brass wakes up to the fact that there's gold out on the Internet? Let's just say that net managers should be ready to stake a company claim. And that means finding an Internet Service Provider (ISP) that can come through with whatever's required. At the very least, corporate networkers need an ISP with enough infrastructure to allow hundreds or thousands of employees to send e-mail, access newsgroups, exchange documents, and reach far-flung servers. More ambitious companies are going to want to put up their own home pages, and some are going to want to transact business over the 'Net.

Tracking down an ISP is the easy part. There are hundreds to choose from. The real trick is sorting through the potential providers to come up with the best choice.

Source: Data Communications (21 November 1995).[13]

According to one Internet directory there are more than 50 different ISPs operating in the UK,[14] but the largest include companies such as BTnet, Unipalm PIPEX, Demon and IBM. Demon, which started business in 1992, now claims to be the leading provider of Internet services in the UK.[15] Unipalm PIPEX claims a similar market share of the corporate market using dedicated leased telephone lines rather than a dial-up service.[16] Some of the major international ISPs include AT&T, CompuServe and Sprint.

■ Specialist on-line service providers

In addition to the ISPs, there are several specialist on-line service organisations who provide both commercial on-line services and access to the Internet. CompuServe[17] and America Online are two such organisations that provide the Internet 'surfer' with some useful landmarks and signposts (*see* Exhibit 8.5).

Exhibit 8.5

FINDING YOUR WAY TO THE ELECTRONIC SHOPPING MALL

On-line services can be viewed as large shopping malls where service providers such as publications, or shopping catalogues, present their products in electronic form. Everything is fairly easy to find and each on-line service tries to cultivate its own look. The Internet is more like a sprawling suburb with few landmarks, making it difficult for users to find their way around.

Source: Financial Times (1 March 1995).[18]

To quote one commentator:[19]

> *'If the Internet is a lawless frontier, then service providers are the new marshals in town.'*

The newness of these marshals is a reference to the fact that, up until 1995, these organisations shunned the Internet. Now, they have all moved to embrace it. As another commentator puts it:[20]

> *'Commercial on-line information services have suffered a high-speed, head-on collision with the Internet.'*

Another company to suffer such a collision was Microsoft, which launched its own proprietary on-line service in 1995 but quickly decided to row in with the industry standards of the Internet, rather than maintaining a separate proprietary network. Another, and potentially much more far-reaching, battle has already begun between the on-line service companies, the ISPs and the traditional phone companies or PTTs (*see* Exhibit 8.6). This battle will eventually determine who controls the Internet and whether the telephone companies are a dominant force in this new medium, or whether they are relegated to being a commodity supplier of bandwidth to other organisations.

■ Marketing on the Internet

Before we explore the capabilities of the World Wide Web, let us examine the capabilities of other parts of the Internet. Keeler (1995)[1] states that the marketing uses of the Internet are fivefold:

- *Sending messages (e-mail).* One of the primary functions of the Internet is to act as a worldwide exchange or clearing house for electronic mail, or e-mail. The Internet itself does not offer e-mail functionality but acts rather like a post office service, or clearing house, for delivering e-mail from one part of the world to another.
- *Transferring files.* Computer files can be transferred from one computer to another

Exhibit 8.6

ISPs VERSUS PTTs

International net managers have good reason to be confused. They keep hearing that the Internet is a global infrastructure that stretches from Tokyo to Timbuktu – and beyond. Yet when they go looking for corporate access to connect up staff all over the world, they find that only a scant handful of service providers can come through with what's needed. But the status quo out in cyberspace is changing fast. Just about every carrier, PTT, and international VAN (Value-added Network) says it's working on global Internet services. Some have already started to deliver, claiming they've got the more typical Internet service providers (ISPs) beat on several counts.

The ISPs, meanwhile, aren't about to sit idly by and get steamrollered by the competition. As expected, the ISPs claim they're the ones with the inside track to the Internet. For starters, they're faster on their feet than the giant carriers and PTTs. Moreover, the ISPs are old hands at the 'Net, and they think they can leverage their technical know-how and operational experience.

Source: Data Communications (21 November 1995).[21]

across the Internet. This is a valuable feature for connecting different parts of the same organisation, or for linking companies to their suppliers or customers.

■ *Monitoring news and opinions.* The Internet is used for on-line discussion and interaction through Bulletin Board Services (BBS) and other discussion groups.

■ *Searching and browsing.* A very large amount of digitised information ranging from books, periodicals, reference works and government publications is available through the Internet.

■ *Posting, hosting and presenting information.* Company reports, marketing messages and information can be posted to a named site on the Internet for others to view.

The case of Juno Online (*see* Exhibit 8.7 overleaf) is an interesting development in Internet marketing which is a combination of advertising and direct mail. The advertising that appears in the corner of the screen is known as a 'banner' and may consist of nothing more than a company logo. Alternatively, some banners invite Internet users to click on an icon in search of a free prize or product information. However, advertising agencies in the US estimate that just 1 per cent of Internet users actually click on the banners.[22]

■ The World Wide Web

The World Wide Web (WWW or Web for short) is the multimedia version of the Internet. It was the recent invention of the 'browser' (*see* Exhibit 8.8 overleaf) which has allowed companies to add colour, graphics, video and other multimedia capabilities to the messages that they leave on the Internet. The numbers of individuals and companies that use the Internet has grown at a phenomenal rate since the Web was established. As a result, the Internet has evolved from being primarily a messaging service to a place for advertising, marketing and selling products and services, and the terms Internet and the Web are now used interchangeably.

Exhibit 8.7

FREE-MAIL

As the morning post too often demonstrates, direct mail advertising is a sloppy business. Without much knowledge of people's likes and dislikes, advertisers resort to the shotgun approach. They send out lots of letters, hoping that some are opened, and maybe even a few read and responded to. It is grossly inefficient: the letters cost a fortune to send, waste time, and consume a lot of trees. The main problems have been that it is hard to find an audience, to work out who is in it, and to discover what they like. Yet on the Internet, people willingly reveal such details as the price of admission to useful sites.

Now Juno Online, a New York company in which DE Shaw, an investment bank, has a $20m stake, has found a way to put the two worlds together. It is offering free e-mail access to anybody in America with a personal computer and modem. In exchange, subscribers part with their demographic details – and put up with advertisements in the corner of their computer screens. Because subscribers know that they will receive advertising anyway, they have a strong interest in describing themselves to Juno as accurately as possible. Unlike direct mail, which may go unopened and unread, advertising on Juno is paid for only when the recipient gets it. And there is a cost saving: Juno, and FreeMark Communications, which launches a rival free e-mail service on May 6th, both reckon they will be around eight times cheaper than direct mail, while offering advertising that consumers are likely to respond to.

Source: The Economist (27 April 1996).[23]

Exhibit 8.8

BROWSERS

The boffins in Switzerland who invented the World Wide Web in 1991 did not see fit to include such frivolities as clickable pictures or sound. It was a tool for scientists, who after all could read. Text was quite good enough, and would avoid wasting the Internet's scarce transmission capacity with graphic files simply for decoration.

It took a 23-year-old programmer at the University of Illinois called Marc Andreessen to cast a vote for the common man. In 1993, he developed Mosaic, a multimedia Web 'browser' that made it easy to view documents on the Web and jump between them. It was the first piece of Internet software to recognise that the network's future lay not with scientists but with ordinary people, who liked their information dressed up in multimedia frills. A year later Mr Andreessen joined up with Jim Clark, a wealthy computer industry entrepreneur, to launch Netscape and jump-start the Internet industry software market.

Source: The Economist (25 May 1996).[24]

The Web consists of hundreds of thousands of pages (known as 'Web sites', 'Web pages', or 'home pages') which are rich in graphics and photographs mixed with text. By clicking on any word in the page that is highlighted, the browser jumps to another linked page using links known as 'hypertext' links (*see* Exhibit 8.9). As individuals jump from page to page on the Web, they are said to 'surf' the Internet.

Exhibit 8.9

HYPERTEXT

World Wide Web pages can be constructed by anyone with a little programming knowledge, and now cover a very wide range of subjects – from the CIA Fact Book and the Hungarian budget to a guide to Dublin pubs and a tour of the Electronic Zoo. The Web's language, HTML (Hypertext Mark-up Language) is used to create documents on the Web.

Source: Whitehorn (1996).[25]

Most major companies in the UK have already established a presence on the World Wide Web and an estimated 100 000 Web sites were in place in the UK in early 1996.[26, 27] The market for creating World Wide Web pages in 1996 was estimated to be worth £30 million, a tenfold increase over the previous year, with many European firms turning to the UK for the necessary skills to create and set up the pages. A European survey of 5000 retailers, banks and commercial organisations shows that the Web is used heavily for a variety of marketing and sales purposes[28] (*see* Table 8.1).

Table 8.1   Business use of the World Wide Web

Business use	%
Information gathering	71
Collaborating with other organisations	54
Marketing	46
Customer service	38
Information publishing	33
Selling products and services	33
Purchasing products and services	23

Source: IMRG (1996).

■ Marketing on the Web

The World Wide Web has extended the marketing potential of the Internet enormously. In addition to the marketing capabilities previously mentioned, the Web also offers:

Advertising

The multimedia capabilities of the Web allow companies to present their products in a much more colourful and graphical format than a standard advertisement. Although potential customers must be attracted to visit your Web site in the first place, the Web can be a cheap means of getting an advertising message across to a large number of people. Small businesses can advertise to a potential market of millions for less than the cost of a single-page advertisement in most magazines.[29] In addition, a recent survey from the

US by researchers AC Nielsen found that the type of person who browses through Web pages is likely to be from the higher socio-economic groups and more attractive to advertisers.[30] Advertising can also be carried out, somewhat strangely, via radio on the Web. For example, Virgin's Web site allows users to listen to Virgin Radio, the first European radio station to broadcast live on the Internet.[31]

Public relations

The Web is being used more and more for a variety of public relations functions such as the posting of notices on new products and the distribution of press releases. Most companies who distribute press releases on the Web will archive these releases and other promotional articles so that users can access them easily again. Other organisations use the Web for sponsoring conferences, industry and sporting events and publications.

Direct sales

Despite some lingering concerns about security, the Web is being used more and more for distributing product information and on-line ordering. For example, Allied Dunbar became the first UK insurance company to put interactive quotations on the Internet in 1995.[32] Computer hardware and software, books, music and vacation/travel-related items are the biggest sellers on the Web, but any product that already has a good image or brand name can be sold over the Internet, with the exception of those items which need to be physically tried such as fashion clothing.[33] US investment broker Fidelity claims that one in twenty of its new clients comes to the firm through the Internet.[34] Exhibit 8.10 provides other examples of companies that are selling successfully. Software programmes known as intelligent agents can also be used to search the Internet for the best deals.[35] This is potentially very good for the customer, but may commoditise the market for sellers.[36]

Exhibit 8.10

SELL, SELL, SELL

Hot Hot Hot (Pasadena, California), a retailer of exotic hot sauces, sold more than $60 000 over the Web last year, representing nearly 25 per cent of its business. It doesn't take an industry luminary to know how compelling numbers like that sound in the corporate board-room.

US manufacturer AMP spends more than $4 million a year to mail out and update some 400 very specialised catalogues containing information on about 134 000 electrical and machine components. About a year ago, while toying with the idea of putting the paper-based catalogues on CD-ROM, Jim Kessler, AMP's vice president of sales and marketing, decided to try to leapfrog to the Internet instead. The benefits of going on the Web were obvious: less cost, more frequent updates, and a glitzy user-friendly way to stay visible to customers. If done right, the project would mean that AMP could move away from its faxback system, which was costing the company $800 000 a year in phone bills alone.

One company which has much to teach others about doing business remotely is Interflora. Interflora set up a central telephone-ordering system eight years ago, and one-third of its business is now accounted for by credit card transactions. Adding an Internet extension to this service was seen as a natural progression for Interflora, which established its first on-line presence with CompuServe just under a year ago. It has since opened another outlet on BarclaySquare and already on-line ordering accounts for 1 per cent of its total turnover. This compares well with the telephone experience eight years ago, and by the year 2000, on-line orders are expected to represent 5 per cent of turnover. The 2800 Interflora florists in the UK and Ireland have found it relatively easy to adopt to the requirements of remote trading.

Sources: Data Communications (21 November 1995),[13] *Datamation* (1 December 1995),[37] *Digital Media* (1996).[38]

Marketing research

One of the more recent uses of the Web is for marketing research, in the form of customer-opinion surveys, product-interest and reaction surveys, as well as experimental discussion or focus group activities.[39] Some companies also ask customers who visit their Web site for personal details which can then be used for direct marketing or polling customer opinion. For example, one UK life assurance company asks its Web visitors for details of their ages, names and addresses.[40] In another recent venture, 13 market-research companies have formed a Web site to provide market analysis to medium-sized businesses.[41]

Creating closer links with customers

The Web can allow companies to gather better information about their customers, and to strengthen the relationship with them (*see* Exhibit 8.11). For example, details of new products or updates to existing services can be communicated to customers by e-mail, with an invitation to get more information by visiting the company's Web site. Some companies specifically ask Web visitors to leave their name and e-mail address so that these communications links can be established. Holiday Inn allows direct booking for its hotels and VISA provides information to help their card customers find the nearest ATM cash machine.[42] General Motors allows customers to design their own car on the Internet[43] and Guinness received an extraordinary hit-rate on its Web site by allowing visitors to download a PC screensaver that was based on a very successful television advertising campaign.[44] Other companies such as the German software company SAP and Microsoft are using the Web as a means of providing on-line customer service and helpdesk support.[45] For example, SAP has a free on-line database of past problems with its software and solutions which customers can search to see if they can find a match with their own problems.

Exhibit 8.11

PINPOINT THE PARCEL

In the brief annals of doing business on the Internet, Federal Express's customer Web site has become a legendary success story. The package delivery giant, which moves 2.4 million pieces every day, put up a server in 1994 on the World Wide Web that gave customers a direct window into FedEx's package-tracking database. By letting 12,000 customers a day click their way through Web pages to pinpoint their parcels – instead of asking a human operator to do it for them – FedEx was soon saving up to $2 million a year by some estimates.

Source: Business Week (26 February 1996).[46]

While few companies have progressed further than creating home pages broadcasting a basic advertising message about their products or services, this is changing. To compete on the Web for people's interest, a company's home page must offer something more than simply an electronic sales message. There are thousands of different pages on the World Wide Web and it is becoming increasingly difficult for companies to attract visitors to explore their own home page and browse through their wares. If companies are to be successful in using the Web as a marketing tool, they will need to integrate it into other marketing media or offer additional functionality to make it attractive for potential customers to visit (*see* Exhibit 8.12).

Exhibit 8.12

ATTRACTING THE INTERNAUT

In traditional media, advertising is everywhere – on TV, in the newspaper, on the sides of buses, through direct telephone marketing, and so on. On the Internet, intrusive or proactive advertising is not permitted and is strongly disliked by the citizens of the network – your potential customers. A Web site is your virtual corporate headquarters, where you can market and sell products and services. The trick is to get Internauts to visit the page.

Source: Ellsworth and Ellsworth (1995).[47]

■ Marketing tips for the Web

Marketing and advertising on the Web are clearly very different to traditional promotional activities. The US technology magazine *Datamation* published a list of ten business tips[48] for companies marketing on the Web (*see* Exhibit 8.13), which provides a good summary of many of the messages given in previous pages.

Exhibit 8.13

TOP TEN TIPS

1 *Make sure your site is scalable.* Don't think in terms of Web pages you simply add and delete. You're committing to a database-driven information store and it is important to link existing databases to the Web and efficiently use existing information.
2 *Make your search engine and database structure flexible and intuitive.* They must be capable of holding all of your content and still give users quick access to what they want.
3 *Content is king.* Graphics attract, but their primary objective is to add value to your customer's on-line experience by delivering value-added content. Product info, news updates and even reference material and documentation are good places to start.
4 *Update often.* Give both customers and browsers reasons to keep coming back. Ideas include special sales offers, premiums, contests or even just news updates.
5 *Don't just sell to customers.* Don't think of the Web as only a place to advertise or promote your company. If you provide valuable information and resources, customers will

keep coming back. (Hint: you'll need more than a picture of your CEO and a recorded message.)

10 *Target the content to your users' specific needs.* Find out what they want by having them register on your site. Get their names, addresses and some information about their jobs and interests.

7 *Make the interface intuitive.* The Web site should be friendly and fast. Efficient service is what the Net is all about.

8 *Location, location, location: traffic drives sales.* If your own site isn't generating enough traffic, consider linking it to those of trade associations, standards committees or other places which people have already discovered. Some companies have grouped together to make a mall-like marketplace on the Web.

9 *Create a sense of community.* Give users a stake in your site. Provide a venue where they can express their ideas.

10 *Get help if all this security and browser technology is not your cup of tea.* Don't be afraid to stick to your core competencies and offload the Web work to service bureaux or consultants who specialise not just in Web development but also in your specific business.

Source: Datamation (1 December 1995).

■ Potential pitfalls of the Net and the Web

Despite their undoubted potential, marketers should also be aware of the disadvantages and pitfalls of the Internet or World Wide Web as a marketing medium. These include:

- *Poor targeting capabilities.* The potential audience may be large but the customer has to search out the company's Web site in order to view the advertising message. As more and more companies begin to advertise on the Internet, the problem of standing out amid all the clutter will pose major challenges to organisations.

- *Cost.* As mentioned above, many home pages offer little more than an electronic version of a newspaper or magazine advertisement. It can cost a considerable amount of money to develop a home page that offers greater functionality and which will stand out among the tens of thousands of others. This in turn will lead to problems of measurement (*see* Exhibit 8.14) and cost effectiveness.

- *Incompatible marketing messages.* Web sites are often created by the IT department rather than the marketing department. This is not necessarily a problem as long as both departments are in touch with each other. Unfortunately, the marketing message that ends up in cyberspace may not necessarily complement the marketing message that is being put out by the rest of the organisation.

- *Immaturity of the Internet medium.* The Internet, and in particular the World Wide Web, has undoubted marketing potential, but will not become a mature, reliable and secure medium for some years to come. At present, it is 'surfed' by a large number of early adopters across the world, but until the speed and reliability of the service are improved, it will not be embraced by the mass market.[49] The general consensus at this point appears to be that the mass market use of the Internet for commercial transactions will not occur until around the turn of the century.[50]

- *Conservative nature of customers.* Research indicates that, even among early adopters,

WHO CAN MEASURE THE NET?

Forget about 'video-on-demand'. The latest buzzword is 'advertising-on-demand'. The target is the Internet – and, in particular, the 5m–8m users of its colourful offspring, the World Wide Web. At last count, in April, there were 25,000 web-sites on the Internet – up from a few hundred a year or so before. The number is doubling every 80 or so days. And most of the growth is coming from companies advertising their wares to on-line users. Surveys show that most people browsing the Web are educated, well-heeled and, once technology makes it feasible, keen to use the Internet for serious shopping.

But companies have been reluctant to commit their advertising dollars. One reason is that there are no independently audited figures for the number of people examining their products, akin to Nielsen TV ratings or Arbitron figures for radio listeners. On the Internet, there is nothing more reliable than a web-site creator's in-house calculations.

Source: The Economist (22 July 1995).[51]

UK attitudes towards transacting financial services across the Internet are highly conservative.[52] Only one-third of Internet users are willing to carry out their banking transactions over the Internet, with security worries as the key stumbling block.

■ *Communications speed.* Realistically, multimedia communications need a bandwidth of at least 2 million bits per second,[53] yet current modem technology has a maximum bandwidth of only 28 800 bits per second. The telecommunications barriers will have to be surmounted before the Internet moves forward from the early adopter stage.

INTERNET COMMERCE

■ Virtual trading

Internet commerce consists of two types of virtual trading. The first, between companies, will become an extension of EDI and is very likely to speed up the pace at which EDI is taken up by smaller organisations.[54] The second type relates to sales to the mass consumer market.

The direct sales potential of the Internet is still unclear because the industry is very immature and the companies that are selling over the Internet are doing it, in general, on an experimental basis. According to Forrester Research, buying and selling of goods through the World Wide Web has yet to progress beyond 'a dozen pizzas and two or three flower bouquets a week'.[55] An example of this is the UK company Argos, described in Exhibit 8.15.

Many people believe that true electronic commerce between companies on the Internet on a large scale will not happen until the turn of the century (*see* Exhibit 8.16). However, despite these caveats, Internet commerce is beginning to take off and many analysts predict that the current limitations of the Internet, in terms of security,

Exhibit 8.15

SO WHERE'S THE RETURN?

While hundreds of companies have rushed to set up their own World Wide Web sites, few are convinced about the value of their Internet presence. Such are the findings of a survey carried out by Hamlin Harkins for the WebSite Internet Consultancy. According to the research, 32.7% of companies questioned already have a Web site, while 27.7% are currently developing or planning to develop one. Yet few organisations that have so far invested in the Internet have seen much in the way of financial return. Argos, for example, has had a Web site for the past ten months but has sold only 22 relatively small items.

The research also found that UK companies are spending an average of £22,708 a year on their sites, and that this investment is expected to increase to an average of £56,000 a year.

Source: Sunday Business ComputerAge (12 May 1996).[56]

Exhibit 8.16

WILL THE INTERNET BE BIG, OR REALLY BIG?

Forrester Research expects consumer purchases over the Internet to grow from $240m in 1994 to $6.9bn by the year 2000 – yet the international research firm Input says the 2000 figure 'will potentially exceed $200bn'.

Source: Financial Times (1 November 1995).

reliability and maturity of the service, will soon be solved and that millions of individuals and corporations will be buying, selling, broking and trading over this medium.[57]

In the UK, a poll carried out in 1995 found that more than 150 000 people have already used the Internet to purchase products and services. An example of one of the first well-known direct sales services was J. Sainsbury's WineDirect[58] which could be accessed from the UK's first Internet shopping centre, BarclaySquare[59] (*see* Exhibit 8.17). The figure for the number of Internet sales in the US and Canada is around 2.5 million.[60]

Exhibit 8.17

SHOPPING IN CYBERSPACE

Welcome to BarclaySquare, the UK's leading on-line shopping centre. Jointly developed by Barclays Merchant Services, a member of the Barclays Bank Group and Interactive Telephony Limited who own and developed the Supernet on-line network, BarclaySquare was launched on the 31st May 1995. Try out Cybershopping in one of our stores with complete security and watch this space for further major store openings.

Source: BarclaySquare, http://www.itl.net/barclaysquare.

■ Internet payment mechanisms and security

A major constraint on the growth of Internet commerce is the security of electronic payments. Security First Network Bank (SFNB), the world's first 'virtual bank',[61] had to devise a series of security procedures that would not only keep unwanted fraudsters out, but would also satisfy the bank's regulating body which granted SFNB its banking licence.[62, 63] In the UK, despite the success of the industry body APACS (Association for Payment Clearing Services) in combating credit card fraud, there is still considerable scope for electronic fraud which is dampening consumer confidence in electronic commerce.[64] The first electronic payments for products and services over the Internet were conventional ones. Subscribers transferred monthly fees for a service from their bank account into the account of the selling party. However, such payments were expensive and could take a long time to process. Subsequent developments included the use of credit cards which enabled faster and cheaper payments, but with the inherent danger of transmitting credit card details over the Internet. Criminals have been known to scan the Internet for credit card number details. The use of encryption of credit-card details has not provided a complete solution to this problem, as small-value payments are still relatively expensive to process. In early 1996, the two major credit-card organisations, VISA and Mastercard, agreed to join forces to come up with a technical standard for safeguarding credit card purchases made over open networks such as the Internet.[65] However, agreement on standards between two major competing organisations can be fraught with difficulties.[66]

INTERACTIVE TELEVISION

■ Interactive television applications

The world is already familiar with one form of multimedia – the television. But television, as we currently know it, is not interactive. It is a 'dumb' machine that is only capable of receiving information, not of transmission. Interactive television is a very different concept as it allows the viewer to send signals back to the service provider. The creation of a truly interactive relationship with customers in the home will open up a very powerful channel through which organisations can provide a whole range of services. Because the penetration rate for televisions is so high compared to PCs (*see* Table 8.2), it would create a very large market for a range of services, such as:

- video-on-demand
- home shopping services
- home banking services.

PC penetration is increasing and 1995 estimates suggest that 27 per cent of Swedish households now have PCs (5 per cent of households have modems), compared to 25 per cent of UK households (2 per cent with modems).[67] The blurring of the distinction between the PC and TV may also mean that interactive television services will be available from the home PC in the not-too-distant future.

Table 8.2 Penetration rates for TVs and PCs

Country	Number of people per TV receiver (1991)	% of households owning PCs (1992)
US	1.2	16
Japan	1.6	12
Germany	1.8	16
Finland	2.0	16
Netherlands	2.1	25
Sweden	2.2	12
UK	2.3	18
Norway	2.4	16
France	2.5	14

Source: The Economist Pocket World in Figures (1996).[68]

■ Video-on-demand

An interactive facility such as video on demand would provide customers with instantaneous access to a particular movie, simply by making the choice from a menu on the television screen. The customer could stop, rewind or fast-forward the movie in the same fashion as if it were a video in a videocassette recorder (VCR). The technical issues relate to the fact that the video is not sitting in a VCR underneath the television, but in a machine several hundred, or thousand, miles away. Despite the fact that there are more than 50 trials in operation around the world,[69] video-on-demand is unlikely to become a reality in Europe until early in the twenty-first century.[70]

A cheaper and easier service to deliver is 'near-video-on-demand'. This has already been adopted by some satellite television companies. This is a variation of the 'pay-per-view' services that are already offered by many cable television companies. Near-video-on-demand will play the same movie on different channels, but starting 15 or 30 minutes apart. After selecting a movie, customers are told how long they have to wait before the movie starts.

■ Home shopping services

Most people are already familiar with the concept of home shopping through the shopping channels that are available from some cable television services. However, the home shopping service that is currently offered is a very inflexible one. The viewer can only react to a particular advertisement by phoning a number that is displayed on the screen. The home shopping that can be offered via interactive television services offers greater opportunities for the viewer and for the marketer. By scrolling through on-line catalogues, interactive television will allow viewers to request more information on products and order the product they require. The three largest cable companies in the UK – TeleWest, Nynex and Bell Cablemedia – have set up a research programme to design interactive services, including providing easy access to the Internet.[71]

■ Home banking services

According to a MORI poll in 1994, only one in five people would use home banking.[72] However, most commentators believe that home banking is now reaching the point of no return.[73] Denmark's Lan & Spar Bank became Scandinavia's first financial services company to offer a home banking service to its customers in 1994. Within two years, 10 per cent of its customer base were using the service.[74] The main driver of growth in home banking is the penetration of home PCs.

■ The future of interactive television

Interactive television is attractive from both a marketing manager's and a consumer's point of view and is the subject of massive investment by the major telecommunications and entertainment companies (*see* Exhibit 8.18). However, to date, only a few countries have moved interactive television beyond the trial stage and it is likely to take considerably longer for these technologies to mature than people originally thought.[75]

Exhibit 8.18

THE BATTLE FOR THE LIVING ROOM

Many large corporations – telephone and cable companies, publishers and broadcasters, film makers and software developers among them – have a financial interest in creating a market in the UK. They are squaring up for what some commentators have called 'the battle for the living room'. But they have yet to pull together all the pieces to be able to offer these services. Meanwhile interactive services based on the Internet and other on-line networks are growing so fast that they could have taken a large part of the market before the interactive TV medium has matured. Huge investment is being poured into the UK's technology infrastructure to support interactive TV, but the commercial side of the strategy is still hazy.

Source: Financial Times (6 December 1996).[76]

However, the UK is reckoned to be as advanced as any other country. NatWest Bank and BT started the UK's move into interactive television in 1995 when it rolled out a trial home banking service to 250 homes in the Cambridge area[77] in conjunction with the local cable television companies. Other services provided in the Cambridge trial include home shopping and video-on-demand.[78]

There are similar trials being conducted all over Europe. In the Netherlands, a joint-venture organisation has been set up between Philips and KPN which has already finished technical trials of an interactive television service. Deutsche Telekom, which has a near monopoly of the German cable market, has a range of trials underway in Berlin, Hamburg, Cologne, Nuremberg, Leipzig and Stuttgart. Elsewhere, Hong Kong Telecom and Singapore Telecom are involved in similar ventures in the Far East,[79] while Telecom Australia and News Corporation are testing various services in Canberra. In Belgium, the national operator Belgacom is running a video-on-demand trial.[80]

The main issue for companies to address is whether to access homes via telephone or cable. Because many cable companies have an optical-fibre network linking into the customers' homes, the amount of data, and the breadth of services that they can deliver, is so much greater than the service that can be offered across a telephone network. However, in the UK, BT's telephone network covers the entire country, whereas a home shopping service via cable would require the agreement of many or all the cable companies.

ANIMATION AND VIRTUAL REALITY

■ Animation

Animation is a type of multimedia that has become increasingly popular in advertising. The techniques and the technologies that have been used in movies such as *Jurassic Park* are now being employed in the advertising industry. The characters that used to be drawn by hand for television advertisements are now being generated by computer (with the aid of humans, it must be added) and animation sequences that would have taken weeks, or months, for a human to generate unaided, can now be created using a PC or workstation in a matter of hours. The computer has not replaced the creative thought processes and skills of the human but, rather, the PC has become another tool for the creative advertiser.

■ Virtual reality

Perhaps the ultimate in multimedia is virtual reality. As Exhibit 8.19 shows, virtual reality is considerably different to the high-quality animation that can be seen in advertisements. Virtual reality is not just confined to science fiction as some of the world's larger companies are currently employing virtual reality for marketing research and product development.

Exhibit 8.19

THE DIFFERENCE BETWEEN ANIMATION AND VIRTUAL REALITY

Where does animation end and virtual reality begin? The extraordinary realistic animation used in such movies as *Jurassic Park* and *Toy Story* isn't virtual reality, no matter how temptingly real the scenes look. Every time you watch *Jurassic Park*, you're seeing the same set of viewpoints – the ones that Steven Spielberg chose for you. By contrast, virtual reality is a 'place' that you can enter, move through, and interact with at will. What you see in a VR system is not a set of stored images, but rather a view – computed on the fly – onto a database of 3-D object data that describes the geometry and attributes of a virtual world. The virtual reality software has to read your current position in virtual space, determine what objects should be visible from this viewpoint, read their co-ordinates from the database, and transform them into perspective. And, as if that's not hard enough, the software also has to render all the objects in real time – between 10 and 30 times per second, or around 50 milliseconds per frame. In contrast, an animation is a fixed sequence of pre-rendered images that were rendered off-line and not in real time.

Source: Byte (July 1996).[81]

There are two different types of virtual reality: *immersive* and *non-immersive*. Immersive virtual reality, often employing the use of a headset and gloves wired up to a computer, gives the user the impression that he or she is operating in a three-dimensional (3D) virtual world. The non-immersive kind involves the creation of a 3D world inside a computer, but viewed in 2D on a computer screen. This is sometimes referred to as 3D modelling and is used in computer-aided design (CAD). The use of virtual reality in marketing is still in the early stages, but it clearly offers great potential (*see* Exhibit 8.20).

Exhibit 8.20

WHAT IS VR GOOD FOR?

VR is a good gimmick; there's no sense in being precious about this. There are lots of applications, such as point-of-sale displays, trade-show booths, and other advertising or publicity related activities, where VR is an end in itself – the novelty of the medium sells the message. You probably won't buy a house solely on the strength of a VR walk-through, but the novelty of it might tempt you to go view the real thing.

Source: Byte (July 1996).[82]

CD-ROM

■ What is a CD-ROM?

CD-ROM stands for compact disk – read-only memory. It is a thin plastic disk covered with a coating onto which digital data has been encoded. The read only refers to the fact that once information is recorded on the disk, it can not be re-recorded and the disk is only used to retrieve information. It is sometimes referred to as an optical storage medium, because it uses a laser beam of light to pick up the digital information from a track of pits which have been etched into the disk. When the disk is loaded into a computer and the disk is spun at a high speed, the laser reflects off it, reading each pit as a '0' and each intervening flat surface as a '1'. This digitised information is then used to recreate the text or visual images stored on the disk, similar to the audio CDs that are used for home entertainment. Practically all new PCs sold nowadays have a CD-ROM drive fitted as standard.

CD-ROMs have been with us since the mid-1980s but have only recently been recognised as a valuable marketing tool. A single CD-ROM can hold 540 megabytes of data, which is roughly equivalent to all 20 volumes of the *Oxford English Dictionary* or half a million pages of text, making it a very efficient means of storing data. The following are just some of the ways CD-ROMs can be used for marketing purposes:

■ *For market research.* Many CD-ROMs are purchased with market-research information stored on them. Nearly all providers of information services have embraced this technology and provide their information in digital form on a CD-ROM in preference to 'hard copy' or paper format. Most publications also store back copies on CD-ROM, with the additional advantage that the articles contained on the disk can be searched quickly for particular subjects or even words.

■ *As a promotional tool.* Companies can provide information on their products and services on a disk and distribute them to potential customers. These can be much more effective than traditional promotional material such as brochures, because they can contain colour, graphs, charts and pictures as well as plain text. These images can be linked together when the CD-ROM is played to give a powerful multimedia presentation. CD-ROMs can be distributed at trade shows and promotions, or can be posted out on a regular basis to retailers (*see* Exhibit 8.21) at a fraction of the cost to send equivalent merchandising material in hard copy.

Exhibit 8.21

ALL THAT JAZZ

Philips Media has helped the distribution division of the Polygram record label create a CD-ROM disk called *The Electronic New Release Book*. The disk, which will be regularly distributed to music retailers, holds sound samples, video clips, and cover art of all new releases. The disk also includes all product set-up and merchandising information. Retailers can view the information by pointing and clicking on album titles, which reveal more in-depth data. The disk is organised by release date, but record store personnel can zero in on material from pop, country, jazz or other categories they choose.

Source: Keeler (1995).[1]

■ *As an integral part of the product or service.* For example, the production of user manuals is now rapidly being replaced by CD-ROM technology where software is sold without accompanying manuals, but with a CD-ROM included instead. Exhibit 8.22 provides another example of a CD-ROM being used as an integral part of an investment service.

Exhibit 8.22

THE DEATH OF PAPER?

Financial institutions looking for an additional edge over their competitors are expanding their use of the Internet as a marketing tool. Paper reports are being ditched in favour of a device that allows institutions to talk to their customers via video presentations and Internet links.

Instead of ploughing through cumbersome quarterly reports investors can use a new CD-ROM to check out their investment portfolio on a computer screen and click onto the information they want to view in more detail. They can also get a unique glimpse of their fund manager talking on video about his philosophy, objectives and investment style. Company and fund information is then updated every quarter via the Internet.

Multimedia design company Delve, has spent £150,000 developing the Delve Report in association with Global Asset Management (GAM). Delve product designer Jonty Huwitz commented: 'Suddenly investors are getting to meet the people who are investing their money face to face'.

▶

Jeffrey Ginsberg, GAM's technical marketing director says the company, which has $8.5 billion under management, intends to use the new technology to communicate with its whole client base. He said: 'The actual CD contains elements you can not provide in hard copy, like the digital video of the fund managers concerned. The Internet has a problem with digital video because the amount of data it requires is so large it is slow to transmit. Therefore the advantage of joining the two technologies is that the CD can provide high quality video and the Internet can update the information on a regular basis. It's the best of both worlds.'

Source: Sunday Business (5 May 1996).[83]

CONCLUSION

Cybermarketing is a new phrase which has been coined to describe the new methods of marketing using multimedia, Internet, World Wide Web, interactive television, animation, virtual reality and CD-ROM. Multimedia is the combination of many different formats, such as text, pictures, animation, narrative, video and music, into a single medium and the past few years have seen tremendous advances in the use of multimedia. The explosion of the Internet has caught most marketers by surprise and, while it is a major threat for organisations still working on the basis of old channel and industry structures, it offers enormous potential to creative marketers who can market their products and services on it. However, marketing in cyberspace is not without its pitfalls. Marketers will need to adopt a different mindset to attract customers to visit them in cyberspace. The Internet itself is a relatively immature medium and Internet commerce will take some years to establish itself as a mainstream activity. The development of interactive TV also holds huge potential, but is still very much a developing technology and will require considerably more investment before it can be commercialised. Companies are already providing this investment in what has been described as 'the battle for the living room'. Animation and virtual reality are also examples of the new ways in which marketers can create powerful visual images and structures to market their products. The very high memory and suitability for multimedia applications makes CD-ROMs another technology with a great deal of potential for marketers.

ASSIGNMENT QUESTIONS

1 What is meant by multimedia?
2 In what ways can multimedia be used to market products and services creatively?
3 What are the advantages of marketing products on the Internet and the World Wide Web?
4 What are the main risks associated with marketing products on the World Wide Web?
5 Explain the future threats and opportunities that interactive TV poses to a major retailer.
6 How could CD-ROMs be used as part of a marketing campaign?

INTERNET AUCTIONS

US airlines made net profits of $2.4bn last year – the biggest in the industry's history. But how much more would they have made if only they had filled those rows of empty seats? Thanks to record passenger numbers, US airlines filled a higher proportion of seats last year than at any time since the second world war. Even so, over the year, they sold only 66% of flight capacity on domestic flights. According to one Wall Street analyst, profits could have soared to more than $8bn if the airlines had been able to fill their aircraft. Now some airlines are experimenting with ways of doing exactly that – by auctioning their empty seats in cyberspace.

In the past few weeks, American Airlines has conducted auctions on the Internet in which it attracted 2,000 bids for 20 pairs of round-trip tickets to destinations in the US and over-seas. Last night, marking the 15th anniversary of its frequent flyer programme, American Airlines opened another Internet seat auction, this time inviting people to submit their bids in frequent flyer miles instead of cash. American Airlines describes these auctions as exper-imental, and the proceeds are going to charity. But the company says it is only a matter of time before it puts its auctions into commercial use.

American Airlines is not the only carrier experimenting with seat auctions. The Hong Kong based Cathay Pacific is conducting its third Internet auction in the US, offering 387 tickets on its services from the US to Hong Kong. Cathay says the response to the latest auction has been 'phenomenal' – more than 10,000 bids have been received so far. It expects proceeds from the three auctions to total $325,000, most of which will translate into profit.

Electronic media could bring significant changes to the way airline tickets are sold – par-ticularly in the US where access to these media is greatest. Mr Julius Maltidus, analyst at Salomon Brothers, says they could bring a third revolution to the US airline industry, com-parable to those prompted by the introduction of jet aircraft in late 1950s and by deregulation in 1978. For airlines, part of the appeal of selling tickets through electronic media is the chance to cut travel agents' commissions. These cost US airlines $6.4bn in 1995, amount-ing to 9 per cent of the industry's total operating costs. A bigger opportunity for change lies on the revenue side of the equation because electronic media such as the Internet will make it possible for airlines to fill unsold seats by auctioning them. If the idea catches on, passengers who need to make firm plans will continue to make reservations in the usual way. However, a day or two before departure, when airline managers can be certain how many unsold seats will remain, the empty seats on a given flight will be auctioned off. The winners may end up paying only a fraction of the full fare. But as additional passengers are carried at little extra cost to the airline, nearly all the money they pay will flow through into profit. One danger for airlines is that some passengers who normally pay full fare will wait for the auc-tion to get their seat at a lower price. But even allowing for a 25% fall in the average fare paid, 100% passenger loadings would quadruple net profits.

On a more practical level, there is also the question of passenger acceptance. While low fares may be popular, crowded aircraft are not. 'Passengers may start to shy away from full flights. I mean, I hate it when those middle seats are full. Don't you?'

Source: Adapted from 'Passengers take a seat at the Internet auction', *Financial Times*, 17 June 1996.

Questions

1 What are the main marketing issues associated with auctioning seats on the Internet?

2 Why is yield management (maximising the number of fee-paying seats) so critical in the airline industry?

3 'While low fares may be popular, crowded aircraft are not.' Discuss.

4 As a marketing manager for an airline, how would you view the balance between the following different distribution channels: travel agent, direct sales, direct via Internet?

References

1 Keeler, L. (1995). *Cybermarketing*. New York: Amacom.

2 Ryan, M. (1995). 'The power of multimedia in Financial Services', Newsletter, Andersen Consulting, Dublin, Summer.

3 Beofor, W. (1995). 'Multimedia and the money men', *Computer Weekly*, 30 November.

4 MacLeod, M. (1996). 'Positive feedback from trial', *Financial Times*, 6 March.

5 Manchester, P. (1995). 'New way to sell cars', *Financial Times*, 7 June.

6 Client Focus Systems (1996). 'Interactive dealing service set up', *Client Focus Systems*, February.

7 Cane, A. (1996). 'Barclays unveils share dealing by video link', *Financial Times*, 4 January.

8 http://info.isoc.org/guest/zakon/internet/history/hit.html

9 The Economist (1995). 'The Internet survey', *The Economist*, 1 July.

10 Faughan, L. (1996). 'And now the Intranet', *Business and Finance*, 26 May.

11 PC User (1995). 'Accessing the Internet', *PC User*, 18–31 October.

12 Kehoe, L. (1995). 'How to join the on-line revolution', *Financial Times*, 1 March.

13 Gareiss, R. (1995). 'The online corporation: choosing the right Internet service provider', *Data Communications*, 21 November.

14 http://www.yahoo.com

15 http://www.demon.net

16 http://www.uunet.pipex.com

17 Green, H. (1996). 'AOL in line for on-line service monopoly', *Sunday Business*, 2 June.

18 Foremski, T. (1995). 'Fresh salvos in the marketing war', *Financial Times*, 1 March.

19 Spar, D. and Bussang, J.J. (1996). 'Ruling the Net', *Harvard Business Review*, May–June.

20 Kehoe, L. (1996). 'If you can't beat the Net, join it', *Financial Times*, 6 March.

21 Greenfield, D. (1995). 'Internet access: the international angle', *Data Communications*, 21 November.

22 Griffith, V. (1996). 'New-look banners', *Financial Times*, 8 August.

23 The Economist (1996). 'Free-mail', *The Economist*, 27 April.

24 The Economist (1996). 'A survey of the software industry', *The Economist*, 25 May.

25 Whitehorn, A. (ed.) (1996). *Multimedia: The Complete Guide*. London: Dorling Kindersley.

26 *Digital Media* (1996). 'Telcos underestimate Internet, report says', *Digital Media*, Issue 1, published by Euromoney Publications.

27 Computing (1996). 'UK Internet provision will be billion pound market by 2000', *Computing*, 18 January.

28 Lambeth, J. (1996). 'Business fails to make net profit', *Computer Weekly*, 18 July.

29 Kehoe, L. (1995). 'Internet brings global network to the home office', *Financial Times*, 6 December.

30 http://www.nielsen.com/home/press/uk (1996). 'AC Nielsen study sheds new light on purchasing behaviour of Internet users', 9 May.

31 Vadon, R. (1996). 'A radio renaissance worldwide', *Financial Times*, 8 July.

32 Kelly, S. (1996). 'Ringing in the changes', *Computer Weekly*, 30 May.

33 Richardson, M.A. (1996). *How the Internet is Affecting Business*. Datapro Information Services, July.

34 McGookin, S. (1996). '"Direct Age" is dawning', *Financial Times*, 10 June.

35 Houlder, V. (1996). 'Fingers that shop around', *Financial Times*, 24 September.

36 Partridge, C. (1996). 'Secret agent', *Computing*, 1 August.

37 McCarthy, V. (1995). 'The web: open for business', *Datamation*, 1 December.

38 Jones, P. (1996). 'Blooming business benefits', *Digital Media*, Issue 1.

39 Ellsworth, J.H. and Ellsworth, M.V. (1995). *Marketing on the Internet*. New York: John Wiley.

40 Client Focus Systems (1996). 'Are you being surfed', *Client Focus Systems*, February.
41 Clement, D. (1996). 'Analysis on the Web – and on the cheap', *Sunday Business ComputerAge*, 7 July.
42 The Economist (1995). Op. cit., 1 July.
43 http://www.gm.com
44 Jones, P. (1996). 'Directions in the digital desert', *Digital Media,* Issue 1.
45 Shillingford, J. (1996). 'Online support helps cut costs', *Sunday Business ComputerAge*, 7 July.
46 Cortese, A. (1996). 'Here comes the intranet', *Business Week*, 26 February.
47 Ellsworth, J.H. and Ellsworth, M.V. (1995). Op. cit.
48 McCarthy, V. (1995). 'Ten top business tips for your Web project', *Datamation*, 1 December.
49 Hewson, D. (1996) 'You'll drop before you shop on the Net', *Sunday Times*, 16 June.
50 Lambeth, J. (1996). Op. cit.
51 The Economist (1995). 'Who can measure the 'net?', *The Economist*, 22 July.
52 Insurance Technology Report (1996). 'Net not ready for transactions', *Insurance Technology Report*, June.
53 Manchester, P. (1995). 'Bandwidth gap needs bridging', *Financial Times*, 3 October.
54 Newing, R. (1996). 'Electronic shopping on the Web', *Financial Times*, 3 July.
55 Kavanagh, J. (1995). 'Purchases on the Internet "could potentially reach $200 billion by year 2000"', *Financial Times*, 1 November.
56 Oldroyd, R. (1996). 'Web entrants getting little return on outlay', *Sunday Business ComputerAge*, 12 May.
57 http://info.broker.isi.edu/fast/articles/EC-on-Internet. *Electronic Commerce on the Internet*.
58 http://www.j-sainsbury.co.uk/wine-direct/shop
59 http://www.barclaysquare.co.uk
60 http://www.commerce.net/pr/. 'CommerceNet/Nielsen announce Internet survey results', 30 October (1995).
61 Gandy, T. (1995). 'Banking in e-space', *The Banker*, December.
62 White, L. (1995). 'Network first', *Computer Weekly*, 23 November.
63 George, T. (1995). 'Security for the future', *Banking Technology*, December.
64 Burke, J. (1996). 'How to fake a credit card in one minute', *Sunday Times*, 30 June.
65 Taylor, P. (1996). 'Fresh opportunities in a vibrant marketplace', *Financial Times*, 6 March.
66 The Economist (1995). 'Card-sharkers and cyberwars', *The Economist*, 7 October.
67 Houlder, V. (1996). 'One race, many roads', *Financial Times*, 16 August.
68 *The Economist Pocket World in Figures* (1996). Economist Publications/Hamish Hamilton.
69 Rasmussen, P. (1995). 'Video gameplan', *DEC User*, December.
70 Shillingford, J. (1995). 'Key technical trials face delays', *Financial Times*, 3 October.
71 Snoddy, R. (1996). 'Saturation point looms', *Financial Times*, 6 March.
72 Whitmore, A. and Jones, L. (1994). *Consumers' Attitudes to Home Finance and Technology*. ICL Financial Services and MORI, July.
73 Gordon, N. (1996). 'Homes for orphans', *The Banker*, January.
74 MacConville, D. (1996). 'Danes ahead on home banking', *Direct Delivery International*, March.
75 The Economist (1995). 'Multimedia's no-man's land', *The Economist*, 22 July.
76 Black, G. (1995). 'Interactive TV put to the test', *Financial Times*, 6 December.
77 George, T. (1995). 'NatWest first with cable TV home banking service', *Banking Technology*, March.
78 Andersen Consulting (1996). *List of Interactive TV Trials in the World*. Andersen Consulting.
79 The Economist (1995). 'Tuned out and dropping off', *The Economist*, 4 November.
80 Rasmussen, P. (1995). Op. cit.
81 Pountain, D. (1996). 'Animation is no substitute for virtual reality', *Byte*, July.
82 Pountain, D. (1996). 'VR meets reality', *Byte*, July.
83 Vincent, C. (1996). 'Paper reports head for the bin', *Sunday Business*, 5 May.

THE MARKETING MIX AND INFORMATION TECHNOLOGY

Part III of this book deals with the use of information technology in the marketing mix. Each of the four elements of the marketing mix – product, price, place and promotion – is given its own chapter:

9

PRODUCT

- Technology-driven products and services
- New product design and development
- The product development life cycle
- The use of information technology in manufacturing

OBJECTIVES

After studying this chapter, you will be able to:

- ☐ Understand how information technology is driving new products and services
- ☐ Understand emerging trends in new product design and development
- ☐ Describe the different steps in the product development process
- ☐ Evaluate the role of IT in the product development process
- ☐ Describe the role of IT in a manufacturing environment

TECHNOLOGY-DRIVEN PRODUCTS AND SERVICES

■ Incorporating IT into the product

Today, the increasing use of information technology is leading to greater efficiencies in the design and manufacture of products and services. There is also a much greater range of products available and IT is being incorporated into products and services themselves. New technologies such as high-definition TV (HDTV), mobile telephones and laser disks create large new markets when they are introduced, but IT is also being incorporated into products and services in a more subtle fashion. For example, cars now employ IT to control many functions that were traditionally operated by mechanical means, including ignition control, central locking, braking systems and air conditioning. Washing machines, toys and many household goods contain computer chips which operate and monitor certain functions and even contraceptive products have entered the IT age (*see* Exhibit 9.1). IT is also enabling new services to be provided. Direct banking and insurance services are only possible due to advances in telephone, call centre and database technologies.

Exhibit 9.1

WHEN GREEN MEANS GO FOR IT

It has been heralded as the best development in contraception since the 1960s. After 15 years of research and development Unipath, the healthcare division of Unilever, has launched Persona, its computerised version of the rhythm method. The hand-held device monitors hormone levels in urine and indicates on which days it is possible to have sex without fear of pregnancy. A green light means go and a red light means no. It went on sale in selected branches of Boots last week with little fanfare but the entire stock sold out twice.

Source: *Financial Times* (10 October 1996).[1]

■ Artificial intelligence

Another example of the innovative ways in which new developments in information technology are being incorporated into new products is the increasing range of products that use a type of artificial intelligence called fuzzy logic. Recognising that ordinary computer logic is not sufficient for a wide variety of tasks which require skill or judgement, scientists have developed fuzzy logic which more closely represents human thinking (*see* Exhibit 9.2).

Exhibit 9.2

FUZZY LOGIC

Operations of present computers depend on simple Yes/No logic, namely binary logic, which is widely different from the information processing inherent in human thinking. Therefore, evaluation based on common sense and flexible judgement is considered difficult to achieve by computers.

Fuzzy theory has emerged as a theory suited to represent uncertainty contained in the meaning of each word. Fuzzy artificial intelligence, as an application of this theory, is expected to play an important role in the future establishment of an intimate relationship between men and computers. It is indispensable for configuring human-friendly machines and speech-recognition systems such as nursing and home robots, and for developing artificial intelligence (AI) tools which support man in production control, medical diagnosis, finance and general decision making. In Japan, a technological research association called the Laboratory for International Fuzzy Engineering (LIFE) research is intended to vitalise basic study of fuzzy theory, research on its efficient utilisation by strengthening ties between industrial and academic circles, and to promote international technological exchange. At LIFE's inception in 1989, 48 Japanese companies paid varying fees to join including:

Canon	Konica	NTT
Fuji Electric	Matsushita Electric Industrial	Olympus Optical
Fujitsu	Mazda Motors	Sharp
Hitachi	Minolta	Sony
Honda	Mitsubishi Electric	Sumitomo
IBM Japan	NEC	Toshiba
Kawasaki Steel	Nissan Motors	Toyota Motors

Source: Kosko (1994).[2]

Consider Canon's handheld camera which uses only 13 rules to tune the autofocus on the lens. The fuzzy logic control system requires little memory and uses image sensors to measure picture clarity. The data from the image sensors, combined with these decision rules that drive the new lens settings, help the new system to focus twice as well as other controllers. The list of some of the fuzzy products which have been launched in Japan and Korea in 1992 give some idea of the potential applications (*see* Table 9.1).

Table 9.1 Applications of fuzzy logic

Product	Company	Fuzzy logic rule
Air conditioner	Hitachi	Prevents temperature fluctuations and consumes less power
Anti-lock brakes	Nissan	Controls brakes in hazardous situations based on wheel speed and acceleration
Auto transmission	Honda	Selects gear ratio based on engine load, driving style and road conditions
Copy machine	Canon	Adjusts drum voltage based on picture density, temperature and humidity
Dishwasher	Matsushita	Adjusts cleaning cycle and rinse and wash strategies based on the number of dishes
Elevator control	Fujitec	Reduces waiting time based on passenger traffic
Golf diagnostic system	Maruman Golf	Selects golf club based on golfer's physique and swing
Microwave oven	Hitachi	Sets and tunes power and cooking strategy
Still camera	Canon	Finds subject anywhere in frame and adjusts autofocus
Television	Goldstar	Adjusts screen colour and texture for each frame and stabilises volume based on viewer's room location
Toaster	Sony	Sets toasting time and heat strategy for each type of bread
Video camcorder	Matsushita	Cancels handheld shake and adjusts autofocus

Source: Based on Kosko (1994).[2]

NEW PRODUCT DESIGN AND DEVELOPMENT

■ The demand for new products and shorter product life cycles

One of the key activities which a marketing manager must manage is to ensure a continuous stream of new products going to market. For example, the company 3M has such a commitment to new products that up until 1992 it had a corporate objective that more than 25 per cent of every division's sales must come from products invented in the previous five years. After 1992 it raised the target to 30 per cent of sales coming from products invented in the previous four years. Employees are encouraged to spend up to 15 per cent of company time on 'skunkworks' projects that interest them and which do not require corporate approval. Another company which has turned product innovation into a distinct competitive advantage is Casio, which brings out a regular stream of new competitive products. Rather than postpone profits until the later stages of the product life cycle, Casio aims to make its money on products with very short life cycles. It achieves this by integrating design and development with marketing so that those closest to the market are responsible for developing new products and meeting customers' needs. Increasingly the speed with which companies can get their products to market is becoming a key competitive advantage and information technology is a driving force behind this (*see* Exhibit 9.3).

Exhibit 9.3

DRUGS AND DATA

A senior executive of Eli Lilly, the US drugs company, described his company's business as '50 per cent information technology, 50 per cent pharmaceuticals'. His comment highlights the increasingly crucial role played by computer and telecommunications technologies in the fast-changing, high-pressure world of the global pharmaceutical manufacturers where a day's delay in bringing a product to market can cost $1 million in lost revenues.

Some companies believe they can cut the clinical trial process by half, from 30 months to 15 months, by managing the process better. Traditionally, a clinical trial depended on a lengthy and largely paper-based process which began with a general practitioner filling out a piece of paper after seeing a patient, sending this report back to the company conducting the trial which then had to input the data for analysis. More recently, doctors have been given computers to enter the data directly and clinical research assistants, who normally visit the GPs every six weeks, have been provided with mobile computers and digital telephones so that they can access the latest clinical trial information remotely.

Given the escalating costs and risks involved in new drugs, many pharmaceutical companies are also attempting to manage the spread of risk by forming research partnerships. In these cases, secure telephone links can help geographically remote teams exchange data and work more closely together. Similarly, companies such as SmithKline Beecham have begun to make extensive use of videoconferencing networks. The need to reach out and communicate with existing or potential customers has also encouraged drug companies to become early business adopters of the Internet as a marketing medium. Today, pharmaceutical companies' Web sites are among the best presented and most informative on the Internet.

Source: Financial Times (10 June 1996).[3]

The speed with which organisations can develop products and get them to market is an important competitive weapon, particularly in high-technology or fashion-oriented products. As in the case of Casio, payback and profitability can be increased by extending the front end of the traditional product life cycle. In general, the time to market from product conception to adoption is shortening and organisations are accelerating this trend using new processes facilitated by information technology. In rapidly changing businesses such as telecommunications, the difference in timing can be the difference between success and failure. Ericsson, a leader in telephone-switching equipment, has cut its development time dramatically by using 'concurrent engineering' rather than sequential development. Using this new system has allowed Ericsson to cut the time from order to delivery of a switching system from 6 months to 10 days.[4] The speed of development in this industry is further illustrated by the fact that 30–40 per cent of sales come from products launched over the previous two years. Figure 9.1 provides a graphical representation of how these changes are changing the shape of the traditional product life cycle.

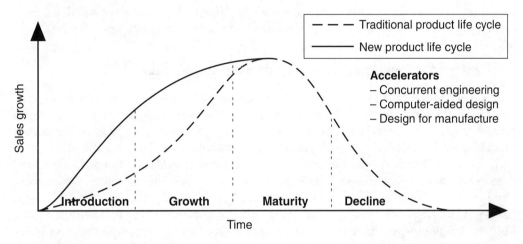

Fig 9.1 New product life cycle

■ Modifying existing products versus developing new products

From a marketing perspective, there is a significant difference between the development of a totally new product and the use of technology to enhance an existing product. Particularly in the highly competitive fast-moving consumer goods (FMCG) industry, it is very difficult to launch totally new products. Most of the successful brands have been established for a long time and the emphasis is on building the existing brand name with improvements to the product or line extensions. The UK's top 20 FMCG products have an average age of 35 years and the launch of new products is difficult and risky. For example, Coca-Cola suffered a major setback in the early 1980s with the launch of its New Coke product and, in response to pressure from consumers, reverted back to the original formulation. On the other hand, the development of its new plastic packaging bottles which had the same shape as the old Coca-Cola glass bottles was very successful. The costs and risks associated with launching a totally new product are much greater than those associated with enhancing existing products.

■ Product versus process development

Marketers and R&D managers also face choices between investing in products or improving their manufacturing processes. Investing in a new manufacturing technology can give a company a cost advantage in the marketplace and is usually less risky. The differences in investment emphasis between countries are illustrated by a study conducted in the 1980s by the Massachusetts Institute of Technology, which found that US companies invested two-thirds of their budget on new products and one-third on process improvement. This was in direct contrast to Japanese companies, while German companies fell between the two with a fifty/fifty ratio between product and process investment. The study concluded that the higher investment in making products more efficiently rather than in totally new products was a significant factor in Japan's better competitive position. It is important to remember that the Japanese have still developed and launched many very successful new products, particularly in home electronics.

■ New product development and design-for-manufacture

Increasingly, organisations are incorporating design-for-manufacture principles into their development efforts. Design for manufacture is an attempt to get away from the traditional product development process, where designs were passed from the design teams to the production unit that had the job of manufacturing them. Difficulties arose when the original design was found to be very expensive or difficult to produce. There are a number of approaches to bridging these gaps between the marketing, engineering and manufacturing functions. Cross-functional teams can be used to integrate design and engineering with the manufacturing process and the customer's requirements. Indeed, leading-edge companies often closely involve their customers in the process. By focusing effort on the design process, potential problems or breakthroughs can be identified before significant costs are committed (*see* Figure 9.2).

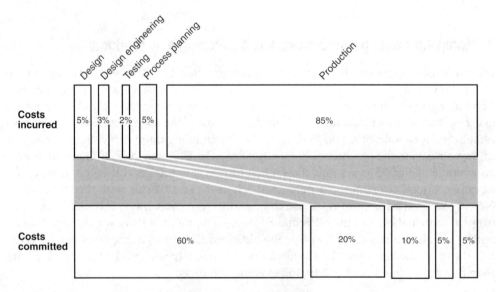

Fig 9.2   Costs committed at different stages of the product development process

Source: Business Week (30 April 1990).[5]

Design-for-manufacture allows leading-edge manufacturing companies to simplify both product and process, leading to:

- *fewer components in the product*. With fewer components, the product is not only easier and less costly to produce; it will probably have greater reliability.
- *fewer steps in the process flow*. With the emphasis on the elimination of unnecessary steps, more value is added to the product. This applies to any process, whether factory operations or office procedures.
- *fewer components in the fixtures and tooling used for machining*. The simplest fixtures and tools require the least time and cost to alter when a machine is changed from producing one item to another.[6]

THE PRODUCT DEVELOPMENT LIFE CYCLE

■ Six stages of product development

The success rate for new products is low and managing the new product development process is a difficult task. Information technology can assist marketers and new product development managers throughout the development process. In order to understand its full impact, we will now look at the role of information technology in the six different stages of the product-development life cycle, as shown in Figure 9.3.

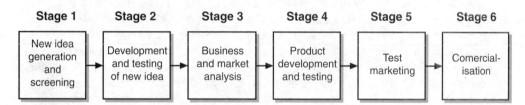

Stage 1	Stage 2	Stage 3	Stage 4	Stage 5	Stage 6
New idea generation and screening	Development and testing of new idea	Business and market analysis	Product development and testing	Test marketing	Comercial-isation

Fig 9.3   Six stages of product development
Source: Based on Kotler *et al*. (1996).[7] Reproduced by permission of Prentice Hall.

Stage 1: New idea generation and screening

Typically, 50 per cent of new ideas are developed internally, 28 per cent come from customers and the remainder come from competitors and distributors.[7] A variety of techniques can be used to generate ideas internally, including employee suggestion schemes and brainstorming sessions. Each year, Toyota gets over 2 million suggestions for improvement from its employees. The screening stage involves taking a number of ideas and eliminating those which are not suitable. Information technology can be used effectively to screen ideas and has a major role to play in the sharing of ideas and obtaining feedback from remote locations. Executives from different offices or countries can be involved in the idea-generation and screening process through the use of videoconferencing, e-mail and groupware. Expert system software can also be used to evaluate each by asking a series of questions on each and attaching a pre-determined weighting to each response. Questions might include:

- What is the product's fit with our existing product line?
- How much will the product be priced at?
- What distribution channels will be used?
- What is the likely volume of sales?
- What is the competition like?

These questions can help executives perform a more rigorous and comprehensive screening of new ideas.

Stage 2: Development and testing of the new idea

Once the idea has passed the screening stage, the next step is to develop and test it. Software tools such as computer-aided design (CAD) programs can be used to design the product and illustrate what it will look like. If the members of a design team are split up and located in different countries, they can stay in touch using video-conferencing and e-mail. Another option which is made available by such technologies as multimedia is to let the customer design the product (*see* Exhibit 9.4).

Exhibit 9.4

LET THE CUSTOMER DESIGN THE PRODUCT

In the US, Andersen Windows uses multimedia applications in retail stores to integrate its customers into its supply chain and, effectively, to sell to a 'market of one'. It has built a system that allows customers to design a 3-D representation of their home, pick the spot where the windows are to be located and experiment with different window-frames. Full motion video runs behind the window to create a more realistic impression. When the order is confirmed, the system generates a parts list that is sent straight back to a production facility. Andersen has ambitions to roll-out the application to all of its distributors. Customers still have to visit the appropriate retail store, but constraints of form have been overcome. All sorts of possibilities are opened-up; similar firms could soon exploit high street based multimedia kiosks to cut out – or disintermediate – the retailer altogether, basing customer service employees at a cheap green-field site. They could source their components globally, depending on which suppliers offer the best value, and have goods delivered to the factory by specialized logistics firms like Federal Express.

Source: Harvard Business Review (March/April 1995).[8]

Stage 3: Business and marketing analysis

Running concurrently with the development of the new idea is the process of business and marketing analysis. Traditionally these activities would have happened sequentially, but it is important that the marketing potential for each idea is continuously evaluated at each stage of the process. Complex IT applications such as data mining can identify if there is a likely demand for the product from existing customers (*see* Chapter 2). In Chapter 3, we examined the use of IT in the six stages of marketing research. Basic software applications such as spreadsheets can also be used to perform the business analysis, sensitivity and 'what if' analysis.

Stage 4: Product development and testing

Once a product concept has been developed and the initial business case has indicated its viability, the next stage is to develop and test the product. IT applications such as virtual reality can be used to prototype the product design so that it meets the needs and requirements of customers better than if the design was created in two dimensions.[9] Building a virtual world inside a computer is useful in a surprisingly wide variety of commercial, industrial and scientific applications. It is easier to control a virtual world than the real one and car manufacturers such as Ford and Rover routinely build virtual models to check ergonomics and help develop a new model before it has been physically built (*see* Exhibit 9.5). Virtual reality can be used to experience a new building design, safely examine a nuclear reactor core or see how a steering assembly withstands a rough country road.

Exhibit 9.5

VIRTUAL PROTOTYPING

One of the key applications for virtual reality is virtual prototyping, particularly engineering design such as cars, factories, aeroplanes, and even buildings, architecture and shop interiors. Often, prototypes of complex mechanical devices can cost as much as the real thing. Companies can save millions by doing it in cyberspace. In 1994, Stephen Wallace, project control manager at Rover, was asked by his managing director to create a prototype of a whole production plant using a virtual reality system. Wallace started prototyping the plant using a non-immersive system in early-1995, preparing for a construction phase that would take the centre into production a year later.

'The building we wanted to use for it was a virtually derelict shell. It was difficult to understand what it would be like when we had done it. We wanted to use it as a showpiece: an example of best practice in terms of facilities,' he says. He used the non-immersion software to visualise elements of the building including desks, the racking that holds all the components, and the areas for the operators. The system picked up some costly mistakes that would have been difficult to rectify. These included the accurate design of safety rails for the supporting columns of the building which had to be reconfigured.

Source: Computer Weekly (18 July 1996).[9]

Stage 5: Test marketing

Companies can decide to introduce a product into the market in one single launch, but in many cases this is considered too risky. Despite the testing that has been conducted in the earlier stages of the product development process, there is still no guarantee that a product launch will be successful. As we have seen in Chapter 1, the number of new product launches has increased significantly in the past decade and the chances of any new product surviving in such a competitive marketplace have decreased. Companies generally prefer to test-market new products in particular locations which are regarded as representative of the wider market into which the product will be launched.

Monitoring and analysing the sales and marketing information that results from a test-marketing exercise are important. In Chapters 2 and 3, we examined various management and marketing information systems that can gather, analyse and summarise such test-market data and help marketing managers make informed decisions on whether or not to proceed with a full product launch. Sophisticated marketing decision-support systems can combine simulated test-marketing with mathematical modelling of the marketing mix. One of the most important developments in test-marketing is the use of simulated test-marketing (STM), which improves the likelihood of new product success. Clancy and Shulman (1991)[10] believe that STM is the best way of reducing risk when launching a new product or repositioning an existing product and claim it has four main advantages:

- *It reduces risk.* Typically eight out of ten new products fail. An STM costing $100 000 to $150 000 can provide feedback in three to six months, compared to several million dollars to test-market and substantially more to launch nationwide.
- *It increases efficiency.* An STM can help prioritise different projects by providing feedback on which provides the greatest potential return.
- *It maintains security.* Real test-marketing alerts competitors to a company's intentions and allows them to react.
- *It can save company time.* As time has become a key competitive weapon, identifying and serving a customer's needs quickly is critical and an STM test can give results in three to six months as opposed to over a year for a real test.

Choosing the location to test-market a new product is also an important consideration. If the location is not representative of the final market, the product may be well received during test-marketing but fail subsequently. The use of geographic information systems (*see* Chapter 4) and geo-demographic analysis tools has become commonplace in determining the most appropriate locations for test-marketing particular products.

Some of the main features of an STM are illustrated in Exhibit 9.6.

Exhibit 9.6

WHY BOTHER TO TEST-MARKET?

Today's better STMs capture every component in the marketing mix – from media weight and schedule through promotion, pricing, product, and positioning – and assess the effect of any plan on brand awareness through to market share and profitability. But what does such a system actually do? Why would a manager use one? Basically, today's STMs test any plan the marketing manager wishes to consider – even a competitor's plan. The marketer simply enters the plan into the computer and the model forecasts consumer awareness, sales, profits, and much more. Some systems can go beyond the volume forecast. For example, the Litmus system permits marketing management to ask 'what if?' questions such as, 'what would happen if I decreased media spending 25 percent?' or 'what would happen if I increased consumer promotion 10 percent?'. To undertake an STM, a marketer must provide a large number of inputs, most of which come right out of the marketing plan and normally include:

- the market's size in buyers, units and dollars
- advertising copy testing results

- advertising budget for the test product and competitors
- media schedule, by month
- trade promotion, by month
- price
- distribution build (the proportion of store carrying the test product, by month)
- expected marketing costs and margin contribution

This information is used to design a research study to simulate the likely trial and repeat purchase for the new (or re-staged) product.

Source: Clancy and Shulman (1991).[10] Copyright © 1991 by Kevin J. Clancy and Robert Shulman. Reprinted by permission of HarperCollins Publishers, Inc.

Stage 6: Commercialisation

During this stage the marketing and production plans for the full-scale product launch are finalised and implemented. The results from the previous test-marketing phase are critical inputs in refining the plan for commercialisation. They may indicate that certain product features should be altered, or that the emphasis on different distribution channels should change or that the price should be changed. Setting up production facilities and investing heavily in promotional expenditure make the whole process of launching a new product very expensive and anything which can improve the success rate is a worthwhile investment. Table 9.2 provides an example of how one system-created plan achieved the same share objectives with a $19 million investment as the manager's plan with a $27 million investment:

The final stage of the product development process leads us directly into the subject of manufacturing and the use of IT in the manufacturing process.

Table 9.2   Example of benefits associated with system-generated commercialisation plans

Food product optimisation	Manager-generated plan	System-generated 'optimal' plan
Cost of implementing plan	$27 million	$19 million
Forecasted share of market	13.7%	14.2%
Expected profit/loss (end Year 1)	– $7.9 million	+ $0.2 million
Payback period	38 months	16 months

Source: Clancy and Shulman (1991).[10]

THE USE OF INFORMATION TECHNOLOGY IN MANUFACTURING

■ Information needs

Production departments plan and control the processes used to deliver goods or services. Traditionally, marketing and production functions have operated independently of each other, but this is changing. In order to market products and services effectively, marketing managers need to understand the potential and limitations of their production operations. A marketing manager for a bank who does not understand the way in which services are delivered in a branch may develop unrealistic products and marketing messages. Similarly, in a manufacturing business, the marketing manager must understand the cost drivers and service levels for both purchasing and manufacturing. When we look at the information needs of typical manufacturing and purchasing functions, we can see the key role of information technology in supporting the planning, control and transaction systems (*see* Figure 9.4).

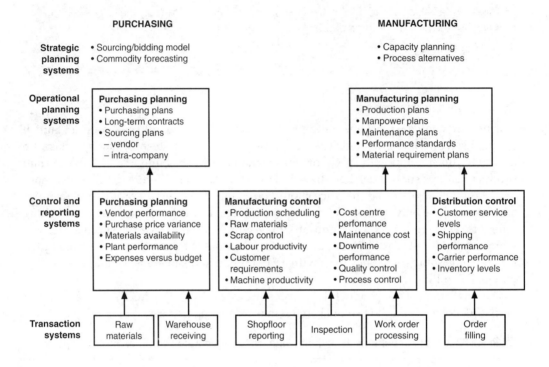

Fig 9.4   Sample information needs for purchasing/manufacturing

Source: Flaatten *et al.* (1989).[11]

■ Computer-integrated manufacturing (CIM)

Computer-integrated manufacturing is a concept describing how computers can be used in factory automation. The basic principles are similar to those for applying information technology to any other areas of the business and consist of:

- *Simplifying the process before starting to automate it*. Any steps in the production, product design or planning processes which are unnecessary should be redesigned for simplicity.
- *Automating the simplified processes*. Automation is achieved using computers and robots which are controlled by information technology.
- *Integrating the resulting processes*. Integration of production and support processes is achieved using computers, telecommunications and IT.

Some of the applications which can be part of a computer-integrated manufacturing program or used on their own include:

- *Computer-aided design (CAD)*. CAD programs help design products using 3-D perspectives of the product. Designers can view the design from any angle and obtain customer feedback on how it looks. CAD programs can be used to test different product designs based on the characteristics of the materials used without building the products.
- *Materials requirement planning (MRP) and manufacturing resource planning (MRPII)*. MRP is used to plan the types of materials required in the production process with the aid of computers. MRPII helps integrate MRP with production scheduling and shopfloor control.
- *Computer-aided manufacturing (CAM)*. CAM is used to manufacture products and can have a number of components including shopfloor control (monitoring and controlling the production process in a factory), process control (directly controlling a physical process), machine control (directly controlling machines) and robots (controlling a machine with human-like capabilities).

The benefits of computer-integrated manufacturing include:

- higher levels of efficiency and productivity through process simplification, better production scheduling, planning and workload balancing.
- increased utilisation of production facilities and better quality through continuous monitoring, feedback and control of factory operations, equipment and robots.
- lower investment in inventories and work in progress through just-in-time policies, better planning and control of production and finished goods requirements.
- higher customer service by reducing out-of-stock situations and producing high-quality products that better meet customer requirements.

CONCLUSION

Technology is driving both the creation of new products and markets and increased efficiencies in the production of existing products. New technologies such as high-definition television (HDTV) and new applications of artificial intelligence such as fuzzy logic will continue to create new markets. Managing a stream of new products is one of the key activities of a marketing manager and the speed with which companies can get their products to market is becoming a key competitive weapon. The time to market for new products is shortening as organisations employ new processes, facilitated by information technology to accelerate the product-development cycle. The costs and risks of developing totally new products are much greater than those of improving existing products or investing in line extensions.

Another key investment decision is how much to invest in either product or process development. Throughout the product-development life cycle, a variety of IT applications can be used to improve the quality and value of the products developed and get them to market faster than the competition. Computer simulation and virtual reality software can be used to prototype and test new products. The production of goods and services is already heavily dependent on information technology applications such as computer-aided design, materials requirements planning, manufacturing resource planning, computer-aided manufacturing and other technologies known collectively as CIM (computer-integrated manufacturing).

ASSIGNMENT QUESTIONS

1 Describe how technology is driving the development of new products and services.

2 Comment on the relative advantages of investing in product versus process development.

3 What do you understand by the term 'design for manufacture'?

4 Briefly describe the product-development life cycle.

5 Discuss the role of IT in manufacturing.

Case study

GENERAL ELECTRIC

It took seven years for General Electric, the US industrial group, to bring to market its F-class gas turbine, which is now being installed in power stations throughout the world. Its successor, the H-class gas turbine, will come to market in half the time, even though it incorporates more new technology, including a revolutionary way of using steam to cool the fast-spinning rotor blades. The speed at which GE is developing the new turbine is a reflection of the rapid advance of research and development tools, notably computer modelling, and of an overhaul of GE's research efforts ordered five years ago by Jack Welch, the group's chairman and chief executive officer. Welch, who took over in 1981, has included R&D in his wider-ranging efforts to extract bigger profits from the company's acknowledged technological and industrial prowess. Even the group's legendary research and development centre, home of two Nobel prize-winners, has not been spared from the demands of change.

'It was a culture shock for some of us,' says Gene Kimura, manager of the mechanical systems laboratory, one of 13 units at the R&D centre. 'But it was absolutely necessary that the company got value for money.' The centre, built in wooded hills in New York state, is GE's equivalent to AT&T's Bell Laboratories. Until the 1950s, 75 per cent of its funds came from group headquarters and most of the rest from US government programmes. Many of its researchers became remote from commercial realities. For some the site seemed more like a university campus than a factory – except that the salaries were higher.

In the early 1990s, Welch decided that this had to change. The group cut its contribution to the central laboratories' budget to 25 per cent, leaving GE's 13 operating divisions to make up the difference – and demand commercially relevant research in return. Now the operating divisions pay 40 per cent of the costs. The remaining 35 per cent is split between the government and Lockheed, the aerospace company which acquired the former GE aerospace business in 1994 in a take-over of Martin Marietta, the defence contractor.

GE also laid down rules for how these funds should be spent – 15 per cent on improving current products, 35 per cent on developing successors, 35 per cent next generation products, and 15 per cent on blue-sky ideas. The central laboratories have an annual budget of just under $400m (£250m) a year, about 20 per cent of GE's total R&D spending. They produce about a quarter of the group's patents and about half its scientific papers. The new financing arrangements have given priority to the needs of operating divisions. The change was reinforced by a management restructuring at the central laboratories in 1993, which saw the appointment of 13 business managers – one for each division – to monitor R&D work done for their divisions. They have tried to ensure that the traditional strong links between technical staff at the laboratories and at the divisions have been matched by an equally tough commercial tie. At the same time, GE threw out a hierarchical system in which laboratory managers reported to branch managers who in turn were answerable to more senior executives. In its place, GE introduced a four-man technical council, headed by Lonnie Edelheit, the senior vice president in charge of corporate R&D. Kimura says that as well as cutting office bureaucracy, the new system created more flexible ways for ideas to be passed between laboratories and discussed among different teams of researchers. 'At the top, things are mushy, which is great for communication.'

Teamwork, says Kimura, is important in commercial research. 'It's a culture we have to create. This isn't a university. We can't have people who stay in their labs and come out and give a paper once a year.' For example, developing aero engines required expertise in high temperature materials, fluid dynamics, emissions, manufacturing techniques and information technology. Hand-in-hand with organisational change at the laboratories has come a rapid advance in research technology, particularly in computer modelling. Sophisticated hardware and software enable researchers to produce ever more accurate computer simulations of products. The techniques help virtually all products, but are particularly useful for large items such as power turbines which are very expensive to construct in physical prototype. Kimura says: 'IT management is critical to our future.'

Yet, even the overhaul of R&D management and the introduction of the latest R&D tools have not been enough to save GE last year from an embarrassing and expensive technical problem. The group's F-class turbines developed faults which only became apparent after the first machines went into service with customers. Some turbine sections had to be flown back for repairs while others were put right by roving teams of GE engineers. The problems cost the group at least $100m. Ironically, the faults were not caused by any high-technology features but by the rotors rubbing against the turbine casing at high temperatures. Kimura says valuable lessons have been learnt. 'We have learnt how to improve the management of launching new products. We put a lot of emphasis on using the latest design tools. We should have paid more attention to traditional fatigue tests.'

Source: Adapted from S. Wagstyl, 'Blade Runner', *Financial Times*, 23 July 1996.

Questions

1 'In the early 1990s, Welch decided that this had to change.' What were the main driving forces for changing the way in which R&D was carried out at GE's research centre?

2 How did IT play a part in improving the R&D and product-development effort at GE?

3 Describe how you think researchers work, collaborate and share ideas in the R&D centre now, paying specific attention to the types of information technology they would employ to assist them in their day-to-day work.

4 How can GE's new R&D capability be used in the marketplace?

5 Discuss the comment from Gene Kimura that 'IT is critical to our future'.

References

1 Jones, H. (1996). 'When green means go for it', *Financial Times*, 10 October.
2 Kosko, B. (1994). *Fuzzy Thinking: The New Science of Fuzzy Logic*. London: HarperCollins.
3 Taylor, P. (1996). 'Increasingly crucial role', *Financial Times*, 10 June.
4 Nilson, T.H. (1995). *Chaos Marketing: How to Win in a Turbulent World*. Maidenhead: McGraw-Hill.
5 *Business Week* (1990). 30 April.
6 Harmon, R.L. and Peterson, L.D. (1990). *Reinventing the Factory*. New York: Free Press.
7 Kotler, P., Armstrong, G., Saunders, J. and Wong, V. (1996). *Principles of Marketing, European Edition*. London: Prentice Hall.
8 Pine, B.J., Peppers, D. and Rogers, M. (1995). 'Do you want to keep your customers forever?', *Harvard Business Review*, March/April.
9 Bradbury, D. (1996). 'Out of this world', *Computer Weekly*, 18 July.
10 Clancy, K.J. and Shulman, R.S. (1991). *The Marketing Revolution*. New York: HarperBusiness.
11 Flaatten, P.O., McCubbrey, D.J., O'Riordan, P.D. and Burgess, K. (1989). *Foundations of Business Systems*. Orlando: Dryden Press.

10

PRICE

- Different approaches to pricing
- The role of information technology in pricing
- Using information technology to estimate demand
- Using information technology to establish costs

OBJECTIVES

After studying this chapter, you will be able to:
- Understand the crucial role of price in the marketing mix
- Describe the different approaches to pricing
- Understand the importance of the demand curve and its effect on price
- Provide a basis for identifying costs of products and services
- Identify the role of information technology in making better pricing decisions

DIFFERENT APPROACHES TO PRICING

The importance of price in the marketing mix

Ever since commerce began, prices were set through a process of bargaining and eventually arriving at a price acceptable to both buyer and seller. Depending on a buyer's bargaining power and negotiation skills, lower prices could be struck for the same product. At the end of the nineteenth century, large retailers started to implement a 'one price policy' where a standard price was charged to all customers for a particular good. This removed the need for store employees to bargain, made life easier for the customer who no longer had to engage in lengthy negotiating sessions and spurred the growth of large retailers such as Sainsbury's, Marks & Spencer and Woolworth's. Today, in many industries, this 'one price policy' model is still the dominant model for setting prices.

Price is a crucial element in the marketing mix for a number of reasons. Unlike the other elements of the marketing mix, price can usually be changed very quickly. While it may take months to prepare and launch a new advertising campaign or years to develop a new distribution channel, a price change can be implemented in a matter of days, or less. The managers of a company may not have much control over other elements of the mix, but they usually have a high degree of discretion on the prices they set.

Perhaps more importantly, price has a critical impact on the total revenue a company generates and an even greater impact on its profitability.

Just how sensitive profitability is to price movements is illustrated in Table 10.1. The example shows the effect on profitability of increasing price by 10 per cent while holding costs constant. If the number of units sold remains the same after a 10 per cent price increase and all costs remain constant, then profitability improves by 67 per cent. This contrasts with a 30 per cent improvement in profitability when the cost of goods sold is reduced by 10 per cent and all other variables are held constant. Our example is slightly artificial, as in the real world we would not expect sales volumes to remain the same after a 10 per cent price increase. As we will see later in this chapter, the skill of the marketing manager is in managing the trade-off between increasing the price and losing sales to a point where the overall profitability of the firm is maximised. The kind of analysis we have just performed is also called sensitivity analysis, as it identifies the variables which have the greatest impact on profitability. One of the advantages of IT is that it enables marketers to perform sensitivity analysis quickly and easily.

Table 10.1 Impact on profitability

Profit and loss statement		Change	Increase in profitability
Units sold	100 000		
Price per unit	£10	10% increase	67%
Total revenue	£1 000 000		
Cost of goods sold (45%)	£450 000	10% decrease	30%
Marketing costs (20%)	£200 000	10% decrease	13%
Research and development (10%)	£100 000	10% decrease	7%
Administrative overhead (10%)	£100 000	10% decrease	7%
Profit before tax (15%)	£150 000		

There are four general approaches which can be taken to pricing:

■ cost-based pricing
■ demand-based pricing
■ competition-based pricing
■ design to price.

■ Cost-based pricing

This involves calculating all the costs of producing and marketing a product and then adding a profit margin to arrive at a price. While in theory cost-based pricing sounds simple, in reality most companies do not know what it costs to produce a product. If a firm has only one product it is relatively simple to calculate product cost, but very few firms make just one product and many manufacture hundreds or even thousands. In service industries the problem is even more difficult. How, for example, does a bank calculate the cost of selling insurance policies through the branch network? Calculating the true cost requires data on the amount of time branch staff spend providing information to customers on each product and such information is difficult to gather accurately. In a manufacturing environment it is possible to calculate the direct labour and raw material costs of producing a product, but it is more difficult to allocate all the indirect costs such as company overheads. Later in this chapter we will examine how some companies are using approaches such as activity-based costing (ABC) to determine more accurately the true cost of producing a product.

■ Demand-based pricing

Rather than base the price of a product on its cost, firms sometimes use a price based on the level of demand for the product. Demand-based pricing results in a higher price for a product when demand is strong and a lower price when demand is weak. For example, night clubs often charge higher prices on Friday and Saturday nights when demand is high. Similarly, hotels often provide discount rates at weekends when there is little or no demand from business travellers. To use this approach the marketer must estimate the amount of product that customers will demand at different prices and then select a price which generates the highest total revenue. The effectiveness of this approach depends on how accurately the marketer can estimate demand. We will address this issue, and the role that IT can play in its resolution, later in the chapter.

■ Competition-based pricing

In competition-based pricing, costs and revenue are considered secondary to competitors' prices. This method is particularly important where products are homogenous or regarded as commodity items. Competition-based pricing strategies include:

- *Penetration pricing.* Penetration pricing occurs when a company, which has large economies of scale, prices below its competitors in order to drive them out of the market by capturing market share.
- *Price skimming.* Price skimming occurs when companies decide to set prices high initially to recoup their investment in research and development and can be regarded as the opposite of a penetration-pricing strategy.
- *Experience-curve pricing.* This is similar to penetration pricing, but the company attempts to exploit its economies gained through experience rather than size. Companies will often price their products below those of competitors in order to move them further along the experience curve and ultimately give them the lowest-cost position in the market.
- *Price signalling.* In this situation, a company lets its competitors know that it plans to defend its prices. The CEO may give interviews outlining his company's strategy and why competitors cannot hope to match it. If the price signalling is backed up by efficient low-cost production facilities, the competitors may not believe that they could win a price war and avoid reducing prices.

There are also several price adjustment strategies to account for different consumer segments and situations:

- *Discount and allowance pricing.* These include cash discounts, quantity discounts, seasonal discounts and allowances.
- *Segmented pricing.* This is used to set different prices for different customers, product forms, places or times.

- *Psychological pricing*. This is used to adjust price to communicate a product's intended position more effectively. Examples include the pricing of many high-priced luxury goods.
- *Promotional pricing*. This includes loss-leader pricing and special event pricing.
- *Value pricing*. This aims to achieve the right combination of quality and good service at a fair price.
- *Geographical pricing*. Geographical pricing includes uniformly delivered pricing, zone pricing, and freight-absorption-based pricing.
- *International pricing*. This is used to adjust prices to different conditions and expectations in different world markets (*see* Table 10.2).

Table 10.2   International price differences

Product	US price	Price elsewhere
Levi jeans	$30	$88 (Paris)
McDonald's Big Mac	$2.25	$5.75 (Moscow)
Pink Floyd CD	$14.99	$22 (EU)
Gucci handbag	$240	$60 (Italy)

Source: Kotler *et al*. (1996).[1] Reproduced by permission of Prentice Hall.

Alternative pricing options available to companies based on their price relative to the competition and the value of their offerings are illustrated in Figure 10.1. Many luxury goods manufacturers such as BMW or Mercedes are positioned in the top right box with a premier market offering. When Toyota attacked the high end of the car market with its Lexus cars, it provided a high-value offering but with an average price relative to the competition in order to penetrate the market. Marketing managers who provide a high-quality offering but at a low price are missing an opportunity to maximise the firm's profits.

PRICE RELATIVE TO THE COMPETITION

		Low	Average	High
	High	Under-priced offering	Ideal for market penetration	Premier market offering
VALUE OF OFFERING	**Average**	Real bargain for the customer	Average market competition	Probably overpriced
	Low	'Cheap goods' offering	Dissatisfied customers likely	Make the sale and run

Fig 10.1   Alternative pricing options

■ Design to price

Another approach to pricing which is becomingly popular is 'design to price' or target costing. It is a classic application of marketing principles, as the customer drives the design of the product and its eventual pricing. Rather than designing a product, calculating production costs and then deciding a price, the consumer is involved in the process from a very early stage. The marketing department conducts extensive market research on different product concepts and the price customers are prepared to pay for them. Having agreed the product concept and price, the company then designs a product to meet the market requirements (*see* Exhibit 10.1).

■ Information for pricing

Regardless of which price approach is used, pricing decisions should be based on accurate information and research on the marketplace and internal costs. However, despite the importance of information in making pricing decisions, in practice many companies do not approach pricing in a very systematic way and some of the commonest mistakes are described below:

- *Pricing based purely on cost*. Cost does not always equate to value. In consumer luxuries such as perfumes and designer clothes, price can be used to communicate exclusivity or very high quality. In such industries a low price based on costs is often associated with second-rate products.
- *Not revising prices quickly enough to reflect market changes*. Companies can lose sales by not reacting quickly to changes in the marketplace.
- *Pricing strategies which are out of step with the rest of the marketing mix*. Where a company is charging a premium price for its product, such as a Rolex watch, it would be inappropriate for the image of the product to distribute it through supermarkets or

advertise it using mass media. In such cases, the distribution channel and promotion campaign should reflect the exclusive image which the product is trying to portray.

■ *Prices which do not take into account different levels of demand.* As we will see later when we examine the demand curve and demand elasticity, different customer segments may be prepared to pay different prices for a similar product. While marketers tend to be aware of situations where prices have been set too high, resulting in lower than expected demand, there are also situations where setting the price too low can result in lost profits (*see* Exhibit 10.2).

In a survey of US companies, Clancy and Shulman (1991)[2] found that many made pricing decisions without any serious formal research. They found that only about 8 per cent of companies were sophisticated players with a serious pricing strategy based on primary research (*see* Figure 10.2). About 4 per cent were radical empiricists with plenty of research but no clear pricing strategy. Some 47 per cent were gamblers with a serious pricing strategy but little or no research to back it up; and the remaining 41 per cent fell into the losers' category, with neither strategy nor research capabilities.

■ Other factors affecting price

A number of other internal and external factors affect pricing decisions. The internal factors include a company's marketing objectives, its marketing mix and its pricing objectives. Common pricing objectives include pricing for survival, pricing to maximise current profits and pricing to maintain market-share leadership. There are also external factors which influence the decisions, such as economic conditions and government actions. In the end, customers decide if the price has been set at the correct level. They measure the price against the perceived value of the product and if the price is more than the perceived value then they will not buy.

	Serious strategy	Little or no strategy
Serious research	Sophisticated players (8%)	Radical empiricists (4%)
Little or no research	Gamblers (47%)	Losers (41%)

Fig 10.2 Strategy/research pricing matrix

Source: Clancy and Shulman (1991).[2] Copyright © 1991 by Kevin J. Clancy and Robert Shulman. Reprinted by permission of HarperCollins Publishers, Inc.

MINI-PRICING

When British Leyland launched the Mini car in the 1960s it was an immediate hit and demand rapidly outstripped supply. The car was designed to tap into a mass market of people that could not afford a car and people who wanted a second car, and was sold at a price significantly lower than the competition. During this period British Leyland was only marginally profitable despite the very high sales of the Mini. If they had priced the Mini £100 higher they would have had approximately £300 million in additional revenue on sales of three million units to invest in research and development and to invest in more efficient production capacity. The argument was that, because the car caught the imagination of the buying public by its styling, customers would have been prepared to pay the £100 premium. In the event the Mini only delayed the financial collapse of the group in the early 1970s. Despite British Leyland getting all the other elements of the marketing mix right, this strategic pricing failure was a contributing factor to the company's demise.

■ Price wars

Price wars are usually started because of excess capacity in an industry. Industries such as steel manufacturing, airlines and shipping, where capacity is fixed and profitability is driven by capacity utilisation, are particularly prone to price wars. Competitors who are losing market share often launch price wars to regain share. A price war should not be undertaken lightly and can be dangerous to corporate health. A drop of a single percentage point in price can cut profitability by more than 12 per cent.[3] One of the reasons for price wars can be 'misreads' where a company incorrectly interprets the movement in a competitor's prices. It is critical to have complete control of the facts and to have a very clear understanding of what the competition is actually doing with its prices, and this requires a formal mechanism to track the prices of competitors.

THE ROLE OF INFORMATION TECHNOLOGY IN PRICING

■ Pricing actions

Clancy and Shulman (1991)[2] identified six actions which companies need to take in order to be successful in their pricing strategies:

1 Examine the environment
2 Tie pricing to the target market, competitive positioning and product
3 Examine many alternative pricing strategies
4 Study manufacturing and distribution costs and their relationship to product demand
5 Undertake serious pricing research to develop a price elasticity curve that shows how sales change as price goes up or down
6 Select the optimal price based on the best strategy, costs and price elasticity curve.

Information technology can assist in all six of these actions. For example, a major car-rental company in the US has developed a decision-support system which allows its marketing staff to analyse changes in competitor prices quickly.[4] The system scans price data from the company's five main competitors for more than 160 locations across the US and Canada, across six car classes, twelve regional market segments and five potential rental segments. Data is collected on a daily basis and significant changes or exceptional movements reported to the marketing department. The reports allow pricing analysts to view the information by competitor or by geographic area. The primary benefit of the system is that it allows the pricing analysts to spend more time making pricing decisions and less time being submerged in a sea of data. The company can also adapt pricing strategies for local areas. Exhibit 10.3 provides an example of one product that is used to examine the environment and report back on shifts in market share and price.

Exhibit 10.3

COVER STORY

In 1988, Information Resources Inc. introduced 'CoverStory', a software product that assists consumer packaged goods marketing executives to investigate, analyse and present IRI's syndicated scanner data. CoverStory automatically analyses data and writes an English language memo such as 'During the four weeks ending June 26, 1988, volume in the Total Frozen Pizza category stood at 31.1 million consumer units – up 0.7 percent from the prior year. Pillsbury's share of the category was 29.1, which is an increase of 5.7 share points from last year but a loss of 3.1 points since last period.' Developed by Professors John Little of MIT and Leonard Lodish of Wharton, CoverStory extracts the most important information, as defined by the user, from the IRI database and delivers it in memo format, supported by tables and graphs. It identifies shifts in price, merchandising, and distribution associated with share gains and losses. It also identifies competitors that are gaining and losing share. Dr. Little says that consumer packaged goods manufacturers purchase 1,000 times more syndicated data than they have in the past. Nielsen Market Research planned to release a similar programme in the near future. This will be an update of ScanFact, which provides specific sales and marketing information from 3,000 stores in fifty markets in a matter of minutes but which unlike CoverStory, does not analyse the data.

Source: Clancy and Shulman (1991).[2] Copyright © 1991 by Kevin J. Clancy and Robert Shulman. Reprinted by permission of HarperCollins Publishers, Inc.

The study of manufacturing and distribution costs can be carried out using spreadsheets and other analytical tools. Using these tools, sensitivity analysis can be carried out to assesses how changes in different variables affect revenue. If sales are 20 per cent below the forecasts, will the product still be profitable? What effect will a price drop of 10 per cent have on profitability? Exhibit 10.4 shows how another IT application can be used to examine alternative pricing strategies.

■ Using IT to speed up pricing decisions

One of the main impacts of IT is the faster speed with which pricing decisions can be made and implemented. A good example is the retail trade, where traditionally

Exhibit 10.4

HEALTH CHECK

A host of programs promise to analyse and improve your business. None, however, take the unique approach of Business Resource Software's computer program called Business Insight. The program weights hundreds of numeric and non-numeric factors that enter into any business venture, including 'hard' data such as sales projections and 'soft' data such as buyer perception, management quality, and product life cycle. From a broader perspective, the program can suggest the best approach to starting a company or analyse product development issues within a large organisation. Even though your business may not be in trouble, Business Insight can provide new insights into its structure and health. Entering data is simple. The program walks you through an extensive series of questions, such as a product's price, the company's revenue objectives and promotional strategy, and the required return on investment. The revenue-objectives question, for example, requires a first-year estimate of company product revenues. Another group of queries focuses on the various stages of a product's life cycle. Not every question has to be answered, but the more information the program has to work with, the better the final analysis will be. Once this data-entry phase is complete, Business Insight analyses the case using its internal rules.

Source: Lotus Magazine (January 1991).[5]

changing prices took a long time to implement. Head office would decide on a price change which would then be sent to the individual stores in the form of a paper-based price list. If products had been individually labelled, the price stickers would have to be removed and replaced with the new prices. IT enables the process to be carried out in a shorter time and with less manual effort. Once the marketing manager has decided on a price change, the new price is keyed into the central computer system and is usually downloaded that night to the stores. The next morning the store manager receives a report which indicates all the prices that have been changed and the new price stickers are also printed. It is important to synchronise the price changes on the shelf and at the checkout. As Exhibit 10.5 shows, this does not always happen but, if done correctly, the time required to change prices is significantly reduced, providing an important competitive advantage in the highly competitive retail industry.

Exhibit 10.5

BAR-CODE BOO-BOOS

Six thousand complaints about discrepancies between bar-code prices and shelf prices were made to the Institute of Trading Standards (ITSA) in the last 12 months. Martin Fisher, pricing specialist for the Institute of Trading Standards, said: 'Such discrepancies crop up quite often. Sometimes, head office decides on a price change, changes the prices on the computer and does not inform stores in time for them to change the shelf price.' The price held on the computer is the one recorded by the till when a bar code on a product is scanned at the supermarket checkout.

Source: Sunday Business (5 May 1996).[6]

New developments are underway which should make the whole process even faster and more accurate. Electronic displays on each shelf showing the name and price of each product would remove the need for any manual intervention once the new price has been set. Once the price has been changed at head office, it could be updated simultaneously on both the electronic shelf display and the computer which stores the prices for the checkouts. Many new retailing systems also allow different prices to be set for different stores. Based on demographic analysis and an understanding of the demand curves in different store locations, higher prices can be set in more affluent areas. Let us now discuss demand curves and the price elasticity of demand in more detail.

USING INFORMATION TECHNOLOGY TO ESTIMATE DEMAND

■ The demand curve

One of the key responsibilities of the marketing manager is to determine the demand for a product as accurately as possible. The marketer uses market research and forecasting techniques to establish the relationship between a product's price and demand. For most products there is an inverse relationship between the price and the quantity demanded; as the price goes up the quantity demanded goes down and vice versa. The classic demand curve illustrated in Figure 10.3 graphs the quantity of products expected to be sold at different prices if other factors remain constant. Because demand depends on other factors in the marketing mix, such as advertising, product quality and distribution channels, a change in any of these factors can cause a shift from demand curve D_1 to D_2. This will lead to an increase in the quantity sold at price P, from Q_1 to Q_2.

Every product has its own demand curve and many are very unlike the classic demand curve in Figure 10.3. Luxury goods such as perfumes and jewellery often sell

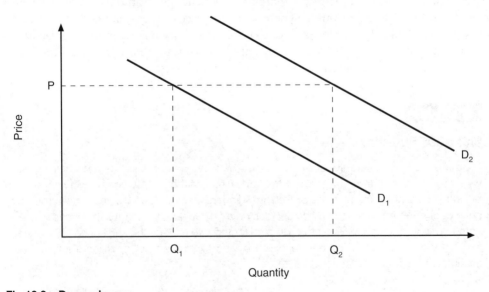

Fig 10.3 Demand curve

better at higher prices and would lose some of their appeal at lower prices. Drawing an accurate demand curve for a product requires information on historical purchasing patterns. The availability of large amounts of scanning data, such as price and quantity sold from many different retail stores, can be used to calculate and graph the demand curve for products.

■ Price elasticity of demand

In order to establish the demand curve, the price elasticity of demand must be estimated. This is a measure of the sensitivity of demand to changes in price and, if marketers can establish this sensitivity, they can set prices more profitably. The price elasticity of demand is described by the following formula:

$$\text{Price elasticity of demand} = \frac{\% \text{ change in quantity demanded}}{\% \text{ change in price}}$$

If demand falls by 10 per cent when a seller raises its price by 2 per cent, the price elasticity of demand is –5 and demand is said to be elastic. If demand falls by 2 per cent with a 2 per cent increase in price, then elasticity is –1. In this case, the seller's total revenue stays the same, as the drop in volume is compensated for by the higher prices.

■ Factors influencing price elasticity

When the unique attributes of a product are easily recognisable, the level of differentiation is increased and customer demand becomes less price sensitive. Consumers are also more sensitive to price when they are aware of substitutes. The size of the expenditure is also important, as customers will be more sensitive to the price of expensive products. When it is difficult to compare prices between competing products because of different pack sizes or product bundlings, then customers are less sensitive to price. Where customers have already made a large 'sunk' investment in a product such as an expensive fountain pen or photocopier, they are less sensitive to the price of the consumables such as refills and paper. This characteristic is often used by the marketer, as in the case of shavers where the profit margin of the actual shaver is relatively low compared to the replacement blades. It also occurs in the mobile phone business where phone companies offer very cheap mobile phones in anticipation of earning profits on the resulting phone calls. Consumers are also less sensitive in the case of image or exclusive products, where a higher price signifies that the product is of higher quality.

■ Yield management

One of the most powerful applications of the demand curve is the concept of maximising revenue across all customers. It is moving away from the 'one price for all' concept to true demand-based pricing. In many ways, this trend is being driven by IT which allows companies to develop and market product offerings at different prices. Marketing managers are now faced with a much more complex task of identifying a range of product or service options targeted at different customers and charging different prices.

Probably the most sophisticated use of this technique is in the airline industry where 'yield management' is supported by complex computer software. The system works by calculating different prices depending on the length of the stay, the time of week the person wishes to travel and the flight times. The airline's objective is to identify and target the business traveller who is less price sensitive than the tourist traveller. Early-morning flights are more expensive, as are tickets purchased at short notice. Tickets which include a weekend stopover are usually cheaper, as business people like to return home at the weekend. All of these conditions help the airline identify the business traveller, whom they can charge a premium for effectively the same service. Efficient yield management has been estimated to have increased the revenues of US airlines by 5–10 per cent.[7] Yield management is critical in improving profitability, particularly where airlines are locked into a high cost structure or have a complex airline network. Although some customers end up paying more for travelling at peak times of the day or flying on more congested aircraft, consumers are generally better off financially. A wider range of fares can be made available to cater for different customer requirements and flights are offered that would not otherwise be viable.

USING INFORMATION TECHNOLOGY TO ESTABLISH COSTS

■ Management accounting systems

The price of a product or service must take account of the cost of producing it. This does not mean that pricing is simply a matter of adding a given margin to the cost of production, although many companies take this approach. Rather, the perceived value of the product and the marketing view of what the consumer is prepared to pay must also be factored into the equation. As we discussed previously, the pricing of expensive perfumes is not directly related to cost. However, the starting point must always be cost. Otherwise, companies will cross-subsidise one product with another and can easily end up in a situation where they are generating large sales (and losses) on the subsidised products, while losing out to the competition on the profitable products.

Nearly all of a company's activities exist to support the production of goods and services and should be considered in product costs. One of the key sources of product-cost information is the firm's management accounting system, which uses a series of assumptions and rules for overhead allocation to determine the cost of producing a product. Traditional product costing allocates overhead costs to each product based on volume or some similar measure such as percentage of direct materials consumed or percentage of machine hours used. Many of the overhead costs in business can not be allocated on such a basis as they are not directly related to volume. An example of how this can lead to incorrect pricing is shown in Exhibit 10.6.

The usefulness of the management accounting system can therefore be called into question. Johnson and Kaplan (1987)[8] concluded that in many organisations the traditional accounting systems had lost their relevance and could not be relied on for making well-informed pricing decisions (*see* Exhibit 10.7).

Exhibit 10.6

THE SAME BUT DIFFERENT

Consider a firm with two products. Product A represents 80 per cent of volume; Product B 20 per cent. Both products take the same amount of operator and machine time to produce. On this basis, overheads were allocated on the same basis as production volumes, with Product A attracting 80 per cent of overheads and Product B 20 per cent. The products were marketed on the basis of cost plus margin.

Closer examination of the two products revealed that the machines that manufacture Product B have a longer set-up time than those for Product A. In addition, Product B required more time to procure materials, had greater customer-support needs, a greater number of sales visits for each sale and greater quality and conformance costs. When the costs were properly analysed, Product B was much more expensive to produce and sell than was originally believed. The result: Product B was being sold below cost and was being cross-subsidised by Product A.

Exhibit 10.7

RELEVANCE LOST: ACCOUNTING BYPASSED

The organisation's management accounting system serves as a vital two-way communication link between senior and subordinate managers. It is the means by which senior executives communicate the organisation's goals and objectives to subordinate and decentralised managers. In the reverse direction, the management accounting system is the channel by which information about the firm's product performance and production efficiencies is reported to upper levels of management. Further, managerial compensation and promotion decisions are usually based on the numbers reported by the management accounting system.

With these vital roles for planning and control information and for communication, motivation and evaluation, the organisation's management accounting system is a necessary component in the firm's strategy to achieve competitive success. An excellent management accounting system will not by itself guarantee success in today's economy – ultimately, success depends on products that meets customers' needs, on efficient production and distribution systems, and on effective marketing efforts. But an ineffective management accounting system can undermine superior product development, process improvement, and marketing efforts. Where an ineffective management accounting system prevails, the best outcome occurs when managers understand the irrelevance of the system and bypass it by developing personalised information systems. But managers unwittingly court trouble if they do not recognise an inadequate system and erroneously rely on it for managerial control information and product decisions.

Source: Johnson and Kaplan (1987).[8]

■ Activity-based costing (ABC) systems

One solution to the problems facing traditional management accounting systems is activity-based costing (ABC). The concept behind ABC is to allocate overhead costs to the activities that generate the cost. The costs in these 'activity pools' are then further allocated or traced to individual products based on the level of activity associated with the product. Because ABC is more concerned with identifying activities that cause cost, it is able to deal more easily with non-volume-related overheads. Using ABC information, marketing managers are better positioned to consider options such as dropping unprofitable products or raising the prices of existing products.

Searching an organisation for all the information about the direct and indirect costs of a product or service can be a major undertaking. Creating an IT system to track cost-contributing activities and presenting the information to management is equally challenging. In many cases, the old accounting system is replaced and new measurement and incentive systems are tied to the new ABC figures. When an ABC system is implemented, managers can use it to answer many questions, including the following:

- What does a given product or process cost?
- What are the non-value-adding activities that contribute to its current cost?
- If a given distribution channel or market is unprofitable, where can the company reduce costs to make it profitable?
- If the company eliminates an unprofitable product or customer, how much will it save in costs?
- If the company lowers the price of a product to increase sales volume, what will be the impact on the cost per unit?
- What can the company do during the design and engineering stages of a product to avoid unnecessary costs in the first place?

Many companies have used ABC in one-time profitability studies to help them decide which products or customers to keep. But ABC can be much more than an accounting technique that shows how much profit individual products are really making or losing. When ABC is woven into critical management systems, it can serve as a powerful tool for continuously rethinking and improving not only products and services but also processes and marketing strategies (*see* Exhibit 10.8).

Exhibit 10.8

THE ABC OF THE AUTOMOBILE INDUSTRY

Chrysler, which has $52 billion in revenues and 123,000 employees, turned to ABC to help transform a bureaucratic organisation set in its ways. Chrysler estimates that, since it began implementing ABC in 1991, the system has generated hundreds of millions of dollars in benefits by helping simplify product designs and eliminate unproductive, inefficient, or redundant activities. The benefits have been 10 to 20 times greater than the company's investment in the programme. At some sites, the savings have been 50 to 100 times the implementation cost. The main purpose of the old cost accounting system had been to help the finance department monitor operations and value inventory. However, outside of finance, few people believed the old system provided an accurate picture of the company's costs. The cost accounting system could not report costs by process, much less separate value-added from non-value-added activities. When Chrysler first introduced ABC they quickly discovered that many employees from front-line workers to senior managers to entire departments resisted. Chrysler had a long history of flavour of the month performance improvement programmes that never seemed to deliver what they promised and were replaced as soon as a new programme came along. After some initial struggles Chrysler overcame internal resistance in ways that serve as a model for other companies. First, they persuaded employees to give ABC a fair shake and ultimately, to embrace the system. Second, they mounted major programmes to educate employees at all levels in the principles and mechanics of ABC. Third, they began with one plant and then rolled out the programme throughout the organisation, making sure that local managers were involved and that there were visible successes. Finally, once ABC had been introduced at a facility, they quickly dumped the old accounting system.

Source: Ness and Cucuzza (1995).[9]

CONCLUSION

Price is one of the key elements of the marketing mix as it has such a powerful effect on profitability, can be changed quickly and management has a great deal of control over it. There are four general approaches which can be taken to pricing: the cost-based approach, demand-based pricing, competition-based pricing and design to price. Despite the importance of price, many organisations do not have a clear pricing strategy based on research. An important part of setting a price for a product is the establishment of a demand curve which maps the relationship between price and demand. This allows the marketer to establish the price elasticity of demand, which measures the percentage change in quantity demanded relative to a given percentage change in price. If marketers can determine the price elasticity of demand then they can set much more accurate and profitable prices. Another key element of pricing is the establishment of product costs. One approach to costing which has proved very effective is activity-based costing, which seeks to establish a more accurate cost for producing any particular product or service.

ASSIGNMENT QUESTIONS

1 Comment on why price is such a crucial element of the marketing mix.
2 Outline the different pricing approaches available to a marketing manager.
3 How do you go about constructing a demand curve for a medium-priced automobile and how would IT help?
4 What is the role of IT in identifying the true cost of products or services?
5 What other industries could benefit from the introduction of yield-management systems?

WORLD PAPER PULP MARKET

Mr Roger Wright, a UK paper industry consultant, has a vivid metaphor for the world's wood pulp producers: 'They're too old for bungee jumping,' he says, 'so the pulp market is the nearest experience they can get.' No image better captures the recent performance of pulp, the main raw material in paper – except that, unlike bungee jumpers, pulp producers cannot rely on a rubber cord to save them as they plunge to earth. The scramble to limit the damage was apparent this week as mills in Scandinavia, North America and Brazil slashed list prices by 15–20 per cent, bringing them close to the level at which business was being done in the spot market. Northern bleached softwood kraft (NBSK), the industry's bench-mark product, now sells for about US$725 a tonne, or 27 per cent lower than the record price of $1,000 which producers tried unsuccessfully to impose on the market last October. One mill after another plans to trim output over the next few months. According to the publication *Pulp and Paper Week*, Canadian mills have announced temporary closures equal to 137,000 tonnes so far this year, or about 1.7 per cent of annual market pulp ship-ments. 'In the next few months, we're going to see unprecedented cuts in production,' says Mr Wright. The shutdowns reinforce pulp's reputation as one of the most volatile commodi-ties. At the end of 1993, NBSK prices were below $400 a tonne. No one predicted that they would double over the next 18 months. The structure of the pulp market is a recipe for sharp price movements. It is a global business with about four-fifths of all market pulp exported from the country where it is produced. No single producer has more than a 6 per cent share.

Most mills' production costs are still well covered by these lower pulp prices. With the exception of Finnish producers, mills usually respond to sagging demand by fighting for market share rather than trimming capacity. The latest meltdown stems from pulp producers' tardiness in responding to last summer's sudden reversal in paper markets. Demand for some grades of paper has softened, especially in Asia. Some producers blame a price war between Indonesian pulp mills and Georgia-Pacific, the big US forest products company, for triggering the precipitous drop in prices. Inventories ballooned: worldwide pulp stocks exploded by 50 per cent in the final three months of last year to 3.1 million tonnes at the end of December. Producers compounded their problems by bringing new capacity on stream. Supplies grew 4.8 per cent in the year to November, with much of the increase coming from new producers, especially in Indonesia. Mr Wright, who believes that prices may be heading back towards $400 a tonne, says that 'even if demand does bounce back, there's enough supply'. Others predict that the market is close to bottoming out. Their case rests on a combination of pro-duction cuts and an improvement in the paper market. One Vancouver-based trader expects that the recent hefty drop in paper prices will stimulate consumption. He adds that China has reportedly resumed large scale paper imports. UPM-Kymmene of Finland, Europe's largest pulp and paper group, is also upbeat. It expects production rates to be back to normal after March. The company, which only operated at 70 per cent of its fine paper capacity in the final months of last year, says paper merchants are working off most of their inventories.

Most analysts take a gloomier view, saying slower economic growth in Europe and uncer-tainty over the outlook for the US economy means de-stocking could continue into the second and third quarters. The expectation of even lower prices also means that buyers are reluctant to step forward. For now the priority is damage control. Mr George Landegger, chairman of Parson and Whittemore, a big North American producer, told the Canadian Pulp and Paper Association's annual meeting last week that pulp mills would have to cut production immediately to 78 per cent of capacity – equal to a three week across the board shutdown – to achieve market equilibrium by March 31. To bring supply into line with demand by mid-year, the mills could ease to an 85 per cent operating rate. Most Nordic producers and hardwood pulp mills in Spain and Portugal are now running at or below those rates. But mills in the US and Canada, which make up more than half of world output, are still operating in the upper 80s. Bungee-jumping may be their sport of choice.

Source: Adapted from B. Simon and C. Brown-Humes, 'Pressing down on the pulp matter', *Financial Times*, 8 February 1996.

Questions

1 How important is price relative to the other elements of the marketing mix in the pulp business?

2 'Others predict that the market is close to bottoming out. Their case rests on a combination of production cuts and an improvement in the paper market.' Discuss.

3 Comment on other industries which may have similar characteristics to the pulp industry.

4 As a marketing manager for a pulp manufacturer, what steps would you take to lessen your company's exposure to price competition?

5 Describe the different strategies which different companies take to competing in the pulp market.

References

[1] Kotler, P., Armstrong, G., Saunders, J. and Wong, V. (1996). *Principles of Marketing, European Edition.* London: Prentice Hall.

[2] Clancy, K.J. and Shulman, R.S. (1991). *The Marketing Revolution.* New York: Harper Perennial.

[3] Garda, R.A. and Marn, M.V. (1993). 'Price wars', *McKinsey Quarterly,* No. 3.

[4] O'Connor, J. (1994). Unpublished research.

[5] Ray, G. (1991). 'Business insight: check your company's health', *Lotus Magazine*, January.

[6] Sunday Business (1996). 'Barcode updates short-change consumers', *Sunday Business*, 5 May.

[7] Cross, R. and Schemerhorn, R. (1989). 'Managing uncertainty', *Airline Business*, November.

[8] Johnson, R.S. and Kaplan, T.H. (1987). *Relevance Lost: The Rise and Fall of Management Accounting.* Boston: Harvard Business School Press.

[9] Ness, J.A. and Cucuzza, T.G. (1995). 'Tapping the full potential of ABC', *Harvard Business Review*, July–August.

PLACE

- The role of distribution in the marketing mix
- Managing multiple distribution channels
- Direct sales channels
- Indirect sales channels
- Emerging distribution channels

OBJECTIVES

After studying this chapter, you will be able to:

☐ Understand the role of distribution channels in the marketing mix

☐ Identify some of the key trends in distribution channels

☐ Identify how companies should approach evaluating different channels

☐ Describe the characteristics of the different channels

☐ Understand how IT is changing the relationships between channels

THE ROLE OF DISTRIBUTION IN THE MARKETING MIX

The role of distribution

The 'place' element of the marketing mix is concerned with the way in which products get to consumers and choices about whether companies should market directly to the customer or go through indirect channels. Channel-management decisions affect pricing, product management, brand image and promotion decisions. Kotler (1983)[1] defines a distribution channel as:

> 'the set of firms and individuals that take title, or assist in transferring title, to the particular good or service as it moves from the producer to the consumer.'

One of the features of channel decisions is that new channels take a very long time to develop. Traditionally, the firm with well-entrenched distribution channels dominated the market and created very high barriers to entry for newcomers. For example, one of the biggest barriers to entry in petrol retailing is the presence of large networks of petrol forecourts, most of which are tied to one of the major oil companies. Over the last 10 to 15 years, the oil companies have moved from using independent garages to directly owning garages. This has allowed them to standardise forecourt layouts and service quality and develop very important forecourt retail businesses. It also gives them control of the distribution channel and makes it very difficult for other oil companies to enter the market. The history of General Motors' distribution network in Exhibit 11.1 illustrates the importance of distribution channel management very well.

Exhibit 11.1

SLOAN RANGERS

One of the most far reaching innovations introduced by Alfred Sloan at General Motors was a new approach to motor dealers. In the 1920s and 1930s, General Motors overtook Ford as the world's largest car maker through an innovative approach to organisation and marketing. Recognising the efficiencies and improved innovation associated with decentralised structures, General Motors was organised around the operating divisions such as Chevrolet, Buick, Oldsmobile, Cadillac and Pontiac. On the marketing front, GM recognised the changing consumer tastes away from a demand for a standard car such as the Ford Model T and the trend towards targeting different cars at different income groups. Recognising the critical importance of the dealer network, GM actively developed a series of partnership agreements with dealers. Some of the innovations introduced included:

- In 1927, GM established an organisation called the Motors Accounting Company which developed a standardised accounting system applicable to all dealers. It sent staff into the field to help install it and establish an audit system.
- In 1929, the Motors Holding Division was established to provide capital to dealers. Through this company, GM obtained a clearer knowledge of dealers' problems and of the retail market and consumer preferences.
- In 1930, General Motors made it a policy to help the dealer dispose of his excess stock at the end of the year.
- In 1934, the General Motors Dealer Council was established to meet with corporate executives and work out policies to improve dealer relations.
- In 1938 the Dealer Relations Board was established to enable dealers with complaints to appeal directly to the top executives of the company.

Source: Sloan (1963).[3]

When a manufacturer uses an intermediary, it gives up some control over how its product is marketed and sold. It also relinquishes profit which could be gained by selling directly to the end-consumer. It even loses control over the customer relationship (*see* Exhibit 11.2 overleaf). Why would any manufacturer be willing to give up this control? There are a number of reasons. In some cases, a manufacturer will not have the financial resources to set up a distribution network to reach a mass market. Where a manufacturer produces a single product, it is rarely feasible to stock a store with only a single product. For example, it would be inefficient for Coca-Cola to open a chain of retail outlets just selling its own drinks. In addition, manufacturing a product requires a different set of skills to running a retail store and retailing margins are often lower than those from manufacturing.

Exhibit 11.2

WHO CONTROLS THE CUSTOMER?

A key issue emerging in the information age is 'Who controls the customer?' Because they provide many key functions that involve direct customer contact (such as locations for storage of product or selling agents who can reach customers effectively), a firm's traditional channels of distribution are well positioned to compete for ultimate control of the customer. However, in the information age, a new type of firm will emerge – a 'customer information firm' (CIF). These firms will collect information from customers and transmit it directly or indirectly to manufacturers. Customers will order from the CIFs and manufacturers will provide products to them.

Whether the customer information firm of the future will be a manufacturer or distributor of today, or an entirely new entity, is an open question. The closest analogy to the CIF is the retailer. The retailer makes it efficient for the customer to shop; its stores can contain as many as 50,000 items from hundreds of manufacturers. The CIF can perform the same function, except that the customer purchases via computer technology and the information about the transaction is captured and processed so that it can be used to design one-on-one product and promotion offerings. Furthermore, the CIF will not necessarily hold products in a warehouse but will drop ship to the customer wherever it is economically efficient. Inventories, to the extent they will still exist will reside only in one location, the manufacturer's warehouse. However, as production is linked more closely with demand, the manufacturer will be able to produce after the order is received, thus reducing finished goods inventory carrying costs to zero – just-in-time at the consumer level.

Thus, the channel of distribution in the future will be focused on product flows and the efficient logistical management of products and more on information management. The emerging 'retailers' are likely to be firms that manage not simply products but information for both consumers and producers.

Source: Blattberg and Glazer (1994).[4]

■ The changing role of distribution channels

New technology changes are creating turmoil in the area of distribution. Direct marketing and telemarketing are allowing organisations such as the Virgin Group to bypass traditional channels and build relationships directly with their customers (*see* Exhibit 11.3).

Exhibit 11.3

PUTTING A ROCKET UP THE PENSIONS INDUSTRY

Virgin Direct, the financial services arm of the £1.6 billion Virgin Group, has launched a personal pension which it claims will 'put a rocket up the pensions industry'. Rowan Gormley, managing director of Virgin Direct, said: 'The pension rules are fine, the tax breaks are spectacular – the problem is the industry. It has hijacked the personal pension for its own gain.' Virgin staff will offer advice over the phone on the Virgin Personal Pension, which is one of the cheapest on the market. New customers pay a 1% annual management fee and a £2 charge per payment. There are no policy fees, no front-end-loaded charges and no bid–offer spread. Policy holders can also change or stop payments at no extra cost.

Source: *Sunday Times* (20 October 1996).[2]

As we have seen, choosing a distribution channel is a strategic decision with major investment implications. In some businesses, such as the airline industry, it is more profitable if customers order directly from the airline rather than going through travel agents. There are major drawbacks, however. If the same airline promotes its direct channel heavily, travel agents may recommend other airlines in retaliation. The case of The Body Shop in Exhibit 11.4 provides another good example of these drawbacks.

Exhibit 11.4

BODY SHOPPING

Early in 1996, 30 Body Shop franchisees trooped into the Army & Navy club in Piccadilly in London. It was an unruly group of clashing personalities and opinions, but all had one thing at stake – their livelihood. Amongst other grievances about inaccurate and misleading profit projections, the franchisees are concerned about plans by Body Shop to introduce Body Shop Direct, a home shopping arm it has been piloting since 1993. Faced with saturation in the number of British stores, Body Shop is planning to boost sales by setting up networks of agents who will operate rather like the people who run Tupperware parties. They will sell Body Shop beauty products directly in people's homes. The franchisees are concerned the plan will bite into their sales, and this is a big concern with Body Shop's latest figures showing that profits are stagnant in Britain. The group said in a recent letter to Body Shop: 'There are four key principles enshrined in the existing agreement – exclusivity, renewability, mutuality and transferability. We need to establish that these principles will be honoured in any new agreement.' The letter speaks of Body Shop's moral obligation to respect the contracts under which the franchisees bought into the business. But Body Shop wants the group to sign new agreements to pave the way for Body Shop Direct, agreements the group members have so far refused to sign. For the Body Shop the contract wrangling comes at a time when it desperately needs to build its business.

Source: *Sunday Times* (29 September 1996).[5]

MANAGING MULTIPLE DISTRIBUTION CHANNELS

■ Hybrid marketing

Traditionally, companies went to market through a relatively limited number of channels and rarely used a combination of direct sales and third-party distributors. Increasingly there is a trend towards using a number of different channels simultaneously to target different market segments. Many banks are now using telephone call centres and tele-banking in parallel with normal branch operations and ATMs. Some are also extending the channels into providing on-line banking over the Internet. Each of these channels has its own set of advantages and disadvantages. Moriarty and Moran (1990)[6] coined the term 'hybrid marketing' to describe the situation where companies use a number of different channels to go to market. They cite the example of IBM, which started to expand in the late 1970s from just using a direct salesforce to new channels such as dealers, value-added resellers (VARs), catalogue operations, direct mail and telemarketing. In less than 10 years, it doubled its salesforce and added 18 new channels to communicate with customers. Apple Computer, which originally distributed its products through an independent dealer network, had to employ national account managers to deal with large corporate customers. The advantages of employing a hybrid marketing system include increased coverage and customised approaches. In adding a new channel companies must have a clear understanding of how it will affect their overall marketing strategy. Moriarty and Moran developed a simple matrix (*see* Figure 11.1) to illustrate the elements of a hybrid marketing system which can identify points of overlap, gaps and areas of potential conflict between different channels. For example, where a bank uses direct mail to generate leads, a smooth handover is required to the direct salesforce where the leads are qualified.

		Generation of leads	Qualification of leads	Sales calls	Closing the sale	Provision of post-sales support	Ongoing management of the account
Direct channels	Direct sales-forces						
	Telemarketing						
	Direct mail						
Indirect channels	Retail stores						
	Distributors						
Emerging channels	ATMs						
	Kiosks						

Fig 11.1   Elements of a hybrid marketing system

Source: Based on Moriarty and Moran (1990).[6] Adapted and reprinted by permission of *Harvard Business Review*. From 'Managing hybrid marketing systems' by R.T. Moriarty and U. Moran, November/December 1990. Copyright © 1990 by the President and Fellows of Harvard College; all rights reserved.

As Moriarty and Moran describe it, the coordination of multiple distribution channels can be a complex business which relies on IT for its successful management:

> 'Once a hybrid system is up and running, its smooth functioning depends not only on management of conflict but also on coordination across the channels and across each selling task within the channels. Each unit involved in bridging the gap between the company and the customer must "hand off" all relevant information concerning the customer and the progress of the sale to the next appropriate units.'

Moriarty and Moran then introduce the concept of marketing and sales productivity (MSP) systems (*see* Exhibit 11.5). In reality, these MSPs are either part of the MkIS concept that was developed in Chapter 3 or an extension to the concept of database marketing that we discussed in Chapter 8. The point remains, however, that the use of databases can have a profound impact on the effectiveness and efficiency of marketing staff.

Exhibit 11.5

MSP SYSTEMS

'A recent technical tool called a marketing and sales productivity (MSP) system can be invaluable in coordinating customer hand-offs. Beyond this, an MSP system can help a company combine and manage distinct marketing approaches to produce customised hybrid channels. An MSP system helps serve customers by identifying and coordinating the marketing methods best suited to each customer's needs. In other words, it allows the development of customised channels and service for specific customer segments. An MSP system consists of a central marketing database containing essential information on customer, prospects, products, marketing programmes, and methods. All marketing units regularly update the database. At any point, it is possible to determine previous customer contacts, prices quoted, special customer characteristics or needs, and other information. These systems can significantly lower marketing costs and increase marketing effectiveness by acting as a central nervous system that coordinates the channels and marketing tasks within a hybrid system. With a fully integrated MSP system, it is now possible to know how much it costs to acquire and maintain a customer which is essential data in understanding a company's marketing productivity.

Source: Moriarty and Moran (1990).[6] Adapted and reprinted by permission of *Harvard Business Review*. From 'Managing hybrid marketing systems' by R.T. Moriarty and U. Moran, November/December 1990. Copyright © 1990 by the President and Fellows of Harvard College; all rights reserved.

DIRECT SALES CHANNELS

■ Direct salesforces

Direct salesforces are examples of direct sales channels where sales 'reps' or account managers work a given geographical territory and cover a number of clients or accounts within that area. In many instances, these sales reps spend considerable time 'on the road' travelling from client to client or from city to city. The allocation of territories to particular sales reps can be automated using statistical techniques to optimise the ratio of time spent with clients to time spent on the road. Geographic information systems (GIS) are also used by marketing or sales managers in territory allocation.

Traditionally sales reps operated with limited additional IT support, but in recent times IT has been employed with some success to improve their productivity. Applications of IT to improve the productivity of the salesforce are sometimes referred to as salesforce automation (SFA) applications which we will examine in more detail in Chapter 13.

■ Telemarketing

In Chapter 5, we introduced the concept of telemarketing and direct mail as part of our discussion on database marketing. Telemarketing is another example of a direct sales channel and refers to the use of the telephone and associated technologies for marketing purposes. The advantages of telemarketing are its flexibility, its interactive nature, its immediacy and the opportunity to make a high-impact personal contact. It has suffered somewhat in the past from misuse and 'cold calling' and some of its disadvantages include a high cost per call, its association with pressure selling and its lack of a visual presentation.

Telemarketing can be described as either *inbound* or *outbound*. If a woman hears a direct-response advertisement on the radio for cheap car insurance for women drivers and phones the (freephone) telephone number mentioned at the end of the slot (and often repeated several times to make sure you get the message), her call will be received by an *inbound* telemarketing group in the insurance company. Twelve months later, if the insurance company phones the same customer to remind her that her insurance is due for renewal, the insurance company is employing *outbound* telemarketing.

Companies are increasingly outsourcing their call handling to external organisations who have a greater capacity to handle very high response rates. Some organisations have even expanded from providing a call handling service internally to providing the service for other companies (*see* Exhibit 11.6). The management of telephone call centres and the technology used to handle large volumes of calls is a major topic in its own right and greater coverage of the subject is provided in Chapter 13.

Exhibit 11.6

A SIDELINE TO ELECTRICITY

As a sideline to electricity, London Electricity now sells helpdesk services. Its centralised customer service centre proved such a success that it set up a bureau service, and now its first client, Total Gas Marketing, is using London Electricity to service responses to one of its advertising campaigns.

Graeme Boyd, Total Gas Marketing's sales and marketing manager, willingly recommends the service. 'We understand that this was the first time that London Electricity has used the Customer Enquiry Centre for an external organisation. We were pleased with the speed of response and the comprehensive IT and telecoms approach London Electricity was able to provide.'

Source: Financial Times (6 March 1996).[7]

■ Direct mail

Direct-mail advertising is used to send advertising material directly to the prospective customer, usually in the form of mailshots, catalogues or door-to-door distribution. Although direct mail has received bad publicity through the proliferation of unsolicited 'junk mail', it has a number of advantages:

- it is more targeted than traditional media advertising (*see* Figure 11.2)
- in many cases, it is also cheaper than traditional advertising
- its effectiveness can be measured.

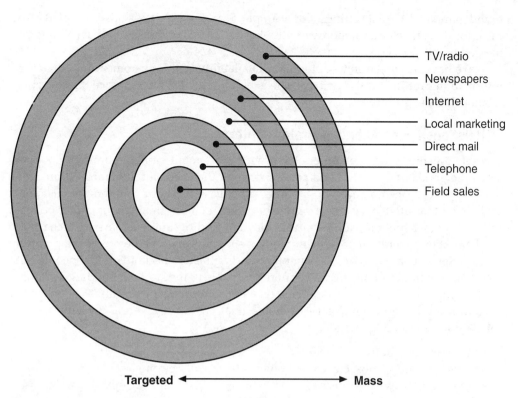

Fig 11.2 Degrees of targeting of advertising messages

INDIRECT SALES CHANNELS

■ Retailers and electronic point-of-sale (EPoS) systems

Indirect sales channels include retail stores such as supermarkets as well as dealers, value-added resellers (VARs) and wholesalers. The retail industry in general, and supermarkets in particular, have invested heavily in IT over the last number of years. One of the most significant changes has been the implementation of electronic point-of-sale (EPoS) bar-code-scanning systems which now provide retailers with levels of sales information to which they previously did not have access. As Parkinson (1994)[8] points out:

> 'Developments in EPoS technology in the supermarket have created a massive flow of raw data. Customer purchasing behaviour is now captured regularly, and as a matter of course, in many purchase transactions where credit cards or other affinity cards are used.'

Where credit cards are used and payments are made electronically, the process is referred to as EFTPoS (electronic funds transfer at point of sale). EPoS and EFTPoS applications are not just confined to supermarkets. Mobile EFTPoS applications can be found in many different settings. For example, Scandinavian taxis have accepted credit cards for several years and, more recently, Australian taxi organisations have also implemented mobile EFTPoS systems.[9]

As we have discussed in Chapter 5, the availability of this customer and purchasing information captured at the point of sale is helping retailers to embrace the concept of relationship marketing.

■ Relationship marketing in a retail context

The relationship which customers have with most retail stores is limited. Shoppers select the goods they require and pay for them at the checkout. It is rarely a proactive one-to-one relationship based on lifetime value. Fast checkout counters for customers with fewer than 10 items is one example of where retailers are reviewing their policies. Using customer lifetime value analysis they are finding that customers purchasing a small number of items are usually infrequent shoppers and yet they receive a premium service. Retailers are now refocusing on providing faster checkouts to the people with full shopping trolleys who are much more profitable to the store. In building a stronger relationship with long-term customers, retailers are borrowing a number of best practices from other service industries.[10] Some relationship marketing initiatives which retailers are conducting include:

- clubs offered by individual retailers
- affinity subgroup clubs, e.g. for pet owners or cookery enthusiasts
- store-branded payment cards aligned to the main payment organisations, e.g. Visa
- different levels of benefits to lock into, e.g. gold coffee lounges, speedy car parking and checkout procedures
- the equivalent of 'relationship billing', giving for example personalised cash register receipts, added-value information about price savings, spend by category or compared to last month or the year to date
- the food equivalent of private banking with privileged services and advice, 24-hour helplines etc.
- customisation of information (e.g. recipe construction, health analysis, calorie quantification, ready-meal tailoring, dinner party service).

Technology and the use of customer information will be critical in developing relationships with millions of customers, as the following comments illustrate:

> *'The strategic assets of retailers in the future will not be bricks and mortar or lorries but the structure and ability to collect, analyse and make use of data.'*
>
> Peter Dettman, ICA[10]

> *'The winners will crack the data mountain.'*
>
> Richard Piper, Europanel[10]

> *'The mountain of data produced in retail has not always assisted management decision making because it has illustrated what has sold and not why.'*
>
> Terry Leahy, Tesco[10]

Table 11.1 provides a summary of the technology initiatives that are being used in the retail business.

Table 11.1 Technology initiatives in retailing

Initiative	Application	Benefits to retailer	Benefits to consumer	Importance by 2005
Personal shopping assistant	Handheld electronic device providing consumers with general shopping information and listings of prices and promotional offerings	Allows personal communication with customers	Electronic comparative shopping	Medium
Shopper identification systems	Electronic tagging system allowing individual shoppers to be identified and shopper movements to be traced	More refined information on consumers	Potentially better service if retailer reacts to findings	Low but increasing
Intelligent labelling	Electronic labels for display at the shelf edge or on individual items	Greater flexibility to change prices and descriptions	Enhanced information	Low
Advanced checkout	Self-scanning by consumers and magic tunnels	Improve service	Eliminates queuing at the checkout area	Medium but increasing
Electronic money	Introduction of new electronic banking system involving some form of e-money for low-value transactions	Reduction in costs associated with cash handling	Increased security	Medium but increasing
Checkout management systems	Computerised system for queue management	Improved customer service and labour productivity	Shorter queue times	High
Videocart	Videoscreen on the shopping cart to provide customers with information during the shopping trip	Additional opportunity to communicate with customers	More information but potentially invasive	Low
Information kiosks	Combination of interactive and multimedia technologies to provide information	Ability to communicate interactively in a cost-efficient way	Added service which overcomes store access difficulties	Medium but increasing

Source: Based on Coopers & Lybrand (1996).[10]

EMERGING DISTRIBUTION CHANNELS

■ Virtual retailing

Today a shopping trip involves deciding what to purchase, travelling to the store, selecting items for purchase, taking them to the checkout, queuing, paying for the goods, putting them in bags and then taking them home. It can be a lot of work and many consumers consider shopping an unpleasant experience. Virtual retailing allows consumers to select the items they require, pay electronically and have the goods delivered when it is convenient. Selecting the goods can be done from work, a hotel, at home or even in the car. It is being made possible by the proliferation of networks and computing technology and, although currently in its infancy, it is expected to grow rapidly over the next few years.[11] Virtual retailing is also referred to as the electronic marketplace, electronic mall or interactive television and is built on the information superhighway which we discussed in Chapter 6. In today's retail world, up to 20 per cent of the price of a product goes to covering the costs of running retail stores, which represents a very significant opportunity for virtual retailing. The implications for retailers will be enormous as location no longer becomes a barrier to entry.

■ Automated teller machines (ATMs) and multimedia kiosks

More than 60 per cent of adults in industrialised countries carry an ATM card, according to the market research company Gallup.[12] And as Table 11.2 shows, there are nearly 150 000 such machines already installed across Europe – one for every 3000 people. On average, more than 3000 withdrawals are made from each machine every month.[13]

Table 11.2   Top ATM installations in Europe (1995)

Country	Installations	% of total
Germany	27 510	19%
Spain	25 069	17%
France	20 533	14%
UK	20 165	14%
Italy	18 672	13%
Netherlands	5 023	3%
Turkey	4 279	3%
Portugal	4 215	3%
Switzerland	3 391	2%
Austria	3 327	2%
Belgium	3 275	2%
Finland	2 833	2%
Sweden	2 294	2%
Denmark	2 021	2%
Norway	1 741	1%
Other	2 339	1%
Total	**146 687**	**100%**

Source: Retail Banking Research Ltd (1995).[14]

ATMs are more than simply a means of withdrawing cash or making routine transactions. Many banks have added new marketing functions to their ATM networks. In the future, the humble ATM and the more modern multimedia kiosk are likely to become one and the same machine.

Multimedia kiosks are unmanned outlets designed to provide product information, customer service and sales functions through the use of multimedia. Although the outlet itself may be unmanned, the kiosk can provide a teleconference or videoconference link to a call centre where human operators can answer more complex questions than the kiosk is designed to handle. Multimedia kiosks have become popular in the financial services industry and already, automated teller machines (ATMs) are beginning to offer multimedia functionality. In the US, for example, 4 per cent of ATMs offered full-motion video by the end of 1995.[15] Citibank's French customers have access to Citibanking, a 24-hour multilingual service, either through the Citiphone service or through ATMs.[16] UK banks like NatWest and Italian banks like Banca Commerciale Italiana and San Paolo Bank are all exploring the possibilities offered by multimedia kiosks.[17] For Italian banks, the proposition is perhaps more attractive than for those in the UK, as banks are more regional with smaller branch networks. Multimedia kiosks offer the possibility to increase coverage without having to invest heavily in the traditional 'bricks and mortar' which constitute so much of the average bank's cost base. However, there are drawbacks to the widespread use of multimedia kiosks in banking, as Exhibit 11.7 illustrates.

Forrester Research has concluded that today's kiosks provide poor customer service and that their appeal will be limited to those customers who are happy to carry out complex transactions, requiring personal information, in public places. If a customer has a PC at work or home, why would he or she prefer to come into a bank to use the kiosk, if the facility can be provided remotely?

Exhibit 11.7

THE MARKETING KIOSK

In all probability there is a role for the marketing kiosk. After all, banks need to explore any opportunity to present their offerings to existing and potential customers, particularly as they now see so few of them face to face in the branch. The challenge for banks is to capture the consumer's attention and then retain it by whatever means necessary. If multimedia kiosks can achieve this even for a relatively small proportion of customers, then banks are likely to continue to pursue this route.

However, it is hard to imagine that multimedia-enabled kiosks and terminals will ever become commonplace. There is a role for such devices but they are likely to address niche areas, with a much greater uptake of multimedia for use in the home rather than in public or in branch locations. As with other emerging financial delivery channels, its future remains unclear, but today's innovators are likely to be the ones ultimately to make full use of the medium.

Source: Banking Technology (July–August 1996).[15]

Other applications of kiosk technology include the provision of tickets and information in the travel industry.[18] Kiosks can be used for providing train and airline tickets to customers, either as a means of improving customer service or as part of a premium service where, for example, airline frequent fliers can use a card to provide kiosk access.

CONCLUSION

Traditionally, companies used either a direct salesforce or an indirect channel to distribute their products and services. Rarely were both types of channel used. This situation has changed and companies now go to market through a multitude of different distribution channels. The management of these multiple channels, referred to as 'hybrid marketing', can be a major challenge. The associated applications of IT, sometimes referred to as marketing and sales productivity (MSP) systems, are further examples of the MkIS database marketing concepts that we discussed in previous chapters.

IT has been employed effectively in the operational support of both direct and indirect channels. Many of the activities carried out by direct salesforce staff have been automated and telephone technology is becoming increasingly popular as companies bypass the traditional delivery channels and sell directly to customers. Direct mail is another example of a direct channel which is supported by IT. Indirect channels such as supermarkets routinely employ electronic point-of-sale (EPoS) systems to gather vast quantities of customer and transactional data, which is subsequently used to build relationships with customers. Supermarkets and other retail stores are also experimenting with a variety of new and emerging delivery channels, such as multimedia kiosks and virtual retailing.

ASSIGNMENT QUESTIONS

1 Comment on the role of distribution channels in the marketing mix.

2 Why should a manufacturer consider using an intermediary?

3 What do you understand by the term 'hybrid marketing'?

4 Why are EPoS systems important to the retail marketing manager?

Case study

DUNLOP-ENERKA

Netherlands-based Dunlop-Enerka produces conveyor belts for mining and manufacturing companies around the world. In Europe, 80% of its orders require customization, cutting and splicing lengths of belt to fit customers' needs. This has presented a problem both for Dunlop-Enerka, which sells directly to the original equipment manufacturers, and for its distributors, which handle maintenance, repair and operating-supply sales. Traditionally, the company tried to solve the problem by stocking huge quantities of belts of various sizes in locations throughout the continent. But the result was burdensome inventory costs.

In 1990, Dunlop-Enerka's managers decided to develop a support system for its European operations. To secure the participation of its distributors, the company began by pledging its own resources. It created a shared multilingual system called Dunlocomm, bought and installed computer monitors at all the participating distributors' sites, and provided free systems training for the distributors' personnel. Dunlocomm monitors the inventory in stock at the company's warehouses and at the distributors' sites on a daily basis. When a distributor requires an out-of-stock belt, it can use the system to locate the nearest source and arrange, by phone or fax, for its delivery the next day. To allay the distributors' fears that they would be unable to get the equipment they needed, Dunlop-Enerka guaranteed the availability of all the stocks listed on Dunlocomm. If a distributor needed a belt that was supposed to be in stock but wasn't, Dunlop-Enerka would customize the order from its own inventory and guarantee delivery within 24 hours. Reassured by these pledges and guarantees, distributors throughout Europe agreed to list their inventories on Dunlocomm. Initially, distributors' inventories dropped precipitously – causing Dunlop-Enerka's inventory levels to soar. But over time, the company's inventory dropped by 20%. The result: thanks to lower costs and faster inventory turns, Dunlop-Enerka's profit margins have risen by an average of 5% per product line, generating income that the company has chosen to invest in new-product development. Product innovations funded by these investments, have increased Dunlop-Enerka's total sales by 30% over the past five years. Distributors' profits have also risen as their inventories have declined and their ability to provide fast and reliable service has improved.

Source: Adapted from James A. Narus and James C. Anderson, 'Rethinking distribution', *Harvard Business Review*, July–August 1996.

Questions

1 If you were given responsibility for persuading Dunlop-Enerka's distributors to support Dunlocomm, what are the key messages that you would give to the distributors?

2 If you were a distributor and Dunlop-Enerka tried to persuade you to use and support Dunlocomm, what would your chief fears be and what would persuade you to agree?

3 What additional uses of information technology could Dunlop-Enerka and its distributors employ and what would be the benefits of such technology?

Case study

FROM PIPEDREAMS TO PIPELINES

'It's your wife on line three, Roy.'

'Thanks, Al . . . Hi, hon. Sure I can swing by the supermarket. Just let me jot down what you're missing for the barbecue. Soft drinks, barbecue sauce, mayonnaise, and tomato paste. And milk, orange juice, and cereal for breakfast, tomorrow. Oh, cat food, too – about twelve cans. No problem, see you by seven o'clock.'

Roy arrives at the bustling supermarket at 6.15 p.m. and makes his way around the various aisles, pleased to find the barbecue sauces and cereals on sale. Roy returns to the checkout line, suddenly feeling the effects of a very long day. By the time he reaches the cash register, he feels like he's only running on two cylinders. While Roy's energy is flagging, the machinery processing his purchase is humming along at full tilt. And the night is still young for the systems and the teams of people that will take over once the checkout clerk has scanned in the soft drinks and other items Roy needs for his cookout. As the scanning takes place, the details of the transaction are transmitted electronically from the point-of-sale terminal to the in-store inventory and shelf management systems. This in turn triggers a fascinating series of events: First, the in-store systems automatically adjust the inventory balance for the items that have just been scanned. Then, they carry out a series of planning steps to determine whether product needs to be reordered.

By ten o'clock that evening, when Roy is bidding his dinner guests goodnight, the systems have evaluated the inventory of the stores and compared the figure against an ongoing calculated plan for every item in every store, noted any differences between what was expected to happen and what really happened, and adjusted the schedules accordingly. In some cases, items are needed earlier than planned; in other cases, they are needed later. Some of the products, such as Roy's mayonnaise, barbecue sauce, tomato paste, and orange juice, have been scheduled for delivery from the supermarket's retail distribution centre (DC). Others, including the soft drinks and milk that Roy purchased, will be supplied by direct store delivery vendors. And still others, such as Roy's chocolate bars, cereals, and cat food have been planned for shipment directly from the manufacturer. The entire inventory evaluation process and transmission of information has proceeded with the buyers still in control, even though it's happening late at night. The buyers, distribution people, and store operations people have set up rules for replenishing inventories so that well after they have gone home for the day, the latest information can be used to recalculate the schedules for each item in each store throughout the chain.

By 11.00 p.m., the in-store systems have recalculated the entire set of schedules for each item and all stores in the chain. While this schedule extends for many weeks into the future, the focus at the moment is on tomorrow. What items need to be picked up from the distribution centre and sent to which stores? This information is extracted from the system, and pick lists are created, identifying the product's location in the DC, and how much to pick for each of the trucks destined for the specific stores; it is even 'smart' enough to know which stores can be restocked during the day, and which can only be replenished at night because of traffic and other logistical considerations.

Between 2.00 and 3.00 a.m., the trucks have left the DC and are en route to their various destinations. Once at their respective stores, the vehicles are unloaded in shelf sequence, so staff can simply 'walk the aisles' and restock the shelves. By dawn, a number of stores in the chain are already restocked with items from the DC and prepared for a fresh round of customers. So much for the mayonnaise, barbecue sauce, tomato paste, and orange juice. Now consider what happens to the soft drinks and milk, which are handled by the direct store delivery vendors. As the soft drinks and milk were scanned, the system transmitted a message to a geographical 'mailbox' shared by various delivery vendors. As in the case of products from the DC, the system merges data from all of the stores in the chain, and breaks it down by geographic requirements. By 3.00 a.m., people at the direct store delivery operations have begun dialling into the electronic-mails system, and have initiated the process of updating schedules, loading trucks, and delivering to those stores. The information in the system is incredibly precise. For example, a soft drink bottler has received a schedule that not only identifies specific routes and specific stores but lists the products, the aisle, the shelf slot, and the specific quantities for each shelf. The bottler's drivers have hit the road by 5.00 a.m., and by ten o'clock that morning the shelf is replenished, ready for Roy's next barbecue. Total lapsed time from when Roy walked in the door to the time the shelf was replenished? A little more than 12 hours. Roy's shopping cart is now accounted for, except the chocolate bars, cat food, and cereal. These items are distributed through an arrangement that, in today's terms, could only be described as unconventional. A number of different manufacturers and retailers, some of which are competitors, participate in a 'cross-docking' arrangement. Truckloads of product from several different manufacturers, destined for different stores and in some cases different retail chains, enter the cross-docking facility. Trucks destined for a particular store or group of stores and loaded with products from several different manufacturers leave the facility. Inside, products are unloaded, sorted by store, and reloaded; they are not warehoused or stored, but rather move in and out. Consequently, products move from the manufacturer's plant to the store shelves in record time, with only one handling step in between. The only thing that could be more efficient would be stores ordering truckloads of product direct from the manufacturing plants – and few stores have either the movement or the space to do that.

Information, not inventory, drives this facility. Here's what happens when the checkout clerk scans these items. By 11.00 p.m., the information about today's purchases has been used to update the schedules for the cross-docking facility. Some items are needed sooner than planned; others later. The latest information is used to recalculate the schedules, and then, just as in the case of the retail distribution centre, the schedule for tomorrow is extracted and picking lists are produced. The next day, these products are loaded, in the appropriate quantities, onto trucks destined for the cross-docking facility. Trucks from the factory are scheduled to arrive at the cross-docking facility within a two-hour time window. The window is rigorously adhered to in order to ensure that the products can be quickly unloaded and reloaded onto trucks, each of which has a specific delivery route. When the trucks arrive at the stores on their route, the products are unloaded by shelf and slot. Each day, this process is repeated in a remarkable sequence of lean, efficient, responsive replenishment. In addition, some products have been custom-packaged in the cross-docking facility according to the demographics and rate of sale by store. Instead of being forced to accept a two to three week supply of certain products, the stores on the delivery route can expect exactly a one-week supply – information has supplanted the shipping unit or lot size, so that stores can dynamically receive what they need, based on their needs.

Does all this sound like a dream? On the one hand, it is; the system just described eliminates most of the bottlenecks and thereby has the potential to increase profitability. On the other hand, the technology needed to move product so effectively is readily available, and a number of pioneering retailers and manufacturing companies, such as Giant Foods, Kellogg, and Nabisco, are gaining significant strategic and competitive advantages by creating 'information partnerships' that link vendors and retailers in 'pipelines' extending from the raw materials to the ultimate point of consumption. And many other companies, in industries ranging from health and beauty care to consumer electronics, are close to implementing infopartnering arrangements through what is know as an 'Efficient Consumer Response' (ECR) system that will slash logistics costs and boost customer service levels. Mass merchandisers and price clubs, too, are in hot pursuit of information partnerships, positioning themselves for the enormous benefits that accrue from gathering demographic and geographic data with every purchase and converting it into 'actionable information.' Aside from the obvious benefits derived from a smoothly operating distribution system, the potential savings in costs are staggering. Consider the grocery industry, which is on the cutting edge of the infopartnering revolution. According to a number of studies undertaken by various independent researchers and funded by industry trade associations, grocery supply chain participants can save an estimated $30 to $50 billion annually in reduced inventory costs across the entire distribution pipeline, and drug store health and beauty care segments can save an estimated $7 billion.

Source: A.J. Martin (1994) *Infopartnering: The Ultimate Strategy for Achieving Efficient Consumer Response*. Reprinted by permission of John Wiley & Sons, Inc.

Questions

1 Comment on the role of information technology in the above scenario.

2 Draw a flowchart depicting the steps taken from when a product is purchased to when the shelves are restocked.

3 Why are information partnerships important?

4 Comment on the type of relationship which retailers need to develop with their suppliers to make this system work.

5 What are the benefits of efficient consumer response?

References

1 Kotler, P. (1983). *Principles of Marketing*. 2nd edn, Englewood Cliffs: Prentice-Hall International.

2 Caine, N. (1996). 'Millions face pensions "misery gap"', *Sunday Times*, 20 October.

3 Sloan, A. (1963). *My Years with General Motors*. New York: Doubleday.

4 Blattberg, R.C., Glazer, R. and Little, (1994). *The Marketing Information Revolution*. Boston: Harvard University Press.

5 Bernoth, A. (1996). 'Body shopping', *Sunday Times*, 29 September.

6 Moriarty, R.T. and Moran, U. (1990). 'Managing hybrid marketing systems', *Harvard Business Review*, November–December.

7 Gooding, C. (1996). 'Customer services shake-up sparked electricity sideline', *Financial Times,* 6 March.

8 Parkinson, S.T. (1994). 'Computers in marketing'. In Baker, M.J. (ed.) *The Marketing Book*. 3rd edn, Oxford: Butterworth-Heinemann.

9 Electronic Payments International (1995). 'Taxis to try mobile EFTPoS', *Electronic Payments International*, March.

10 Coopers & Lybrand (1996). *The Future for the Food Store: Challenges and Alternatives, A Study Conducted for The Coca-Cola Retailing Research Group – Europe*. London: Coopers & Lybrand.

11 Schneider, F. (1994). *Virtual Retailing, International Trends in Retailing*. Arthur Andersen and Andersen Consulting, July.

12 Glaskin, M. (1994). 'Smart card meets ingenious terminal', *Financial Times,* 15 November.

13 Electronic Payments International (1996). 'Sweden heads ATM league table', *Electronic Payments International*, April.

14 Retail Banking Research Ltd (1995). *ATMS and Cash Dispensers 1995*, London: Retail Banking Research Ltd.

15 Whybrow, M. (1996). 'Nipped in the bud', *Banking Technology,* July–August.

16 Black, G. (1995). 'PC technology transforms teller machines', *Financial Times,* 5 July.

17 Dempsey, M. (1995). 'The jury is still out', *Financial Times*, 5 July.

18 Guptill, B. and Thomson, W. (1995). 'Full-service applications for travel ticket kiosks', *Gartner Group,* 30 June.

12

PROMOTION

- The role of promotion in the marketing mix
- Advertising media
- The impact of information technology on advertising
- Sales promotions

OBJECTIVES

After studying this chapter, you will be able to:

- [ ] Understand the role of promotion in the marketing mix
- [ ] Identify some of the key trends in promotion
- [ ] Describe the different media which can be used in the promotional mix
- [ ] Understand the role of IT in advertising
- [ ] Understand the role of loyalty cards and affinity cards in building customer loyalty

THE ROLE OF PROMOTION IN THE MARKETING MIX

The promotion mix

Having developed a product, agreed its price and selected the most appropriate distribution channel, an organisation must promote it to potential buyers. A small local shop will rely on a good location and an attractive sign to bring in customers. It may decide to advertise on local radio or deliver flyers to local households to expand its trade. Larger stores may advertise on TV to attract customers outside of their immediate catchment area. Large manufacturing companies, particularly in fast-moving consumer goods (FMCG), rely heavily on television advertising to attract customers.

Companies can choose from a variety of different communication channels and will rarely rely on just one. The particular combination of methods which a company uses to promote its products is called the promotional mix and the four possible ingredients of the mix are advertising, personal selling, sales promotions and public relations.

Advertising

Advertising is a paid form of non-personal communication about an organisation and its products. Messages are transmitted to a target audience through a medium such as television, radio, newspaper, magazine, catalogue, direct mail, public transport or out-door display. Advertising is a flexible means of reaching both large target audiences and small, precisely defined segments. It can be a cost-effective method of targeting poten-tial customers on a repeat basis. In addition, the visibility that an organisation achieves through advertising can enhance its public image. On the negative side, the financial outlay can be very high, even though the cost per person reached is low. In addition, advertising rarely provides feedback and measuring its effect on sales is difficult. This is reflected in the oft-repeated comment that half of all advertising expenditure is wasted; the problem is that nobody knows which half.

Personal selling

Personal selling involves informing customers and persuading them to purchase prod-ucts through personal communication. There is a wide variety of personal selling roles, including direct calls by a salesperson and telephone sales. Personal selling is usually more expensive than advertising but often has a greater impact on customers and pro-vides immediate feedback. In Chapter 13 we look at the use of direct salesforces in greater detail.

Sales promotion

Sales promotions act as short-term incentives to distributors and salespeople to stock products and to customers to buy them. Examples include coupons, bonuses and con-tests used to increase the sales of a product. As we will see later in this chapter, sales promotions have benefited greatly from the use of IT.

Public relations

Publicity is a non-personal communication transmitted free of charge through mass media. Examples include newspaper, radio or TV stories about personnel changes in an organisation, the opening of new stores or the launch of new products. While the trans-mission of the story can be free, there are costs involved in preparing press releases and the biggest risk is losing control of the message.

In the remainder of this chapter, we will focus on the use of IT in advertising and sales promotions. Personal selling is given more detailed treatment in Chapter 13. Of all the elements of the promotional mix, public relations is the one least affected by IT. However, there are still examples of the use of information technology here. For exam-ple, Hewlett-Packard was one of the first companies to launch its own press releases and news information onto a news bulletin board which was shared with several hundred publications worldwide.[1]

ADVERTISING MEDIA

■ The changing nature of advertising

Each day consumers are bombarded with advertising messages for all kinds of products through many different advertising media, ranging from TV to direct mail. Traditional mass marketing used a small group of advertisements on a limited number of media to reach as many people as possible. Developments in alternative media channels and the use of customer databases have enabled marketers to create individualised advertisements based on the customer's behaviour and preferences. While traditional media such as TV are still important, a whole range of other options such as the Internet, CD-ROMs and interactive television are becoming available. This has caused marketing departments to explore ways of developing customised statements and small press runs, highly tailored to the customer. The variety of different options open to marketers will increase dramatically and marketing departments will have to develop new capabilities in these areas. One of the biggest trends in advertising is the fragmentation of media. Marketers for FMCG goods can no longer rely on the effectiveness of large advertising budgets which promote their products on TV (*see* Exhibit 12.1) and the job of reaching customers has become much more complex.

Exhibit 12.1

MARKETING BREAKTHROUGH 2000

The American consumer giant, Procter & Gamble (P&G), is cutting back its spending on advertising to pay for a new wave of lower prices on some of its best-known brands. The company plans on reducing the level of marketing support from a quarter of net sales to a fifth or less by the end of the decade. P&G spends $8.3 billion (£5.4 billion) worldwide on marketing, and the cuts could deprive the advertising world of more than $1.6 billion a year in revenue. In Britain this will translate into an average 10% cut in TV advertising budgets this year. The internal memo, called Marketing Breakthrough 2000, confirms the company's drive to reduce prices. 'In many markets our major competitor is own label,' the memo says. 'We're reducing our selling prices so that our premium versus private label is less of a barrier to the growth of our brands.' The memo to regional managers around the world also instructs them to 'become true experts in non-TV media'. P&G, along with fellow consumer goods manufacturers such as Unilever and Colgate-Palmolive, spends the vast majority of its advertising budget on TV. The impact of P&G's new marketing style will therefore be a double blow for the TV industry. The effects are already being felt across Europe. P&G recently cancelled all its brand advertising on London's weekday channel, Carlton – usually it spends an estimated £1.5m a month.

Source: Sunday Times (18 February 1996).[2]

■ Developing an advertising campaign

An advertising campaign consists of designing a series of advertisements and placing them in various advertising media to reach a particular target market. In general, the following guidelines can be used to develop an advertising campaign for most types of organisation:

- identify and analyse advertising target market
- define advertising objectives
- determine advertising budget
- develop media plan

- create advertising messages
- execute campaign
- evaluate advertising effectiveness.

Each of the steps can use IT to a certain degree. For example, there are applications available to maximise the effectiveness of media planning, even if these applications have not always been embraced enthusiastically by the advertising community (*see* Exhibit 12.2).

Exhibit 12.2

MEDIA PLANNING IS TOO SCARY

More than a decade ago, one major New York advertising agency introduced a computer model to the media department. If you set the media programme's objectives, the model would search through millions of combinations to tell you what media to buy. The first time the agency tested the model against the media planners, the model's recommendations were 22 percent more efficient than the planners. The model routinely beat the planners by 10 percent or more, but it was never adopted. The agency does not use it today because people feel it's too unorthodox, too scary, too threatening – because they feel marketing is an art, not a science.

Source: Clancy and Shulman (1991).[3] Copyright © 1991 by Kevin J. Clancy and Robert Shulman. Reprinted by permission of HarperCollins Publishers, Inc.

In developing an advertising plan there are various media available to the marketer, each with its own particular characteristics. The final choice of media will depend on a number of factors, including the nature of the message to be communicated and the financial resources available. Some of the main characteristics of the different types of media are illustrated in Table 12.1.[4]

THE IMPACT OF INFORMATION TECHNOLOGY ON ADVERTISING

■ Growth of direct mail

Direct mail's share of advertising expenditure in the UK has steadily increased over the years. Between 1988 and 1992, its share rose from 7 per cent to 11 per cent, mainly at the expense of press advertising which dropped from 60 per cent to 55 per cent over the same period. The average household in the UK now receives between six and seven pieces of direct mail every month.[5] The more highly targeted groups, typically ABs and those over 35, receive significantly more and there is evidence to suggest that particular segments of the market are already being overtargeted. For example, 84 per cent of the 'grey' market (those over 55) consider the level of targeting to be excessive.[6] Other findings from such surveys give the following picture:

- 95 per cent consider telemarketing to be unethical
- 76 per cent consider direct mail to be unethical
- 71 per cent consider the sale of lists between companies to be unethical behaviour

Table 12.1 Characteristics of different advertising media

Medium	Types	Factors affecting rates	Advantages	Disadvantages
TV	• Broadcast • Satellite • Cable	• Time of day • Audience size • Length of spot • Volume and frequency discounts	• Reaches large audience • Low cost per exposure • Highly visible • High prestige • Geographic and socio-economic selectivity	• High monetary costs • Highly perishable message • Size of audience not guaranteed • Amount of prime time limited
Radio	• AM • FM	• Time of day • Audience size • Length of spot • Volume and frequency discounts	• Low-cost broadcast medium • Message can be quickly changed • Geographic selectivity • Socio-economic selectivity	• Provides only audio message • Short message life • Listeners' attention limited because of other activities while listening
Internet	• Web page • E-mail address		• Message can be changed quickly • Interactive • Visual presentation	• Difficult to get browsers to Web site
Newspaper	• National • Local • Morning • Evening • Sunday supplement • Weekly • Special	• Volume and frequency • Number of colours • Position in paper • Circulation level	• Almost everyone reads a newspaper • Selective for socio-economic groups • Geographic flexibility • Short lead time • Frequent publication • Merchandising services	• Short life • Limited reproduction capabilities • Large advertising volume limits exposure to any one advertisement

Table 12.1 *continued*

Medium	Types	Factors affecting rates	Advantages	Disadvantages
Magazine	• Consumer • Farm • Business etc.	• Circulation level • Cost of publishing • Type of audience • Volume and frequency • Size and position • Number of colours • Regional issues	• Socio-economic selectivity • Good reproduction • Long life • Prestige • Read in leisurely manner	• High absolute monetary cost • Long lead time
Direct mail	• Letters • Catalogues • Price lists • Calendars • Brochures • Coupons • Circulars • Newsletters • Postcards • Booklets • Samples	• Cost of mailing lists • Postage • Production costs	• Highly selective • Little wasted circulation • Circulation controlled by advertiser • Personal • Stimulates action • Relatively easy to measure performance • Hidden from competitors	• Expensive • No editorial matter to attract readers • Considered junk mail by many • Criticised as invasion of privacy
Outdoor	• Posters • Painted displays • Spectaculars • Poster vans	• Location • Length of time • Land rental costs • Cost of production • Intensity of traffic	• Allows for repetition • Low cost • Message can be placed close to point of sale • Geographic selectivity • 24 hours a day	• Message must be short and simple • No socio-economic selectivity • Seldom attracts readers' full attention • Criticised for being traffic hazard and blight on countryside

Table 12.1 *continued*

Medium	Types	Factors affecting rates	Advantages	Disadvantages
Inside public transport	• Buses • Underground	• Number of passengers • Size and position	• Low cost • Captive audience • Geographic selectivity	• Does not secure quick results
Outside public transport	• Buses • Taxis	• Number of advertisements • Size and position	• Low cost • Geographic selectivity • Reaches broad, diverse audience	• Lacks socio-economic selectivity • Does not have high impact on readers

Source: Based on Sally Dibb, Lyndon Simkin, William M. Pride and O.C. Ferrell, *Marketing: Concepts and Strategies*, Second European Edition. Copyright © 1994 by Houghton Mifflin Company. Adapted with permission.

- 67 per cent of respondents do not consider that direct communications provide information
- 47 per cent consider direct marketing to be an invasion of their privacy.

As the amount of material dropping through the letterbox increases, the chances of it being read decreases. There is some evidence that people react well to material that is of interest or directly relevant to them and that the key to successful direct-mail advertising is very close analysis of the target audience (*see* Exhibit 12.3). The ability to target customers closely is dependent on building an accurate database with sufficient information to identify key customer groups. Some commentators argue that when direct mail is more clearly targeted on customers' real needs, the situation will improve.[6] Customers should then see a reduction in the amount of unsolicited mail they receive and advertisers should see a corresponding increase in response rates.

Exhibit 12.3

HITTING THE TARGET

Marketing managers need to be able to show that they are advertising in the best places to increase sales, that their products are offered at the best prices to maximise income and profit, and that their budget is being targeted at the best prospects. If prospects can be identified as a class, the sales force may be directed towards them, while the less-costly telesales operation handles the others. Statistics can also refine direct marketing by making direct mail more appropriate and helping companies find out what sort of people are likely to welcome their direct mail. Statistics may be able to indicate whether age, sex or location is the most important aspect among prospects, whether they are equally important or whether it is a particular combination which is important. Answers to these questions could reduce the field of prospects and thus the amount of money wasted on misdirected marketing prospects.

Source: Financial Times (3 April 1996).[7]

Direct mail should not simply be seen as a stand-alone means of communicating with a customer. All forms of communication with a customer offer the opportunity to include a marketing message. Companies that have regular correspondence with customers, by way of monthly statements for example, can tailor marketing messages for inclusion with the correspondence.

■ Direct-response advertising

If the marketing message is sent directly to the customer by a means other than through the post, the process is better known as direct-response advertising. The message can be delivered via television, radio, newspapers or magazines and customers are asked to respond directly to a specified telephone number or address. Direct-response advertising has increased in popularity as a marketing tool in the 1990s. In 1994, approximately 20 per cent of commercials on television carried a telephone response number, a substantial increase on the previous year.[8] The *Sunday Times* dated 15 September 1996 contained 63 half-page or full-page advertisements for companies or products, of which 50 included a telephone number to call, 22 of which were freephone numbers.

However, the subsequent handling of the telephone calls can leave a lot to be desired. Over one-third of telephone calls generated by direct-response advertising on television are not picked up by the company that advertised or by the call handling company acting on its behalf. In the case of call centres, the major problem appears to be the lack of advance warning that they receive on the exact timing of the advertising campaign and their inability to staff up for the ensuing deluge of phone calls. Some television channels such as Channel 4 in the UK are now allowing call handling centres direct access to their advertising schedules so that they can make the appropriate arrangements for staffing.

A good example of how direct-response television advertising has been used to build up a database of customer information comes from the drinks company Britvic (*see* Exhibit 12.4). Other examples of direct-response television advertising include Martini's 'beautiful people' campaign in 1996 ('Are you the best looking person you know? Call 0990 70 71 72 and you could be lucky enough to appear in our new commercial.') where the number of responses ran into the hundreds of thousands.

Exhibit 12.4

PUTTING THE FIZZ INTO THE DATABASE

Four years ago, Tango was just another boring fizzy drink. Now it's one of the most famous brands in the UK, thanks to a brilliant marketing strategy. Steve Kay is the real life Mr Tango who has built the once-ailing soft drink brand into one of the marketing successes of the 1990s. Since Kay took the reigns as marketing director of Britvic Soft Drinks, Tango has become the star performer of its sector – not through its taste but through a marketing approach that can be regarded as ground-breaking or deviant, depending on your point of view. Kay attributes the success of Tango to his ability to keep a finger on the pulse of the 16-to-24-year olds who buy the brand. More than two and a half million people have responded to the phone number flashed at the end of Tango commercials. On a more prosaic level, these have given Britvic a massive database of its customers to target with further promotions.

Source: Sunday Business (5 May 1996).[9]

■ Television advertising

The main IT-driven trends in television advertising are described below:

More targeted messages

Developments in signal compression are paving the way for cable networks to provide increasingly targeted TV for more specific audiences than can be reached today. This offers the potential for cable to become as targeted as radio and magazines. There is currently a very large variety of magazines available for all kinds of specialist groups, ranging from golfers to bonsai tree enthusiasts. Obviously a golf club manufacturer is much more likely to get a positive response to an advertisement if it is advertised in golf magazine than in a national paper. The same applies for television, where specialist channels will develop to cater for niche segments.

Advertising-on-demand

One Japanese manufacturer has been selling VCRs (videocassette recorders) that pause recording during TV commercial breaks. In time, it should be possible for manufacturers to build a television that would automatically suppress advertisements before they appear and give consumers much more control over what they want to watch. For example, the advertising breaks could be replaced by short computer-based learning modules which allow viewers to brush up on their language skills while the TV suppresses the commercials. At the other extreme would be advertising-on-demand, where viewers could control the advertising they wanted to watch. Why would consumers ever want to watch advertising? In some situations, for example where a consumer is considering purchasing a car, they may like to view all recent car advertisements to get an overview of what is available in the market. This already happens on cable TV with the so-called 'infomercials', where companies provide information and promote their products. The loop is closed when viewers are provided with a freephone number to place their orders.

Pay-per-view

One of the biggest threats to advertising-supported television will be pay-per-view cable television (*see* Exhibit 12.5), which offers viewers 'whatever you want, whenever you want it' television. In the future, viewers will be able to access any TV show, documentary or other programme from a central digital library. When TV viewers have the same control over their TV viewing as magazine readers, the advertising industry will lose a major captive audience.

Exhibit 12.5

THE MAKING OF A DIGITAL DEAL

The new BSkyB, Bertelsmann and Canal Plus alliance is planning more than 100 channels of digital satellite TV in Germany this autumn. The alliance which is expected to invest about £300m ($460m) to the venture, believes it is essential to launch a large number of channels swiftly to signal digital television's arrival. The likely plan involves the launch of 20 to 30 distinct channels. Remaining capacity would be used for pay-per-view sport, and services akin to video-on-demand – devoting a large number of channels to a few top films with staggered starts. After Germany, the main target is expected to be Italy, where cable and satellite television is in its infancy and the partners have no complicating partnerships. The alliance recognises partners will honour previous commitments and it is very unlikely it will try and compete in the UK, where BSkyB is the dominant satellite broadcaster, or France, where Canal Plus is the leading pay TV company. The advantages the potential partners could bring to the deal included BSkyB's digital channel capacity, Fox programming from the US and Bertelsmann's pay-TV football rights in Germany.

Source: Financial Times (12 March 1996).[10]

■ Videotex

Videotex, or viewdata, is the term used to describe any two-way system for transmitting text or graphics across a telephone network, for display on a television screen or PC. Typically, these videotex services are provided by the post, telegraph and telephone (PTT) companies. Examples of videotex services include Prestel in the UK and Teletel in France. Prestel was the world's first public videotex service when it was launched in the UK in 1979.[11] It was initially a very popular service, with more than one million customers in the 1980s. Teletel began service in France in 1984 and built up a customer base of three million by 1988.

In general, videotex has been less than commercially successful as a vehicle for marketing promotion. In theory, the videotex proposition looked attractive to potential business customers as it promised to provide the business user with a wide variety of electronic services available from a single terminal. It also promised the business user access to many of those in the PTT's business and residential customer base, who were expected to use the service. All these opportunities would be made available for a relatively low fee.

In practice it worked out quite differently. Videotex was beset by technical problems related to the speed at which information could be accessed and transactions could be carried out. Despite the initial rush of subscribers, the end-consumers did not feel that they received sufficient value to continue paying for the service. Customers also did not want to pay for separate terminals when they already had expensive personal computers on their desks. Other technologies such as CD-ROM began to provide a faster, more reliable service than the videotex service was capable of delivering. By 1989, there were less than 100 000 terminals attached to Prestel, less than one-tenth of the peak customer numbers. In 1994, the service was relaunched as New Prestel with 30 000 customers. In France, the fact that France Telecom had provided the 'Minitel' terminals free of charge to their customers helped to sustain the market. Even now, the installed base of Minitel is formidable. For example, France's largest mail order company, La Redoute, gets 20 per cent of its orders via Minitel.[12]

With the arrival of Internet services via PC, videotex services will not survive in their current format. The superior graphical capabilities and greater array of services available on the Internet will eventually overwhelm the existing videotex services provided by the PTTs who are responding to the changes in the market. In 1995, Deutsche Telekom upgraded its one million videotex customers to full Internet access and signed an agreement with America Online (AOL) and the German publisher Bertelsmann to offer on-line services to European users. Similarly, France Telecom has given Internet access to its 6.5 million Minitel users. Cable & Wireless has gone the furthest in Internet services by setting up its own service to provide transmission capacity to Internet Service Providers (ISPs). It has set up a network of Internet access points in Australia, Bermuda, Germany, Hong Kong, Japan, Sweden and the UK.[13] Even the French will eventually succumb to the Internet. In 1996, there were at least 1000 French-language sites on the Internet and this number will continue to grow.

■ Teletext

Unlike videotex which is transmitted via phone lines, teletext is broadcast with normal television transmissions. In the UK, the BBC offers Ceefax and ITV transmits Teletext UK. Teletext has been more successful than videotex and works very well in complementing other advertising media. While a TV advertisement usually only lasts a minute or less and does not convey much detailed information, the teletext service can provide additional detail. In some situations, TV and print adverts refer the customer to the teletext service for more information. The advantage of teletext is that consumers can access it whenever they want and can control the speed at which they receive information. One of the biggest growth areas is in providing travel information and the service is very effective in listing plane, shipping and rail schedules. Another major growth section has been the advertising of last-minute travel bargains.

While teletext is very effective when customers know what they are looking for, the initial prompt to look for additional information must be provided by traditional TV and print advertising. Its advantages over the Internet are the penetration of TVs and its speed. The advantage of the Internet is that it is two-way communication and it is likely that many companies who have provided information on teletext will eventually migrate to Internet Web sites. Ultimately the two technologies will converge.

■ Newspapers and magazines

Improvements in printing and binding technology are making it easier and more cost effective to customise magazines for selected target audiences. Advertisers can use these customised editions to target advertising messages more selectively. This allows magazines to produce several different editions, each addressing the needs of different constituencies. Magazines are facing competition from on-line computer services. In the future consumers may be able to select articles of interest to them and create their own personal magazine on a computer terminal. This trend is part of a wider technology movement sometimes referred to as the 'electronic newspaper'. In the US over 100 newspapers offer daily information, ranging from traffic reports to soap opera updates. The reports are given to customers using a telephone service and freephone numbers. The *New York Times* and the *Los Angeles Times* fax several-page summaries of the day's top stories to companies in Japan and Russia. Many newspapers and magazines, from the *Financial Times*[14] to *Playboy*,[15] are now posting summary articles on the Internet.

■ Place-based media

Technology developments will allow advertising to be targeted to individual stores on large and small screens. Such advertising can be very effective. For example, an advertisement for baked beans at a store entrance will have a higher impact on the purchase decision than one seen the previous night on television. Research in the 1980s indicated that the average American was exposed to 150 advertisements a day from television, radio, newspapers and magazines. Non-traditional media will significantly increase consumers' exposure to advertising messages (*see* Exhibit 12.6).

Exhibit 12.6

YOU CAN'T HIDE FROM THE ADVERTISERS

Alternative media available in the early 1990s:

- Channel M, a four-screen video wall with top-40 music videos, advertising, and information in Aladdin's Castle Video Arcades. The target is 12-to-24-year-old males.

- Check-out Channel, a television screen at check-out counters with CNN and Headline News talent as anchors. The target is grocery store shoppers, predominantly female.

- Concierge, interactive kiosks in airports that take travel and entertainment reservations and gift orders. The target is adults, twenty-five to forty-nine, taking a dozen or more trips annually.

- Diamond Vision, signs in stadiums, ball parks, and race tracks. The target is sports fans, primarily male.

- Health Club TV, television monitors in health clubs that entertain and inform exercisers. The target is adults, eighteen to forty-nine, with an income of $36,000 or more.

- MallVision, a nine-screen video wall located at the centre or middle court of a shopping mall. The target is shoppers of all ages, including teens.

- Metro Vision, high resolution video monitors in subways, bus stations, and airports, providing general interest subjects and travel information. The target is the working public; people fourteen to thirty-four, especially females.

- Patients Movie Network carries programming in hospitals edited for patients admitted for general procedures. The target is health-conscious adults.

- Videocart, spun off as a separate company by Information Resources Inc., provides shopping carts with video screens. The screen presents advertisements to shoppers as they pass the appropriate shelf in the supermarket and displays other information such as store specials, new products and the like.

- Whittle Communications is augmenting traditional media in doctors' and dentists' offices with news billboards carrying specialised advertising. The company is also introducing special television programmes into professional offices and schools; the programmes are tailored for the audiences and carry commercials.

Source: Clancy and Shulman (1991).[3] Copyright © 1991 by Kevin J. Clancy and Robert Shulman. Reprinted by permission of HarperCollins Publishers, Inc.

■ Internet

As we have already discussed in Chapter 8, the Internet is a recent and very powerful new advertising media. Even small family shops have been able to successfully promote themselves via the Internet.[16] Successes such as these are tempered by the views of some analysts that small retailers will ultimately lose out to Net shopping.[17] There are many different ways in which companies can advertise their products on the Internet, including setting up World Wide Web pages and using the services of companies such as Yahoo which provide Internet services (*see* Exhibit 12.7 overleaf).

Exhibit 12.7

YAHOO BOYS MASTER THE NET

The biggest ideas are the simplest. Jerry Yang an all-American PhD student was playing on the Internet in 1994 and created a catalogue of his favourite sites. Three years on, he and fellow student David Filo expanded the idea, marketed it, won venture capital and created Yahoo, a company now quoted on Nasdaq, and valued at more than $550m. Yahoo (it stands for Yet Another Hierarchical Officious Oracle) has become one of the largest 'search engines' on the World Wide Web, offering 40m Internet users a quick route to finding information. It is also one of the first companies to try to make money through Web advertising and this month launched a British directory. Regionalisation is the key to attracting highly targeted advertising and increasing revenues. In its first four months, Yahoo generated $1.4m in advertising. Yahoo serves up a total of 14m pages each day, enabling it to command premium advertising rates.

Source: *Sunday Times* (27 October 1996).[18]

SALES PROMOTIONS

■ Trends in sales promotions

Over the last 10 to 20 years sales promotions have become an increasingly important element of the marketing mix. In the US in 1977 the ratio between advertising and promotion was 60:40. By 1987 the ratio had been reversed.[19] Not all of these promotions have been successful, as we discovered in Chapter 1 and as the case of Hoover in Exhibit 12.8 illustrates. In the past, promotions served to jump-start sales and rarely involved the use of IT. Many campaigns were aimed at a broad audience, with little differentiation made on the basis of a customer's past activity or behaviour. Customer databases were rarely used as they tended to be out of date or inaccurate.

Using information technology, marketers can now incorporate customer behaviour. Detailed transaction databases using information on previous purchase histories can be used to generate offers aimed at changing customer behaviour. They can be used either to retain existing customers or to acquire new ones. Using the concept of customer life cycle profitability, companies can use promotions that lose money in the short term but generate profitable relationships over the longer term. The modern promotions are more effective because they relate directly to the customer's likes and lifestyle. Major opportunities exist in marketing to the customer when they are about to make a purchase and are most susceptible to a marketing message. This can be called 'just-in-time marketing' and examples include point-of-purchase coupons tailored to the buying preferences of the customer.

Exhibit 12.8

HOOVERING UP THE FREE FLIGHTS

One of the most spectacular corporate disasters in recent years was the UK Hoover promotion in the autumn and winter of 1992–93. The net result of the promotion was a cost to the company of over £20 million plus an effect on reputation which is difficult to evaluate. In contrast, the effect on the executives responsible was very measurable as most of them lost their jobs. The Hoover promotion ran in two stages. Stage one, during the early autumn of 1992, offered customers two free return air tickets to continental Europe if they purchased any Hoover product worth more than £100. Stage two, which began on 1 November, was an offer of two free flights to the United States if the customers purchased a Hoover product worth more than £250. Stage one of the promotion started off fairly well with satisfied customers and little general attention. It was only months after the promotion had ended that adverse comments started to appear. Stage two was almost instantly a news story. The Hoover promotion was not the first of its kind, several companies had run free flight promotions previously but without the attention and side-effects Hoover was soon to experience. The Hoover promotion caught the imagination of people, especially when alert journalists realised that the company had not made any commitments as to how they would send the participants in the promotion over the Atlantic. Then, they started to fuel doubts as to how the details of the promotion were designed. The promotion was created so that prospective participants would be discouraged to go through the whole process. One such aspect was that there were six steps to be taken, five by post, within eight weeks to obtain the free tickets. The customers were expected to tire of the process and not bother to complete the offer. In the case of Hoover that did not happen. In addition, the company also misjudged the way the customers would respond to the offer. Normally one would expect a 5–10 per cent redemption rate; the Hoover promotion went significantly over that.

The end result was that a large number of appliances were sold but the costs to the company proved to be enormous. The attention to detail that is necessary in a turbulent world was missed and safeguards to allow for the unpredictability of the consumers were not installed – actually the reverse, as apparently no tickets at all were purchased prior to the promotion.

Source: Nilson (1995).[19]

■ Loyalty programmes

Another aspect of sales promotions is the use of loyalty programmes to build stronger relationships with existing customers. Having recognised the importance of a core customer group which remains loyal to a brand, many organisations are implementing loyalty programmes to identify and reward these customers. Customer loyalty programmes are not new. For years, savers could collect Green Shield Stamps and motorists have been able to collect Tiger Tokens every time they filled up their car with Esso petrol. A multitude of retailers have offered stamp-based schemes to entice consumers away from the competition and to turn them into loyal customers of their own. Information technology had a very small role in these early programmes, but is increasingly becoming a vital component in developing customer loyalty programmes.

In the UK supermarket industry, Tesco is a leader in the area of loyalty programmes. It launched its Clubcard scheme in February 1995 and in less than 18 months built up a customer base of 8.5 million cardholders.[20] Its 1996 variation of the scheme, Clubcard Plus, went even further by offering customers 5 per cent interest on credit balances on the card while charging 9 per cent on debits (*see* case study at the end of the chapter). This initiative was regarded in the industry as an extremely innovative means of winning customer loyalty. Most of the other large retailers in the UK have followed Tesco's lead by introducing loyalty schemes of their own. Safeway's ABC loyalty card has 3.8 million customers[21] and J. Sainsbury's scheme was launched in June 1996 at an estimated cost of up to £20 million.[22,23] The Sainsbury Reward Card aimed to gain 6 to 7 million users within six months of launch.[24,25] Asda, with the help of GE Capital, the US finance company, is following the example of Sainsbury, Safeway and Tesco (*see* Exhibit 12.9).

Exhibit 12.9

LOYALTY CARD SCHEMES

The databases held by the likes of Tesco and Safeway not only give information on names and addresses but also on spending habits, allowing them to target the biggest spenders and those most loyal to their own brands. Store cards in fashion retailers by contrast are less up to date and hold far less information because shopping trips are less frequent.

Source: Sunday Business Computer Age (5 May 1996).[26]

The reason for the investments is the belief that such facilities will make the customers much more loyal to the store and reduce the need for multimillion pound advertising and discount battles to gain or retain market share. Will it work? It seems to have for Tesco. In 1996, for the first time ever, it moved ahead of Sainsbury's with nearly 23 per cent of the grocery market in the UK, compared to Sainsbury's 19 per cent.[27] Will it continue to work? Inevitably the competition will retaliate, but if it gives Tesco a lead for a couple of years until the next major marketing battle, Tesco will regard it as worth the investment.

Companies need to understand that the loyalty scheme itself is no substitute for a good product or a good brand.[28] They must also understand that a successful loyalty programme will not happen overnight. In addition, investments in analysing the data to develop marketing campaigns must be made to capitalise on information gathered from customers. Other initiatives such as self-scanning in supermarkets can be linked into loyalty schemes.[29,30]

■ Smart cards

The choice of technology is important (*see* Table 6.2 on p. 106 for a more detailed description of different types of plastic cards). While cards with magnetic stripes or bar-codes are less expensive and are supported by existing card readers or bar-code scanners at the point of sale, they often require communication with a central database to download customer information. Smart cards carry the information on a chip inside the card, allowing the retailer to access purchase history instantly. Boots, the UK chemist, was one of the first high-street retailers to use a smart card for its loyalty programme. Although the scheme only began as a trial in 1995, Boots claims that the average value of each transaction by a loyalty card holder has increased from £5 to £7.[31]

Many people are concerned about the amount of personal information that is already accumulating about them on various databases. This issue will certainly increase when smart cards become more pervasive (*see* Exhibit 12.10). There is a growing move to undertake a radical reform of data protection legislation in the UK to offer greater protection to individuals.[32] Ironically, this additional protection may well help to realise the full potential of smart cards. If consumers feel that their actions and transactions are not being uploaded onto some gigantic 'Big Brother' database every time they use a smart card, the acceptability of such cards is likely to increase.

Exhibit 12.10

BIG BROTHER'S LITTLE ELECTRONIC HELPERS

Smart cards of the future should be owned by consumers and not their issuers, says a report by London-based think-tank Demos. Pointing to public suspicion about the accumulation of personal information on smart cards, the report also calls for the establishment of 'data access agencies' equipped with skills and encryption cracking tools to check chip-encoded data. The report warns that the huge potential of these cards will be lost unless public trust can be guaranteed by giving individuals much greater control over personal information. With 84 million magnetic stripe cards already in use, and on average, individuals in Britain appearing on about 200 databases, Demos points to growing fears about how sensitive information could be accessed by employers, financial institutions, government agencies and others.

The report's authors cite research which indicates that four out of five British people feel anxious about how personal information is used and just as many Americans feel that they have lost control over information about themselves. Some fear that sophisticated data mining techniques could turn smart cards into 'Big Brother's little electronic helpers'.

Source: Banking Technology (June 1996).[32]

■ Affinity cards

Many non-banks have started using credit cards as a means of generating customer loyalty (*see* Exhibit 12.11). The rise of affinity card schemes, whereby organisations have co-branded cards with banks, has demonstrated that particular segments of the market can be very successfully targeted. General Motors launched a card in the US in 1992 which proved so successful that it was extended to other countries including the UK, Canada, Australia and Brazil. In the UK, GM generates an annual turnover of £1700 per card, twice the market average. The reason that customers use the card so heavily is that 5 per cent of all transactions carried out using the card is accumulated towards a discount on a Vauxhall or Opel car (GM brands in Europe). In the UK in 1994, over 10 000 card customers redeemed their bonus points against the price of a car.[33] GM is not alone in building up a loyalty scheme – Ford and Barclaycard have also created an alliance to tie in customers to their products.[34]

Exhibit 12.11

CREDIT CAR(D)

A credit card can also be a method of recruiting customers for other products and services. Flemings Save & Prosper offers a low-interest card to a limited number of customers, and Mark Ward-Norbury, senior banking services manager, says: 'We got into credit cards because we saw it as a good way to expand our customer base and to bring in a slightly younger profile of customer.'

An increasing number of issuers outside the financial services sector are teaming up with banks and credit card brands to use cards as a way of attracting customers for their main businesses. The GM/Vauxhall credit card, for example, earns points towards a new Vauxhall as users spend on the card.

Source: Financial Times (4 July 1996).[35]

CONCLUSION

The role of promotion is to communicate with individuals and groups in order to persuade them to purchase an organisation's products. The particular combination of methods which a company uses to promote its products is called the promotional mix and the four possible ingredients are advertising, personal selling, public relations and sales promotions. Advertising is very good at reaching very large audiences but can be expensive. One of the biggest trends in advertising is the fragmentation of media, with a variety of different media becoming available such as the Internet and interactive TV. Personal selling is excellent at customising messages for individuals, but can also be very expensive. Sales promotions in the form of coupons, bonuses and loyalty programmes are also a very important part of the promotional mix and are becoming much more focused using technology. Public relations can be a very cost-effective way of raising the profile of an organisation, but the risk is that the organisation loses control of the message it wants to transmit.

IT is playing an important role in all four elements of the mix. Direct-mail and direct-response advertising are heavily dependent on computer and telephone technology, while the nature of TV advertising is being altered radically by the emergence of advertising-on-demand, pay-per-view and other new technology applications. The growth of IT-enabled loyalty programmes and affinity cards is having a similar impact on sales promotion programmes.

ASSIGNMENT QUESTIONS

1 Describe what is meant by the promotional mix and its four main ingredients.

2 What are the main advertising media and which would be most appropriate for a small local retailer?

3 What is the likely future of videotex and teletext?

4 Describe some of the key changes that are occurring in sales promotions.

5 Evaluate the importance of loyalty cards in increasing customer loyalty.

TESCO AND SAINSBURY'S

Over the past 18 months, Tesco has broken new ground in customer service – winning the loyalty of eight million shoppers with its Clubcard initiative – and has stolen a march in the race to gain market share. Since the launch of the scheme, Tesco edged its market share ahead of Sainsbury's for the first time ever, according to market researcher AGB.

The UK supermarket said that it was extending its successful Clubcard loyalty scheme. Tesco's latest loyalty card innovation looks particularly clever. The superstore chain has reinforced its position as market leader by coming up with a bold new concept: a loyalty/charge card which pays 5 per cent interest on cash balances and charges only 9 per cent on overdrafts. NatWest Bank, which is administering the Tesco scheme, pays just 0.25 per cent gross interest on its interest bearing current account. Tesco's terms are also much better than some building societies. Some industry commentators have likened Tesco's move to a Trojan Horse, in advance of a more aggressive move into financial services. After all, Tesco has the enormous potential to make use of its vast customer base: millions of shoppers make 9m purchases a week at its 545 stores around the country. Tesco says that it has no current plans to obtain a banking licence or to offer the Clubcard as a debit card service outside the Tesco network. Yet it adds that it is always looking for ways to develop the Clubcard. Several other UK retailers, notably Marks & Spencer, offer financial services, as do other continental groups, including the French retailer Carrefour and Ahold of the Netherlands.

Not only does Tesco's new scheme create an impression of superior customer service, it may even boost profits – the evidence from the US is that retailer-branded charge card and credit card customers spend more. Certainly, the worst case scenario seem to be that the scheme will break even and leave customers with a warm fuzzy feeling about the company – and with an even closer tie to prevent them from returning to a rival. Furthermore, it is a clever way of achieving a marketing victory in the extremely competitive food retailing market without cutting prices.

But of course, there had to be a loser. It is less than a month since Sainsbury's announced its own plan to launch a loyalty card. If it turns out to be another conventional loyalty scheme, it will look pretty stale next to Tesco's new plan. Sainsbury's loyalty scheme is based on a £20m investment in smart card technology which was originally conceived as a means of winning back lost ground from Tesco. Sainsbury's will start trialling the 'Multi-card' in the next two months before rolling it out to its 682 supermarkets, Savacentre, Homebase and Texas stores. The smart card will contain a microprocessor and memory which will store personal details about the holder and also record loyalty points that can be redeemed later. Smart cards can also be used to hold cash and details about a customer's credit cards. But Sainsbury's will need to invest millions on: making the cards, issuing machines, new software for its tills, smart card readers for the tills, and extra costs in administration.

Although smart cards cost considerably more to implement than magnetic stripe cards, Sainsbury's could save millions in the long-run because customer data, such as the amount of points collected, can be kept on the card. The company would save on the cost of sending out regular statements, which Tesco currently does.

Source: Adapted from 'Tesco tests current account loyalties', *Financial Times*, 5 June 1996; 'Tesco plans services to challenge banks' and the 'Lex' column, *Financial Times*, 4 June 1996; 'Sainsbury's makes £20m smart move', *Sunday Business ComputerAge*, 12 May 1996; 'City loses its taste for Sainsbury's', *Sunday Business*, 5 May 1996.

Questions

1 Discuss which of the two supermarket chains has the best loyalty scheme and state your reasons for saying so.

2 Will Sainsbury's investment in smart card technology eventually confer any competitive advantage over the Tesco Clubcard Plus loyalty scheme?

3 Which business does Tesco want to be in – food retailing or financial services?

4 What were the marketing reasons behind NatWest's decision to administer the Clubcard Plus scheme on behalf of Tesco?

Case study

SMART PROGRAMME

A unique application of smart card technology was launched in 530 outlets in Scotland in March 1997. The first phase of the programme allows customers to collect and spend SMART points at Commercial Union, Currys, Dixons, Hilton Hotels, John Menzies, The Link, RAC, Shell, Vision Express and Victoria Wine.

Prior research indicated that members of most of the current 140 loyalty card programmes in the UK thought it took too long to collect enough points to gain a worthwhile reward. They were also put off by the inconvenience involved in claiming their rewards and by having to carry so many cards.

The new multi-company SMART programme evolved from the highly successful Shell SMART programme which, since its launch in 1994, has become the biggest smart card-based collection scheme in Europe attracting more than four million card holders. Since signing up to the original SMART scheme in 1995, John Menzies has seen the average purchase of SMART card holders increase by more than £5 per transaction. What makes SMART unique is that you only need one card in your wallet to collect and spend points with ten companies. The microchip on the SMART card allows people to instantly spend the points they have collected with any of the companies in a simple and convenient way, whenever and wherever they choose.

Unlike traditional loyalty cards, smart cards contain a wafer-thin microchip which acts as an electronic purse, storing points when customers make a purchase and emptying them out when points are spent. Microchip technology also means smart cards have the potential to become payment cards or 'keys' to mobile phones, homes or cars. The cards are personalised for each customer and carry the cardholder's name and a unique smart card number. If the card is lost, it can be reissued straight away with the points balance on it. Terminals at any of the participating outlets can also print out a points statement any time a customer visits.

A measure of how far the technology has advanced is that today's SMART card contains as much computing capacity as a small personal computer of the early 1980s. From a customer's perspective, the cards will reward them for shopping with thousands of high-quality reward choices ranging from part-payment for computers at Dixons, a pair of glasses at Vision Express or a free night at a Hilton Hotel. The card also allows customers to exchange points for instant rewards at all the outlets whenever they choose.

As one analyst commented, 'With so many pieces of plastic cluttering up people's wallets, a single card which allows customers to collect points at a variety of retailers has to be the way forward. In the future more and more customers are likely to shift their spending into such multi-partner schemes which allow people to accumulate points more quickly for better rewards.'

Questions

1 From a customer's perspective what are the advantages of this particular scheme compared to traditional loyalty schemes?

2 What drove Shell UK to look for partners to join its SMART card initiative?

3 How can companies which are not involved in the scheme maintain their competitiveness in the marketplace?

4 *Since signing up to the original SMART scheme in 1995, John Menzies has seen the average purchase of SMART card holders increase by more than £5 per transaction.* Comment on this phenomenon.

5 What other potential applications are there for smart card technology?

References

[1] Whitehall, B. (1993). 'A workable alternative to the press release?', *Business Marketing Digest (UK)*, Vol. 18, Part 4.

[2] Mellor, P. (1996). 'P&G slashes advertising to cut price', *Sunday Times*, 18 February.

[3] Clancy, K.J. and Shulman, R.S. (1991). *The Marketing Revolution.* New York: Harper Perennial.

[4] Dibb, S., Simkin, L., Pride, W. and Ferrell, O.C. (1994). *Marketing.* Boston: Houghton Mifflin.

[5] DMIS (1994). *Direct Mail Information Services (DMIS) Report.* London: DMIS.

[6] Evans, M., O'Malley, L. and Patterson, M. (1994). 'Direct marketing: rise and rise or rise and fall?', *Marketing Intelligence and Planning*, Vol. 3, No. 6, August.

[7] Black, G. (1996). 'How to make sense of the numbers', *Financial Times*, 3 April.

[8] Croft, M. (1996). 'Right to reply', *Marketing Week*, 12 July.

[9] Teather, D. (1996). 'Tango & Cash', *Sunday Business*, 5 May.

[10] Snoddy, R. (1996). 'The making of a digital deal', *Financial Times*, 12 March.

[11] Zorkoczy, P. and Heap, N. (1995). *Information Technology, An Introduction.* 4th edn, London: Pitman Publishing.

[12] Salz-Trautman, P. (1996). 'French prove resistant to change', *Digital Media,* Issue 1.

[13] Roussel, A. (1996). 'The Internet strategy for European carriers', *Gartner Group*, 29 March.

[14] http://www.ft.com

[15] http://www.playboy.com

[16] Mgadzah, R. (1996). 'Netting customers', *Computing*, 2 May.

[17] Computing (1995). 'Small retailers lose out to Net shopping', *Computing*, 14 December.

[18] Steiner, R. (1996). 'Yahoo boys master the Net', *Sunday Times*, 27 October.

[19] Nilson, H.T. (1995). *Chaos Marketing: How to Win in a Turbulent World.* Maidenhead: McGraw-Hill.

[20] Brown-Humes, C. (1996). 'Tesco plans services to challenge banks', *Financial Times*, 4 June.

[21] Teather, D. (1996). 'Asda joins queue to offer supermarket credit cards', *Sunday Business ComputerAge*, 5 May.

[22] Burton, G. (1996). 'Sainsbury's shops around for cheap loyalty card technology', *Sunday Business ComputerAge*, 23 June.

[23] Ham, P. (1996). 'Store Wars: now Sainsbury launches loyalty card', *Sunday Times*, 16 June.

[24] Brown-Humes, C. (1996). 'Sainsbury card for customers offers BA link', *Financial Times*, 18 June.

[25] Randall, J. (1996). 'Sainsbury plays its loyalty card', *Sunday Times*, 23 June.

[26] Teather, D. (1996). Op. cit.

[27] Moore, L. (1996). 'City loses its taste for Sainsbury's', *Sunday Business*, 5 May.

[28] Stead, J. (1996). 'Loyalty is back in fashion – at any price', *Sunday Business*, 7 July.

[29] McNevin, A. (1995). 'Loyalty pays', *Computing*, 30 November.

30 Computing (1996). 'Supermarket chain adopts self-scanning', *Computing*, 2 May.
31 Jervis, J. (1996). 'Smart cards are right prescription for Boots', *Computing*, 11 July.
32 Penrose, P. (1996). 'Smart card report calls for data access agencies', *Banking Technology*, June.
33 Gandy, T. (1996). 'Buy drive', *The Banker*, March.
34 Moir, C. (1995). 'Plastic revolution', *Financial Times*, 25 October.
35 Rich, M. (1996). 'Play your cards right', *Financial Times*, 4 July.

MARKETING OPERATIONS AND IMPLEMENTING SYSTEMS

Part IV covers the operational and implementation issues associated with marketing and customer information systems. It contains two chapters:

13

INFORMATION TECHNOLOGY IN SALES AND SERVICE MANAGEMENT

- Sales management
- Salesforce automation (SFA)
- Implementing SFA systems
- Customer service management
- Telephone call centres

OBJECTIVES

After studying this chapter, you will be able to:

☐ Understand the major changes that have taken place in the sales function over the past decade

☐ Describe what is meant by salesforce automation (SFA) and how to implement an SFA programme

☐ Describe the components of a typical SFA system

☐ Understand the growing importance of telephone-based customer service

☐ Explain how information technology is used in telephone call centres

SALES MANAGEMENT

The sales function

The sales function is where the needs of an individual customer are met through the supply of a particular product or service. The other elements of the marketing mix may have created an awareness and desire for a product in the customer's mind, but the sales function converts that desire into an actual transaction. For example, a key part of a bank manager's job is to turn a customer's desire for a mortgage into a sale. There are many ways of making such a sale, including face-to-face meetings with a sales representative or via a conversation with a telesales operator. Both of these are examples of personal selling. Even when a product is bought off the shelf in a supermarket and no personal selling is involved, a salesperson is used by the product manufacturer to ensure that the supermarket stocks the product.

Personal selling is becoming more sophisticated and professional, with salespeople requiring consulting and advisory abilities in addition to their traditional sales skills. A major advantage of personal selling is the fact that sales messages can be adapted to meet the individual needs of each customer. The main disadvantage is the cost of supporting a salesperson. In the UK alone, it is estimated that over 600 000 people are directly employed as salespeople.[1] Given the importance and cost of maintaining a salesforce, many organisations are now using technology to improve their productivity.

■ The changing role of the sales function

One of the greatest changes in the sales function in the past decade has been the move from a product focus to a customer or account focus, with the resulting dramatic changes in the mindset of the sales manager and salespeople. For example, during the 1980s, many sales departments prepared national promotional plans which were used to drive individual sales targets for salespeople, a top-down planning approach. Now there is a much greater focus on understanding the likely buying patterns of individual accounts at a local level and aggregating them into an overall sales plan. With a focus on individual accounts or customers, many companies are spending more time trying to increase the profitability of those accounts rather than trying to increase the overall volume of sales, which may or may not increase profits. In many cases this has only become feasible with the use of IT to enable sales departments to track sales and profitability at an individual customer or account level.

Salespeople have always relied on relationships with their customers, but companies are now moving more towards a team approach to selling where the depth and breadth of that relationship are increased and the chances of follow-on or repeat sales are enhanced. Team selling requires greater coordination and relies heavily on good-quality information to be shared between different members of the sales team. Table 13.1 provides a summary of the major changes that have taken place in the sales function in the past decade.

Table 13.1   The changing focus of the sales function

From (1980s):	To (1990s):
• Product focus	⇒ Customer focus
• Product marketing	⇒ Regional brand marketing
• National promotional plan	⇒ Local account strategy
• Volume focus	⇒ Profitability focus
• 'Sell to' philosophy (push)	⇒ 'Sell through' philosophy (pull)
• Relationship selling	⇒ Relationship- and information-based selling
• Single-brand focus	⇒ Category focus

• Uniform salesforce	⇒ Team selling:
	  – account
	  – category market specialists
	  – merchandising

■ The rise of the mobile salesforce

IT has had a profound impact on the way in which salesforces operate. Mobile phones and voicemail systems mean that salespeople on the road can always be in contact with the head office. The laptop personal computer that can fit into a briefcase or can be carried easily has also created a much more mobile salesforce. Some organisations have taken the process even further by supplying their salesforce with palmtop computers which can fit into a pocket or handbag (*see* Exhibit 13.1).

Exhibit 13.1

A PASSION FOR PALMTOPS

Reed Information Services sells industrial directories across Europe. Its 50-strong UK sales force are based in Sussex but travel the country to demonstrate *Kompass* and *Kelly's* directories. Sales manager Mark Brundrett says his colleagues have a considerable amount of material to heave around. When Reed decided to issue sales staff with a portable computer last year, the choice was influenced by the need for true portability. 'We wanted to give them something they could carry in their pockets and use to record information immediately after a meeting,' he says. The Psion 3a which retails at £399 was Reed's choice. But Brundrett had reservations about how his staff would take to any kind of computers. 'I had some salesmen with a difficult attitude to PCs. I thought that one third of them would like it, one third would be reluctant users and the remaining third would resent this equipment,' he recalls. But Brundrett was pleased to be proved wrong and his sales team have taken to the palmtop computers with a passion.

Source: Financial Times (1 November 1995).[2]

Well-designed laptop software can capture the customer's attention with graphics and interactive features and quickly draw the customer into the sales process. It can increase the overall professionalism of salespeople as they work through the sales cycle with potential customers. Some of the benefits provided by laptop software applications include:

- freeing salespeople from routine office administrative tasks, enabling them to spend more time with customers
- providing better customer service because the salesperson has immediate access to information such as stock levels or quotations and can take decisions on the spot
- providing control over the sales process and capturing information that allows management to measure and monitor sales performance
- helping to create sales opportunities and manage them so that a greater proportion are converted into sales.

However, salesforces have been slow to embrace IT (*see* Exhibit 13.2 overleaf), despite the potential it has for improving sales productivity.

We will now examine some of the issues surrounding salesforce automation, beginning with an explanation of why the sales area has been so reluctant to embrace IT, and finishing with an example from the life assurance industry on the impact of a salesforce automation project on salespeople.

> **Exhibit 13.2**
>
> ### SALES: THE FINAL FRONTIER
>
> If your company is typical, you've long ago automated most parts of the business, including manufacturing, inventory control, purchasing, and accounting. But sales – that's another story. It's a wide open universe of wheeler-dealers with highly personalised, highly variable styles of work that has resisted all but the most basic computerisation.
>
> *Source: Datamation* (1 May 1995).[3]

SALESFORCE AUTOMATION (SFA)

■ The business case for salesforce automation

While FMCG companies rely heavily on promotions and advertising to market their products, industrial goods such as raw materials, major equipment, component parts and industrial services are marketed in a different fashion. Personal selling, using a direct salesforce, is more effective than advertising in business-to-business situations and receives a correspondingly higher share of the overall marketing budget (*see* Figure 13.1).

Because the cost of maintaining a direct salesforce is high, salesforce productivity is an

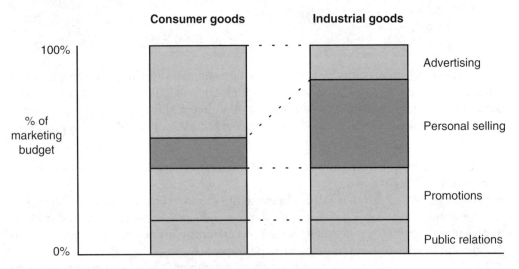

Fig 13.1   Importance of personal selling in industrial marketing

important issue for sales and marketing managers. In many industrial organisations, salesforce costs are the largest single marketing cost. A typical field representative will have a car, mobile phone, expense account and bonus scheme, but there are limits to the number of customers that can be met in any particular day. Many organisations have begun to question the effectiveness of the traditional salesforce and feel that:[4]

- salesforce effectiveness is difficult to measure
- potential business leads slip through the net
- vital customer information remains hidden on scraps of paper or in the salesperson's head
- if a sales representative leaves the company, important customer information also leaves
- salespeople are always busy but the sales results are often mediocre
- bonus schemes fail to encourage sales teams' efforts.

The same organisations have invested in, or are investigating, various means of automating the salesforce to improve productivity and increase sales. The benefits of salesforce automation can be significant. For example, HP Foods, which sells a variety of food products through shops, supermarkets and other retailing outlets, replaced its traditional salesforce of 100 sales representatives with 12 business development executives equipped with mobile phones and computers.[5] The business case for automating the salesforce does not have to stop with the sales representative and, as the case of Campbell Soup in Exhibit 13.3 shows, the benefits are far more wide reaching.

Exhibit 13.3

IN THE SOUP

Campbell Soup is investing $30 million in sales force automation for some 1,000 sales reps, sales administration, marketing, operations and IT employees in the US and Canada. The stakes are high. The New Jersey-based food giant, with customers including supermarket chains, other retailers, and food service vendors like KFC and McDonald's, hopes to save more than $18 million annually through shorter order cycle times, more accurate invoicing, and better control of funds used for product promotions. Campbell's effort cuts across a host of functions: distribution, pricing, invoicing, settlement, and accounting.

Source: Datamation (1 May 1995).[3]

A closer examination of the SFA programme provides a clearer picture of the type of transformation that took place in each of the Campbell Soup organisations (*see* Table 13.2).

IMPLEMENTING SFA SYSTEMS

■ Key success factors

Sales and marketing are littered with examples of failed implementations of salesforce automation projects. In general, salespeople are reluctant to waste time on anything which is unlikely to have a relatively quick payback period. The following factors improve the chances of success on any salesforce automation programme:

Table 13.2   How automation improved sales at Campbell Soup

	Before	After
Product/customer administration	• Paper-based process with data often rekeyed • Customer contract not captured in system causing inaccurate invoices • Redundant information with greater chance of error	⇑ Integrated customer service system results in data being keyed in only once ⇑ Customer contract generated electronically and captured in system ⇑ Elimination of non-value-added tasks across multiple departments
Order control	• Orders not thoroughly checked • Special handling required for urgent orders needed within 48 hours • Customer order-status information very labour intensive • 18 hours from receipt of order to confirm order	⇑ Orders checked up-front to improve process flow and eliminate downstream problems ⇑ All orders immediately processed ⇑ Approved order information available to distribution centre immediately ⇑ Customer enquiries answered immediately using on-line system
Settlement	• Inaccurate invoices lead to penalties, audits etc. • Finance department lacks information to settle disputes • Salespeople spend 40% of time on administrative work	⇑ Accurate invoices significantly reduce penalties ⇑ Finance department can investigate every discrepancy with facts ⇑ Salespeople spend very little time on administration
Accounting	• Transactions feed into a number of different computer systems • Various system updates lead to inconsistent data and confusion • Considerable manual work required to produce MIS reports	⇑ Transactions feed directly into customer service system ⇑ Systems are integrated ⇑ Timely accurate reporting delivered with minimal work

Source: Datamation (1 May 1995).[3]

■ *Involve salespeople in the design.* Salespeople should be involved early in the design of any IT system. The performance and ease of use of the system must be such that salespeople will want to use it rather than being forced to use it. The best way to achieve this is to get them involved in designing the system.

■ *Minimise the 'administration' elements.* Software must be easy to use and have the minimum amount of administrative overhead if salespeople are to spend the maximum amount of time with customers.

■ *Avoid 'big bang' implementations.* Quality of software and ease of use are paramount in persuading a non-automated salesforce to move to a computer-supported operation. Software should be tested on a small 'pilot' group initially before the entire salesforce is converted to the new system. The pilot group should consist of people with a positive attitude towards the new system and who will act as 'champions' during its rollout.

■ *Minimise the impact of 'bad press'.* Bad press from sales representatives can kill an SFA initiative before it has been rolled out to the full salesforce. A clear communications plan and the provision of excellent support are pre-requisites for successful implementation.

■ Supporting the sales representative

As is the case with many IT programmes, the human component of implementing an SFA initiative is frequently underestimated. We will discuss this issue again in Chapter 14, but for the moment, let us examine the following areas of importance in SFA programmes:

Training

Not all salespeople are computer literate and some will be apprehensive about IT-based selling. After all, these people have carried out their duties for years (often decades) without any support other than pen and paper and, more recently, a mobile phone. A training programme must be designed which will cater for those salespeople who are already familiar with PCs, as well as those who are computer illiterate. For people who have never used a personal computer before, at least one week of initial PC orientation is required before they are introduced to sales software on the new system.

Helpdesk support

Invariably, when an SFA programme is launched, there are numerous initial teething problems. Many of these problems will relate to salespeople not understanding how their PCs operate, rather than problems with the technology. The provision of a telephone-based helpdesk will provide a quick response during this initial period. Ideally, the helpdesk operators should be salespeople with strong technical skills, rather than technicians who know the technology but may not appreciate the mindset and issues of the typical salesperson. If salespeople find that their difficulties are not being resolved immediately, they will revert to their old, paper-based work practices and the initiative will fail.

Backup support

A considerable amount of infrastructure and backup are also required to support laptops on a day-to-day basis. This includes the need to maintain and repair PCs that have been damaged in use, the requirement to issue new upgrades of software as products and prices change, and such routine activities as regularly backing up data.

■ Salesforce automation – an example from the life assurance industry

The experiences of some insurance companies that have implemented SFA initiatives bear out these points:

> *'The training cost ended up being at least four times the software development budget.'*

> *'Users must have faith in the helpdesk from the beginning or it will fail.'*

> *'The personnel required to support a laptop strategy must be integrated with the existing business organisation structure – otherwise you end up maintaining two systems and two lines of communication.'*

> *Source*: Casey, A. and Vale, R. (1994).[6]

Life assurance is an industry where several salesforce automation programmes have been implemented – some successfully, others less so. Life assurance and pension products require face-to-face consultation and most life assurance companies employ their own direct salesforces. It is a business which has seen a very large investment in IT to improve salesforce productivity. In the following example we will describe some of the software modules available in a salesforce automation package. Some of these modules will reside on the laptops of the salesforce, others on the central mainframe and some modules can be held on either laptop or mainframe. The various modules and where they reside are illustrated in Figure 13.2.

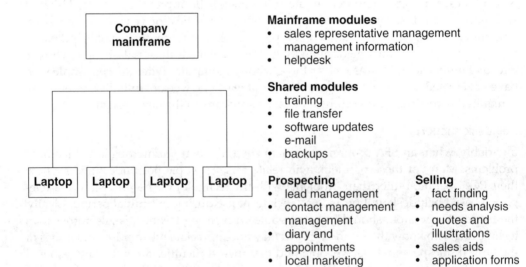

Figure 13.2   Typical location of software modules (life assurance example)

Source: Adapted from Andersen Consulting (1994).

Modules located on salesperson's laptop

The software applications that the sales representatives have on their PCs can be categorised as either *prospecting* applications or *selling* applications. The prospecting applications are unlikely to differ greatly from industry to industry and, typically, a salesperson would have the following modules available on a laptop computer:

- *Lead management*. An estimated 75–90 per cent of sales leads that companies receive from advertising are not followed up.[7] A lead-management module captures all information relating to the development and management of a sales lead. It might include information to support the generation and distribution of leads to the most suitable person on the salesforce, as well as the review and monitoring of leads to ensure that they are followed up promptly.
- *Contact management*. The role of this module is to allow the entry, update and review of all significant contacts with a customer. Whenever the salesperson calls or visits a customer or prospect, the details of the conversation would be captured, allowing an accurate picture of the customer's requirements to be built up over time. One advantage of this module is that, even when salespeople leave the organisation, information on customers is retained.
- *Diary and appointments*. If the contact was significant and warranted a further meeting, the salesperson would make an appointment for a particular date in the future. Most sales software applications will include a diary-management system.
- *Local marketing*. Possible functions of this module include the generation of a list of targets for a particular promotion, letter generation, trend analysis by client group and information on local marketing events.

The modules relating to selling will differ from industry to industry. However, they will typically follow a well-tried sales model which consists of the three main tasks of obtaining information, providing quotations and taking orders. In the life assurance industry, the salesperson will use some or all of the following modules on the laptop computer:

- *Fact finding*. The first task is to complete a financial review or 'fact find' to gather all personal and financial information about the client. This will typically include name and address, employment details, current life and pension provisions, assets, liabilities and cash flows. This data can also be used at a later stage to analyse the company's customer base and design specific promotions.
- *Needs analysis*. The next step in the process is to complete an analysis of a client's needs, based on the information provided by the customer in the 'fact find' stage or based on the customer's own personal preferences.
- *Quotes and illustrations*. The next step in the process is to provide options or quotations to the client. A graphical presentation of the expected returns from investing different amounts of money in a particular finance plan is a very effective sales tool.
- *Sales aids*. These can be used in conjunction with the presentation of a quotation to a customer and might include a short PC-based presentation of how a particular financial product can help a customer deal with such changes as redundancy or bereavement.
- *Application forms*. On acceptance of one or more products, a customised application or proposal form can be printed by the salesperson using a portable printer. The completed application can be transmitted to the insurer either by post or electronically.

Shared modules

Some of the sales system modules will be shared between the salesperson's laptop and the insurer's main computer system. These modules include:

- *Training*. Residing either on the sales manager's or area manager's PC, or accessed from the insurer's mainframe, this module might include training histories of individual salespeople, field visit summaries which log the sales manager's assessment of the salesperson after a field visit, or performance analysis of individual salespeople.
- *Electronic mail*. E-mail can be used to send messages electronically around the sales network. This can be particularly useful in keeping a salesforce mobile and 'on the road'. These modules are often run centrally, with the salesforce having the ability to create messages remotely for transmission later that evening.
- *File transfer*. The file transfer component is used to transfer information from the central computer system to the salesperson's laptop computer and vice versa. The information to be transmitted can include the application or proposal form mentioned above, new sales presentations, corporate selling guidelines or management reports.
- *Software updates*. The file transfer process can also be used to distribute new software, although, given the length of time it can take to send large files electronically over the telephone line, this is typically restricted to small files of data. Pricing updates are often distributed in this fashion.
- *Backups*. As described earlier, backups of data need to be made on a regular basis in case the laptop experiences a technical fault.

Modules located on company mainframe

A variety of different components may reside centrally on the insurer's computer, including the following:

- *Sales representative management*. This component manages all aspects of sales performance. It might include information on sales representative licensing history, client complaints (required by regulation in some countries), laptop equipment inventory, personnel and payroll records.
- *Management information*. Sales software applications must capture the basic data needed to manage the sales process. The indicators that are likely to be monitored include number of applications submitted, product sales mix, commission earned, average case size and sales achievements against targets.
- *Helpdesk*. As discussed previously, central helpdesk support for salespeople is a key function to be managed and delivered centrally.

CUSTOMER SERVICE MANAGEMENT

■ The rise of telephone-based customer service

The use of information technology to improve customer service in Europe is still relatively underdeveloped but is increasing rapidly.[8] Many of the leading companies tend to be subsidiaries of US organisations. Large companies have been faster to use technology and small to medium-sized enterprises (SMEs) tend to use IT to a more limited extent in customer service. However, one technology which is very widely used in customer service today is the telephone. If a customer wants to receive information on a product, place an order or report a problem, he or she is more likely to contact the supplier or manufacturer by telephone than by any other means (*see* Exhibit 13.4). If the query can be dealt with while the customer is on the phone, then the optimum solution has been achieved. The customer is happy because the query has been dealt with promptly and the supplier or manufacturer is happy because the minimum effort has been used.

Exhibit 13.4

TELEPHONE CALLS ON DISPLAY

On entering the UK headquarters of Digital Equipment Corporation in Reading, a suspended electronic display reminds staff how many customers have telephoned Digital during the course of that day. At 9.00 a.m. the neon display had notched nearly 90 calls; by 10.00 a.m. that number had more than trebled. The entire organisation appears to be built around the customer.

Source: King Taylor (1992).[9]

However, successfully resolving a customer's query presupposes the availability of accurate information to deal with the query. It also assumes that the caller can get through to the right person in the organisation with the minimum inconvenience. Quite often the experience from the customer's perspective can be as follows (or similar to Adrian in Exhibit 13.5):

'The phone rings twenty times before somebody answers.'

'They keep passing me around.'

'I keep having to repeat information.'

'They never return my calls.'

Exhibit 13.5

ADRIAN'S GOT A HEADACHE

At 9.00 a.m., Adrian wrote a list of companies that he needed to telephone. He spent the rest of the morning trying to get through. Most lines were constantly engaged. Other times he got through, was put on hold and then forgotten about. One company had a touch-tone answering system which confused him with endless lists of names and coded numbers. Finally, Adrian got through to a company that had installed a Vocalis virtual operator. The phone was answered automatically after two rings and he was able to speak normally and to get the information he required in no time at all. In fact, the Vocalis system gave Adrian everything he needed. Except an aspirin.

Source: Vocalis advertisement (1996).

TELEPHONE CALL CENTRES

■ Growth in call centres

Call centres are big business as customer service moves into the telephone era. Call centre operations are either set up in-house or, increasingly, are being offered as a third-party service by specialist providers. Many organisations realise that they do not have the skills or the resources to manage a telephone-based customer service operation and an increasing number of companies are now making the decision to outsource their call centre operations to third parties with the required scale and expertise (*see* Exhibit 13.6). The US leads the world in call centre implementation, with an estimated 500 000 customer service representatives (CSRs) employed in 25 000 call centres. Across Europe, the same trend is occurring as external providers such as Bertelsmann, Brann and Stream join an ever-increasing number of in-house call centres.

Exhibit 13.6

SUPPORTING THE WORLD IN JAPAN

Decisions Group is a £15m call-centre agency that provides support to Microsoft, the world's biggest software company. Japanese customers for Microsoft Network, an Internet access product, have their queries dealt with by a 100-strong Tokyo centre set up in May 1995 by Decisions Group. Each phone operator works on a PC and talks through user problems on screen. High-technology companies are generating a huge amount of business for call-centre operators. Consumer demand for computer products requires a lot of technical support, which would be prohibitively expensive without the labour-saving attributes of the desktop PC.

Source: Financial Times (19 September 1996).[10]

The UK is the most advanced user of call centres in Europe, but other countries such as Spain, Germany and the Scandinavian countries are catching up fast. For example, Skandia Bank has only one branch in Stockholm but offers a free direct banking service which allows it to offer an interest rate four percentage points higher than that for rival savings accounts.[11] At the forefront of the movement towards call centres are the financial services and utility industries. A good example of a utility company employing call centre technology is Norweb, now part of United Utilities (*see* Exhibit 13.7).[12]

■ Call centre technology

Modern telephone call centres are constructed using a variety of telephone and computer technologies from a range of suppliers. The three main technology components in a call centre are:[13]

- automatic call-distribution (ACD) systems
- voice-response systems
- computer telephony integration (CTI).

Exhibit 13.7

CONVERGING ON BOLTON

Finding a call centre that could cope with 4m calls annually was a priority for Norweb. The UK's north west electricity supplier, recently taken over by sister utility North West Water, has a territory that extends from the Scottish border to north Cheshire. Centralising customer support for its 2.1 million customers in one centre posed specific problems, according to Ken Harrison, Norweb's domestic customer services manager who looks after the new customer service centre at Bolton. 'We had recently centralised into one customer centre in Bolton, from six centres scattered across the north-west. It was important to build a "centre of excellence" to ensure that we delivered the right levels of customer service. We had various goals and aims, some set by the regulator, but we had our own internal goal: to answer 90 per cent of our calls in an average of 20 seconds.' The new Bolton centre, where 200 staff at any one time answer customer queries, runs 10 applications, including the telephone directory, an information system to broadcast the updates in company procedures, and a system to deal with enquiries which anticipates the most likely incoming questions and provides standard answers.

Source: Financial Times (6 March 1996).[12]

Automatic call-distribution (ACD) systems

The key technology component in the call centre is the ACD. This is the modern version of the older PBX (private branch exchange) and PABX (private automatic branch exchange) telephone exchanges and has a far greater range of features. It is designed to receive large volumes of incoming calls, answer the calls automatically, place them in a waiting queue and connect them to the next CSR who becomes available. While callers wait, ACDs can play recorded announcements to encourage callers not to hang up. As well as managing call routing, ACDs provide status information, such as average wait time, so that managers can make decisions about call handling. Information from the ACD is also very useful for tracking promotions, providing information on where calls are originating from and other marketing purposes.

Voice-response systems

One of the major decisions when designing a call centre operation is whether customers are initially routed to a human operator or to a voice-response system. Many companies adopt the latter route in order to keep costs down and in the US this is the preferred method with most calls never reaching a human operator. In Europe, attitudes are different and some industries such as financial services prefer to maintain human contact and give callers the choice of speaking to a customer service representative or having their query dealt with by voice response.

Voice-response systems are referred to as *voice-response unit (VRU)* and *interactive voice response (IVR)*; although both terms are used interchangeably, there is a subtle distinction between the two. VRUs provide a simple recorded message such as the reply that customers typically get when they dial a speaking clock or the local rail timetable. IVRs are interactive, using pre-recorded messages and then accepting responses from touchtone phones to answer queries from callers. For example, if a customer wishes to check a balance on his or her current account, the transaction could be carried out using IVR, as shown in Table 13.3.

Table 13.3   Typical IVR conversation

Caller:	Dials the telephone number
IVR:	Answers with a pre-recorded message such as 'Welcome to ABC Telephone Banking' and requests caller to enter an account code or identification number, e.g. 'Please enter your 6-digit account code'
Caller:	Taps in the account code or identification number using the keys on the telephone pad
IVR:	Requests the caller to enter a personal identification number (PIN) or similar security code, e.g. 'Please enter your 4-digit security code'
Caller:	Taps in the PIN
IVR:	Requests the caller to choose a service by entering the appropriate number, e.g. 'Please select the service you require. Press 1 for balance enquiry, 2 for bill payment . . .'
Caller:	Enters the appropriate number, e.g. 1 for balance enquiry
IVR:	Requests the caller to choose the account type, e.g. 'Please select the account you require balance information on. Press 1 for current account, 2 for savings account . . .'
Caller:	Enters the appropriate number, e.g. 1 for current account
IVR:	Responds with the information, e.g. 'The balance on your current account is . . .'

■ Computer telephony integration (CTI)

The convergence of telephone and computer technology is known as computer telephony integration (CTI). According to a 1996 survey by the *Financial Times*:[14]

> *'The digital worlds of telephony and computing are on a collision course which promises to transform business communications and redefine the relationship between traditional telecommunication equipment vendors, computer and network groups, and software specialists.'*

CTI provides the ability to retrieve customer data and deliver it to the customer service representative (CSR) together with the incoming phone call (*see* Exhibit 13.8).[15] Automatic retrieval of customer data, based on information given to the IVR, reduces both the amount of time a CSR has to spend before addressing the customer's needs and the amount of information the customer has to repeat.

Exhibit 13.8

HOW CAN (CT)I HELP YOU?

'Sony Help Line, can I help you?' 'Philips Quoteline, how can I be of service?' In fact, the room full of people giving these diverse answers to telephone calls are working for a different company altogether: the insurance company Domestic & General, in Wimbledon, South London. D&G is using Computer Telephony Integration (CTI), a powerful combination of

telephony and a computer database. This allows its operators to service insurance policies for more than three dozen different manufacturers, some to extremely tight service level agreements. D&G's automatic call distribution (ACD) system allows staff to identify which helpline the customer has dialled, so that they can respond to policy-holders with the appropriate manufacturer's name.
Source: Financial Times (15 June 1995).[15]

Although CTI was first introduced in 1982 in the UK,[16] it has only matured as a technology in the 1990s. Using CTI, the caller's files can be accessed on screen in a matter of seconds and the caller's query answered. If the CSR cannot deal with the call, it can be diverted to a supervisor. When the call is transferred, the supervisor's screen is automatically filled with that customer's details through the use of CTI. This 'screen popping' reduces the customer's frustration because the same questions that the CSR asked need not be repeated. CTI is a business which will be worth $10–12 billion a year globally by the year 2000 and is transforming the way in which call centres and telemarketing operations are being managed. There are already over 170 different software and CTI solutions available for automating call centres.[17] Exhibit 13.9 provides an example of one organisation that has invested £10 million in call centre technology from a variety of different software and CTI vendors.

Exhibit 13.9

PHONE A LOAN

Barclays is spending more than £10m to upgrade its Barclaycall telephone banking service. The service, which has more than 200,000 customers (up from 30,000 a year ago) will move to a 24-hour operation this year. The bank plans to start selling additional services over the phone, such as overdrafts and loans. It also plans to introduce a telephone banking service geared to small businesses. To cope with these changes, Barclays is planning to increase its use of computer telephony integration (CTI) to enable customer details to be flashed up on the PC screens of the bank's 'telebanking' operators. It is also investigating the use of interactive voice response (IVR), which will help route incoming calls to the right person. And it is considering using voice recognition to handle routine transactions, such as balance enquiries, automatically.

Gary Hoffman, managing director of Barclaycall, says: 'We are integrating some of the telephony components of our existing bank systems including our core accounting systems and customer information systems.'
Source: Sunday Business (5 May 1996).[18]

■ Other call centre components

Other applications of information technology in the call centre include the following:

- *Predictive dialling.* Predictive dialling is an outbound IT application whereby customers or prospective customers are automatically dialled using a list of telephone numbers from a customer database. Predictive dialling also employs statistical techniques in the form of a 'pacing algorithm' to reduce the risk that there will be no free CSRs available to deal with a successfully connected call. The pacing algorithm monitors and controls a number of key variables in the call centre, such as the connect rate, average call length and customer wait time, and can predict when the next outbound call should be made.[19]

- *Tracking software*. Tracking packages normally serve two purposes. The first is to record and track customer interaction with the company, so that every employee has the necessary information to deal with the customer. The second is to track customer problems from initiation to resolution, so that if the problem happens again it can be resolved more quickly.
- *Imaging software*. Imaging software allows CSRs to view documents such as product catalogues, diagrams and customer correspondence. Viewing the actual documents on-line allows the CSR to provide an accurate and up-to-date service.
- *Fax-on-demand*. Fax-on-demand allows information to be faxed automatically to the customer without any human intervention. For example, if a customer needs a company's price list, they phone the company and speak to the IVR, enter the fax number and within minutes the price list is sent electronically from the company's computer system to the customer's fax number without a paper copy of the price list being generated.

Monitoring call centre performance

Regardless of whether an operation is outsourced or in-house, organisations using the telephone as a key customer service tool need to answer the following questions if they are to monitor the level of service they provide:

- How many calls do not get through?
- How long do customers have to wait?
- How many calls did not get through to the right person?
- How many queries were answered correctly first time and how many required one or more follow-up calls to resolve the issue?

Many of these questions can be answered through the combination of computer and telephone technology.

CONCLUSION

In the 1980s, the typical sales function was product focused and structured along product lines or brands. Today, most sales organisations are focusing on customer groups or specific accounts and have moved to information-based selling and team selling. In industrial markets, personal selling has a much more important role to play than in consumer markets. However, despite the move towards information-based selling and the increasingly expensive nature of personal selling, field salesforces have been reluctant to embrace information technology and salesforce automation (SFA). Implementing SFA is not easy and salespeople must be involved in the design of any new sales systems. The importance of the human components such as training, helpdesk and back-up support should not be underestimated and the rollout of new systems should be carried out on a phased basis.

As consumers lead increasingly busy lives, customer service has moved into the age of the telephone. Large, specialist telephone call centres for customer service have become commonplace, often with the operations outsourced to third-party organisations which have the skills and the resources to handle thousands of customer calls every day. The three basic IT components of a telephone call centre are the automatic call-distribution (ACD) systems for managing and routing the incoming calls, voice-response systems which offer the caller the option to talk to a human operator or be connected to an interactive voice-response (IVR) system and computer telephony integration (CTI), which is the hardware and software that optimise the efficiency of the people handling the calls. The full potential of telephone-based customer service is only starting to be realised and companies that are using it are stealing a march on their competitors.

ASSIGNMENT QUESTIONS

1 What have been the major changes in the focus of the sales function over the last decade?

2 What do you understand by salesforce automation (SFA)?

3 How can SFA improve the productivity of the salesforce?

4 Discuss why telephone-based customer service has been growing in importance.

5 Describe the three main technology components of a call centre.

Case study

ROYAL AUTOMOBILE CLUB

The Royal Automobile Club is the second largest motoring organisation in the UK. The largest, the Automobile Association (AA), ruled supreme until 1985 with six million members compared to the RAC's two million. Since then the transformation has been astonishing. The RAC now has 5.2 million members compared to the AA's 7.5 million. Although still some way behind, the RAC is catching up fast. The catalyst for this change was the appointment of Arthur Large as chief executive. In 1985, the RAC was known very much as a gentleman's club, with an institutionalised management structure. Managers were known as superintendent, inspector, chief superintendent and sergeant. Staff saluted their superiors while wearing white gloves and military style uniforms. Arthur Large took a more focused view of the purpose of the RAC. His view was that: 'What the motorist wanted most was for his motoring organisation to answer the phone quickly, to get to him quickly and to re-mobilise him.' He saw his mission of running the RAC as an efficient and profitable business to be clouded by tradition and beset by embedded practices. His objective was to transform the RAC into a business minded organisation.

In 1988, the volume of calls from motorists exceeded the capacity of the RAC's paper-based system. The RAC had little management information coming back from the system and no effective way of controlling the business or monitoring its performance. The RAC divided the country up into 17 autonomous regions each with its own control room.

Members had a card with 34 different emergency phone numbers. Only if they called the right number would they get through to the control area that could help. A number of advisory committees dedicated to changing the whole direction of the company were formed. Recruiting new members, making a profit and becoming a high-tech company were set as the new goals. Corporate objectives and targets were issued to everyone and updated annually. Staff were encouraged to adopt a more informal and friendly style. During Large's tenure at the RAC, unnecessary levels of management were axed. The marketing and sales departments spawned selling teams to sell bulk memberships to car manufacturers, securing deals that would be the basis for phenomenal growth. The personnel department was charged with sorting out internal communication, and management and technical staff brought into reality the idea of a computerised rescue service based on a fully automated and nationally integrated network. The CARS system (Computer Assisted Rescue Service) emerged.

The CARS system allows calls to be handled anywhere in the country. It combines a central computer-based 'command and control' centre supported by 17 regional centres with direct two way communication to the patrolman via mobile data terminals. Wherever the breakdown occurs, the motorist now calls a single freephone number. The motorist's information is recorded directly into CARS, identification of membership, member's location and analysis of the fault are performed and the data relayed to the mobile data terminal in the patrolman's car. It is these mobile terminals that have revolutionised the organisation. Management information is now flowing directly from the sharp end of the business to managers. From being an antiquated organisation the RAC is now probably better organised in its field of operation than any other commercial organisation.

The RAC's Service Managers now have the ability to manage. This in turn has enabled budgetary control to be devolved to the Regional Service Managers who now have control over service costs, the operation of vans and patrolmen and how well these and CSR resources are used.

The RAC's £30 million investment in IT and buildings is beginning to pay off in increased memberships and profits. After an initial loss when the bulk of the investment was made, it generated a £7 million profit in 1990 on a turnover of £155 million whilst the AA made a £4.1 million profit from a turnover of £231 million. Alongside their investment in IT the RAC launched a programme to provide motoring services both to company fleet operators and through agreements with manufacturers on the sale of new cars. This 'Motorman' programme has been pivotal in developing the business of the RAC. The CARS system has proved key to winning many of the new contracts.

Source: Adapted from *Royal Automobile Club 'Computer Assisted Rescue Service'*, Digital Equipment Company (1991).

Questions

1 Describe Arthur Large's marketing philosophy.

2 Which elements of the marketing mix did Arthur Large address with the £30 million investment in IT and buildings?

3 What role did IT play in the RAC's transformation?

4 Describe how telephone calls from customers are handled at the RAC.

5 How did the role of marketing change in the RAC in the years between 1985 and 1990?

Case study

THE ROBECO GROUP

The Robeco Group is a Dutch company which sells participations in a variety of mutual funds. Its value-added offer as compared to other mutual fund management companies is that, in addition, it provides a telephone-based information and consultancy service to its customers. Its customers are frequently small investors who do not have the large amounts of capital that, in the eyes of investment managers, merit particular attention. At Robeco, that attention is available by telephone. Opening an account at Robeco gives a customer access to Robeco's customer service department. The department was conceived as a support unit to customers to answer whatever questions they might have about their account. It is necessary because customers have no face-to-face contact with the company. The customer service department is, today, a fully-fledged investment advisory service.

Customers can call in between the hours of 2 a.m. and 9 p.m. Their calls are answered by any one of a number of qualified investment advisers on duty. Using his own dedicated terminal, the investment adviser has immediate access to all information on the customer's account, including the type of investment he has chosen and the growth of those investments over the last three years. The investment adviser is also equipped to provide full information on each of the company's different investment funds. The return to date, the return over the last year, the selection of shares into which the fund has invested and other similar data are immediately available to the adviser from his terminal and to the customer by telephone. Information on market developments and stock indices can also be brought onto the screen and used to respond to a wide variety of questions. 'The customer can ask us all kinds of questions . . . "Should I sell my stocks; what happened on Wall Street today?"'

Investment advisers are trained to respond not just by repeating the information, but by interpreting the information for the customer. A customer might ask, 'What implications does the end of the Gulf War have on my investments?' or 'I heard that the property market in London has experienced a fall in prices of nearly 20 per cent; what effect will that have on the Rodamco fund?'. Investment advisers are not entirely left on their own to respond to these kinds of questions. Their training permits them to know what kind of information is needed to answer the question; the computer system then gives it to them. The investment adviser responding to the question about London housing will, for example, first look for information about the Rodamco fund; there he might find a full list of items impacting the fund and their estimated degree of impact; he will also find what percentage of the entire portfolio is invested in the London market. He will then look under another subject heading concerning the property market in London to find forecasts concerning the direction it is expected to take in the short and the long term. Putting the two together, he will then be able to respond to the question.

The company has developed an expert system which permits the investment advisers to be even more efficient when it comes to responding to these kinds of questions. It will increase both the accuracy and efficiency of the responses. 'The expert system is for us to give better advice, quicker advice, but the customer will not notice there is an expert assisting the investment advisers. He will just see that he is getting better service.'

With over 350,000 telephone calls coming into each of the company's offices every year, Robeco is already very efficient at providing good service rapidly. Some of these telephone calls must be responded to in writing. The computer helps there too. The investment adviser prepares the letter to the customer. It is immediately registered in his file and transferred by computer with the name and address already on it to the documents department where the necessary documents are stored. The appropriate documents are attached to the now printed-out letter, put in an envelope and popped into the mail. The entire process is accomplished in less than a day.

For the customer who is used to being ignored or forgotten by investment managers, Robeco's service is a welcome change. Because it is by telephone, it provides the additional advantage of being more easily accessible. The customer doesn't have to skip work to keep an appointment with an investment manager who doesn't really care to meet him, nor does he have to 'go into their offices' simply to make a transfer of his investments from one fund to another. Because the information is being interpreted by the investment adviser, he is getting as much advice as he would ever get from an investment manager. He can also call as many times as he wishes and never feel that he is abusing the information service – Robeco is there for that.

Source: Adapted from Horovitz, J. and Panak, M.J. (1992). *Total Customer Satisfaction: Lessons from 50 European Companies with Top Quality Service*. London: Pitman.

Questions

1 How did Robeco use IT to gain a competitive edge in the financial services marketplace?

2 What elements of CTI is Robeco using?

3 What are the key benefits that Robeco customers are receiving now compared to other investment fund customers?

4 Describe the key marketing message that Robeco should communicate to its customers.

5 What additional services might Robeco consider giving its customers over the phone?

References

[1] Cummins, J. (1989). *Sales Promotion*. London: Kogan Page.

[2] Dempsey, M. (1995). 'A passion for palmtops', *Financial Times*, 1 November.

[3] Kay, E. (1995). 'Selling enters the information age', *Datamation*, 1 May.

[4] Marketing (1994). 'Marketing guide: computers in marketing', *Marketing*, 17 March.

[5] Rines, S. (1995). 'Forcing change', *Marketing Week*, 1 March.

[6] Casey, A. and Vale, R. (1994). *Life Design Guidelines*. London: Andersen Consulting.

[7] Donath, B. (1994). 'Roadkill in the back room', *Marketing*, 21 July.

[8] Domegan, C.T and Donaldson, B. (1991). 'Customer service and information technology', *Journal of Information Technology*, Vol. 7, pp. 303–12.

[9] King Taylor, L. (1992). *The Sunday Times Business Skills Series: Quality: Total Customer Service*. London: Century Business.

[10] Dempsey, M. (1996). 'Marketing down the line', *Financial Times*, 19 September.

[11] Gooding, C. (1995). 'A two-way long-term relationship', *Financial Times*, 15 June.

[12] Gooding, C. (1996). 'Handling 4m calls a year', *Financial Times*, 6 March.

[13] http://www.sun.com (1996), 'Integrating computer and telephone technologies'.

[14] Taylor, P. (1996). 'Learning to live together', *Financial Times*, 2 May.

[15] Gooding, C. (1995). 'CTI at Domestic & General', *Financial Times*, 15 June.

[16] Gooding, C. (1995). 'Only speak when you're spoken to', *Financial Times*, 3 May.

[17] Gooding, C. (1996). 'More help to keep the show on the road', *Financial Times*, 6 March.

[18] Sunday Business (1996). 'Barclays spends £10m on telebanking system', *Sunday Business*, 5 May.

[19] Taylor, P. (1996). 'Learning to live together', *Financial Times*, 2 May.

14

IMPLEMENTATION OF MARKETING AND CUSTOMER INFORMATION SYSTEMS

- The systems development life cycle
- Feasibility study
- Requirements analysis
- Design
- Implementation
- Maintenance
- Selecting packaged software
- Key success factors

OBJECTIVES

After studying this chapter, you will be able to:

☐ Understand the characteristics of computer systems development

☐ Identify and describe the key phases and steps in the systems development life cycle

☐ Explain the pros and cons of using a sales or marketing software package

☐ Understand the key success factors in developing computer systems

THE SYSTEMS DEVELOPMENT LIFE CYCLE

■ The nature of computer systems

Information technology can be a major business enabler and source of competitive advantage. More and more, business managers are using IT to change the way they do business and to reengineer business processes. However, before embarking on a major IT project, managers should be aware of the risks involved and the importance of following a recognised systems-implementation methodology. The following characteristics of computer systems development should be kept in mind before starting a project:

- *Complexity.* In a major systems development project several hundred thousand lines of computer code may be written and tested. Several different hardware, software and telecommunications standards have to be integrated.
- *Long elapsed time.* A typical systems development effort can last anywhere from six months to a number of years. It is rarely possible to design, develop, test and install a new computer system in less than six months. The rapidly changing nature of business means that the requirements are likely to change during the project and the project team will have to adapt to these changes.
- *Difficult project management.* Many computer systems do not deliver the required results. We will examine one such situation in a case study at the end of the chapter. The reasons for failure are numerous, but inadequate management of the multitude of strategic, technical, design, operational and change management issues that are inherent in systems development is a major factor.

■ The systems development life cycle

The design and development of any computer system are major undertakings and require a considerable investment in management time and resources. The major issues tend to revolve more around project management and gaining the support and backing of business users than around technical considerations. Successful implementation requires a rigorous approach to be adopted and clear stages of development to be addressed in sequence. Lucas (1985)[1] points out that:

> 'a computer-based information system has a life cycle, just like a living organism or a new product.'

The concept of the life cycle is well understood and accepted. Understanding the life cycle and the particular challenges to be faced at each stage is a critical first step in developing successful computer applications. Flaatten *et al.* (1989)[2] identify five major phases in this systems development life cycle (*see* Figure 14.1).

Within these major phases, there are clearly many more lower-level steps and tasks. Indeed, a variety of systems development methodologies exist which show how to develop a system in great detail. Concentrating on the main building blocks of any systems development life cycle, we can expand the five major phases into a longer list of steps and tasks (*see* Table 14.1).

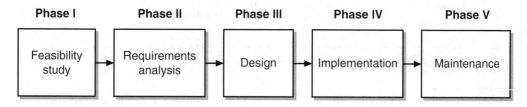

Fig 14.1   Major phases in systems development

Source: Flaatten *et al.* (1989).[2]

Table 14.1   Detailed systems development life cycle

Phase	Steps within each phase	Tasks within each step
I. Feasibility study	1. Project inception	• Conduct high-level investigation
	2. Feasibility study	• Review existing processes and procedures • Evaluate alternative systems • Prepare preliminary cost estimates
	3. Existing systems analysis	• Perform detailed analysis of existing systems, processes and procedures
II. Requirements analysis	4. User requirements analysis	• Identify key users and user requirements • Collect data on volumes, inputs and outputs, files • Set boundaries to system • Design ideal system (without any constraints) • Revise design to make ideal system practical
III. Design	5. Detailed design	• Design technical architecture • Design processing logic • Prepare file design • Identify inputs and outputs
	6. Programming specifications	• Prepare programming specifications • Develop procedures
IV. Implementation	7. Programming and configuration	• Program modules • Install and configure packaged software
	8. Testing	• Conduct unit tests on program modules • Conduct combined module tests (string tests) • Conduct system test on full system • Conduct user acceptance tests
	9. Training	• Develop training materials • Conduct training courses
	10. Conversion and installation	• Convert existing data • Install system
V. Maintenance	11. Maintenance and enhancements	• Perform maintenance • Introduce enhancements

Source: Adapted from Flaatten *et al.* (1989)[2] and Lucas (1985).[1]

The tasks and steps in the life cycle are usually followed sequentially and provide a set of guidelines or a checklist which should be used to manage the implementation of any computer system. The tasks and steps can also be taken and developed further into a more detailed project plan which is tailored for the specific company. We will now look at what needs to be done in each of the phases in more detail.

FEASIBILITY STUDY

■ Project inception

Marketing systems usually begin with an idea or request from top management to do something. That 'something' may be a response to a competitive move such as a rival firm launching a card-based loyalty scheme, or a response to an internally recognised need such as a lack of good marketing or sales information. The idea may be well conceived or may be little more than a whim. The first step is to decide whether this 'something' should be killed at birth, or whether it should be developed into a fully fledged project and ultimately a marketing system. The starting point in the process is usually some form of feasibility study.

■ Feasibility study

The objective of this stage is to determine the viability of the project and prepare the ground for the systems implementation project. There are three main elements to any feasibility study:

- *Review existing processes and procedures.* There is little point in developing a new marketing system without first examining what already exists in the organisation. A preliminary examination of the existing systems will provide the starting point from which any new project can begin. Usually there is some existing capability which can be used as a starting point for the proposed marketing initiative. For example, if the existing sales information is inadequate, it is important to understand what sales information is currently available to marketing managers as the existing system may form the basis for further improvements.
- *Identify alternative systems.* Alternatives may include deciding to modify an existing system rather than starting from scratch, or outsourcing to a third party rather than developing a system in-house. For example, if an organisation wishes to develop a direct marketing capability, it can find a number of third-party organisations that would be happy to provide that service, at the right price. Another major decision at this stage is whether to develop the system from scratch or modify an existing package. We will look at the advantages of modifying an existing package later in this chapter.
- *Prepare preliminary cost estimates.* An initial estimate of the likely costs of the different alternatives is required before a decision can be taken to proceed further. The objective of this step is to provide senior marketing management with a range of alternatives and high-level cost estimates so that they can decide to move to the next step in the process, or abandon the initiative.

■ Existing systems analysis

The objective of this stage is to gather more detailed information on existing processes and procedures. This detailed analysis will provide the background information against which the requirements for the new system can be assessed. This stage involves conducting detailed interviews with existing users on how they use the current system, the procedures which the IT department use to run the system and how information is processed. It usually consists of identifying all of the relevant data and programs used by the existing computer system. The existing hardware architecture and communications links would also be documented.

REQUIREMENTS ANALYSIS

■ User requirements analysis

Once the feasibility study has established that a particular marketing or sales system is appropriate, the next step is to define more precisely a realistic set of requirements for the proposed computer system. It is not sufficient to say: 'We need a better sales information system – please develop one for us.'

A detailed set of requirements must be produced which will drive the development of the system. If the users are simply asked for their requirements, the system developers are likely to end up with a 'wish list' which will take much longer to implement and will be much more expensive to implement than the initial cost estimates. As requirements are identified, the costs and benefits of meeting these requirements should be assessed. Most IT departments employ people known as business analysts who, with the help of the marketing department or other users, can balance the items on the wish list with what is feasible to implement.

Quite often the requirements are prioritised into A, B and C requirements, or some similar categorisation from 'must-haves' to 'nice-to-haves'. The implementation of the 'must-haves' should proceed without delay while the 'nice-to-haves' may be postponed for subsequent projects. The business analyst will also estimate the number of users, number of transactions per day, number and frequency of reports to be printed, number of customers to be held on the database, required response times for queries and so on. This information will be used to select the hardware, software, database and telecommunications infrastructure.

This phase may appear straightforward but very often several iterations are required. There is also the issue of obtaining agreement, or sign-off, from the users of the proposed system and it is imperative to gain sign-off to a clearly defined set of requirements before the design phase begins.[3] Not all systems development projects end in successful implementation. Perhaps the most critical part of any such project is the requirements-analysis phase, where the success or failure of the project is often determined. We will examine one such failure in a case study at the end of this chapter.

DESIGN

■ Detailed design

The objective of this stage is to prepare a detailed functional and technical design of the new system. New business processes and workflows are defined and windows, screens and reports are all specified. Typically, a project team is set up with business users, business analysts and technical analysts. If possible, users should design their own systems with the help of IT staff, rather than the other way around. However, as Exhibit 14.1 shows, users should not be given a completely free hand during the design stage!

Exhibit 14.1

TOO MUCH TO REPORT

One of the most frequent complaints we hear is that users cannot understand reports. Having users actually design a report increases their understanding, which is another good reason for this design approach. Another chronic complaint we hear is that too much data are produced by computer systems. Even if users do design them, they still may be guilty of producing too much information.

Source: Lucas (1985).[1]

Between them, the members of the project team flesh out the details of the system, refine it and make revisions to the overall system specification which makes it acceptable to both the business users who have to use the system and the IT people who have to program, test and implement the system to a given budget and timescale. Typically, there are at least two design documents that are produced during this stage of the project. One is the *functional design document* which outlines, to a considerable level of detail, exactly how the new system will work from a functional or business perspective. A second document, called the *technical design document*, describes the various technical aspects of the system, including processing logic, file design, database design, input and output devices, networks and security requirements.

One of the best ways to get people to understand and buy into the design of any IT system is to show them a prototype of how the system works. Modern computer systems allow prototyping to be carried out faster and more easily than in the past. The design of IT solutions based on packaged systems will often involve a prototyping phase, sometimes called a 'conference room pilot', where marketing staff or business users can see and use the new system. Their feedback is then used to finalise the design of the system.

■ Programming specifications

The objective of this stage is to prepare detailed specifications for the programmers to follow during the implementation phase of the project. Sometimes, this stage is carried out in conjunction with the programming and configuration stage. It is unusual to have all the programming specifications completed before programming starts.

IMPLEMENTATION

■ Programming and configuration

The objective of this stage is to develop the computer code for the proposed system. When people think of the development of computer systems, they often envisage a roomful of programmers sitting in front of screens, tapping line after line of computer code on their keyboards, the result of which is a single, large computer program which sits in the memory of a vast computer in some remote basement, quietly whirring away. The image is not a million miles from reality, although the percentage of the effort associated with generating computer code is relatively small – typically less than 35 per cent of the overall implementation effort. In fact, almost as much time is spent testing the programs as is spent in generating the computer code.

Either as part of the design stage or at the start of the programming stage, a series of programming work units are prepared which are used as the detailed specifications for the computer programmers to use. After the program has been written, the code is often checked by another programmer or supervisor before it is tested.

When a company decides to use packaged software, which we will discuss below, much of this programming work is eliminated. The software is installed and 'configured' to the required specifications. For example, a sales package will have working, fully tested software for managing a salesforce, but the areas and regions of a salesforce need to be defined or 'configured' when the package is installed. Similarly, a marketing information system will have a large number of predefined reports to choose from but, during installation, the exact number and type of reports must be selected.

■ Testing

The objective of this stage is to ensure that the system works exactly as the designers intended. In a large, complex computer system the number of lines of computer code may run into millions and consist of hundreds or possibly thousands of separate programs, each of which performs a particular function within the overall system. A program may consist of ten lines of code or it may contain several hundred. Regardless of the number of lines of computer code, testing the programs is a critical and time-consuming component of the overall systems development life cycle. Software errors can result in unstable computer systems, incorrectly processed transactions and eroded customer confidence. The different types of testing are:

- *Unit testing.* Once an individual program is written by a computer programmer, it is tested on its own and this is known as a unit test.

- *String testing.* Following the unit test, several programs may be tested in a string test to ensure that they work together correctly.

- *System testing.* When all the programs are completed, the final test is carried out on the entire system. System tests must be rigorously carried out over a period of weeks, or even months, to ensure that all parts of the software are working together in the desired fashion.

■ *Acceptance testing*. Even after the system test has been completed, a final acceptance test is carried out. The purpose of this test is to allow the marketing or sales staff who will use the system to operate it before it goes live. Quite often a computer system will work in exactly the way that it has been specified, but when the users get the opportunity to try it out, there are certain aspects which they do not like or wish to change. For example, the response time for conducting an enquiry might match the specification, but marketing managers might not be satisfied with the time taken once they have had the opportunity to use the system for the first time.

■ Training

A critical component of any computer implementation is the training that is provided to the users of the system. More sales and marketing systems fail due to their rejection by the users than due to underlying technical or performance issues. As we discussed in the earlier sections, the design of a new computer system will probably incorporate certain changes in the ways in which people work. For example, at one extreme, an insurance salesforce which may have had little exposure to computers may be required to move to a more automated environment where sales leads and quotations are prepared and tracked on a laptop computer, proposal forms are generated on a portable printer and sales results are uploaded to the head office by means of a modem and mobile phone connection. Such a radical change in work practices may be more than a traditional sales agent can cope with, unless that person has been given the proper training and support as the new sales system is rolled out.

The effort in preparing training material should not be underestimated. A one-day training course may take several weeks to prepare. Some trainees may require one-on-one support in certain situations. Almost all will require more than one course before they are comfortable with the new technology. Helpdesk support must be considered to provide a telephone-based support service for newly trained staff. Another option is to build help functions and tutorials into the system so users can access help on-line. A major growth area is the provision of computer-based training (CBT), which can be very cost effective if there are a large number of users to be trained.

■ Conversion and installation

The objective of this stage is to install the new system and convert the data from existing systems on to the new system. Often, one of the most time-consuming elements of any IT implementation is data conversion. Conversion refers to the stage in the implementation when all the existing marketing data that resides on the company's current computer systems and on paper records is loaded, or converted, to the new system. Conversions need to be carefully planned and in many cases special programs must be written to convert existing data automatically into the correct format for use in the new system.

Installation refers to the loading up of the tested software, and the converted data, on to the new system.

MAINTENANCE

■ Maintenance and enhancements

The systems-development life cycle does not finish when the system has been implemented. The objective of this phase is to ensure that the system operates correctly and that future enhancements are incorporated into it.

Any IT system needs to be maintained and, despite the best efforts of the programmers who have coded and tested the system, some software problems, or 'bugs', will be discovered after the software has been installed. Users will also have minor modifications that they want to make from time to time. Changes in the way the company operates also need to be reflected in the software. If two sales regions are combined, for example, these changes have to be reflected in the system. On an even more regular basis, price changes in supermarkets need to be updated in the system on a daily basis.

These changes and enhancements are usually controlled through the use of a 'change request' mechanism, where users formally request changes to be made and sign off those changes after they have been made by the maintenance team.

SELECTING PACKAGED SOFTWARE

■ Packaged versus custom-built software

An important distinction must be made between *custom-built software* and *packaged software*. The marketing system can be built from scratch to meet the exact needs of the marketing users or, alternatively, an existing computer package can be chosen which meets most of the marketing manager's requirements. As more and more sales and marketing packages become available in the marketplace, and as their reliability and number of features increase, the trend is for companies to choose from the increasingly wide choice of marketing and sales software packages. An example of how one company searched the market for a suitable marketing package and selected one from a list of 35 different vendors is given in Exhibit 14.2.

■ Benefits of packaged software

If a package can be found which meets most of the proposed requirements, it is probably a better option than a customised solution. The benefits of a computer package are as follows:

- *Speed of implementation.* Packaged software typically takes less time to implement than custom-built software. This is because all of the computer code has already been written and tested. This package will need to be 'configured' to meet the exact needs of the marketing organisation, but the configuration is usually straightforward. Only in cases where additional functions or modifications are required will there be a need for programming and testing.
- *Lower risk.* Because the software has already been tested and is probably running

Exhibit 14.2

FROM 35 TO 8 TO 3 TO 2 TO 1

John Laing, the UK construction company, began looking for a replacement for its old marketing system which would retain its best features and give scope to expand its functions. The mainframe database system had been used by all the marketing staff as well as sales staff and many other departments. It contained a mass of information on projects, bids, costings and contracts. A working party of users and computer specialists was set to study the requirements for a new marketing system. First the company invited bidders to attend a briefing on what was wanted. Next it sent out questionnaires to around 35 interested vendors and saw many of the products demonstrated. Then it looked at eight products in greater detail, reducing the field to a shortlist of three. Around 50 users were involved in testing two of the shortlisted systems. This ensured that they chose a system which they wanted and would be keen to use.

Source: Financial Times (1 November 1995).[4]

successfully in other locations, the risk of failure is lower. When choosing a software package, marketing managers must ensure that they arrange a site visit to view the software operating in a live environment and talk to other users of the package.

■ *Reduced costs.* Most of the costs associated with the implementation of any software solution are staff costs, rather than hardware or software costs. Although there is an initial cost associated with purchasing the package software licence and usually an annual ongoing maintenance fee, the overall cost of using a package should be lower than the total cost of implementing the IT solution.

■ *Additional functionality.* Many software packages will offer other features and capabilities which the marketing manager would not necessarily have considered in the initial feasibility study, or even during the design stage.

■ Drawbacks of using packaged software

So far, so good. Why, then, would companies go to the expense of building their own computer systems, rather than relying on a package to fulfil their needs? In the past, the number of software packages was limited and although the number is increasing and their use is becoming more prevalent, there are at least three potential drawbacks to their use:

■ the available packages may not meet the requirements of the marketing manager may require so much modification that a custom-built approach is preferable

■ the company may not wish to become dependent on a software vendor for support and maintenance (an annual maintenance charge of 10–20 per cent of the original licence fee is not uncommon)

■ the company may need to purchase additional hardware, and possibly software, to run the selected software package.

Another consideration is the fact that any software package is unlikely to meet all the company's requirements. The marketing manager must decide which of his or her requirements are absolutely vital, as opposed to 'nice to have'. Armed with this information, IT and marketing can decide what to do when their requirements are not met by the package that they have selected. The choice is threefold:

- *Ignore the requirement.* If the requirement is only 'nice to have', and the costs of modifying the package appear too great, the marketing manager may well decide to drop that particular requirement from the list. It is quite common to bring a 'wish list' of requirements into a software package-selection exercise, only to see several of the requirements eliminated at a later stage. The choice of a computer package always involves trade-offs between costs and benefits.
- *Change the software package.* If the requirement is absolutely essential, then a modification will be required to the package and the effort involved can be estimated by the package supplier or the company's own IT people. Many modern packages are built in a structured, modular fashion whereby the package can be modified by 'configuring' certain tables within the package, rather than rewriting the underlying computer code. However, there may come a point when the extent of the modifications outweighs the advantages of using a software package in the first instance and it may make more sense to build a customised system.
- *Change the way the organisation does business.* This may appear an unusual response, but it is quite a common and viable option in many circumstances. The nature of modern software packages is that they have certain practices, or workflows, embedded in them which often represent 'best practice'. For example, a lead-management system may require salespeople to be much more rigorous in their approach to qualifying and following up on sales leads. If the salesforce can be persuaded that this change in work practices is a good thing, then it makes sense to change work practices, rather than simply automating those that exist.

KEY SUCCESS FACTORS

■ Achieving a successful implementation

Following the phases, steps and tasks outlined above or using some other systems development methodology is not enough to guarantee the success of a new sales and marketing system. At least three other elements must be in place, which are:

- senior management sponsorship and support
- good project management
- the involvement of marketing and sales users.

Senior management sponsorship and support

While small-scale IT projects can often be delivered with little senior-level involvement or sponsorship, large-scale IT systems are different because they typically involve reengineering internal business processes and procedures and changing the way people go about their day-to-day work. Often, they will also have an impact on the way the company interacts with its suppliers and customers. Without active involvement and support from senior levels within the organisation, such large-scale projects will fail to achieve their full objectives. For major projects many organisations will appoint a senior executive or director as the official project sponsor, with full responsibility for the successful implementation of the project. In some cases, the project sponsor will act in this capacity on a full-time basis.

Good project management

On an ongoing basis throughout the project, the following management activities will increase the overall chances of success:

■ *Tracking and resolving issues*. During a project, a multitude of different issues will arise. These issues may be technical or may relate to aspects of the business which need to be resolved by marketing managers or general business managers. A clear system is required for logging, tracking and addressing issues which might otherwise remain unresolved and cause problems when the system is rolled out to the marketing users.

■ *Monitoring project progress and risk*. Another integral component of good project management is the ongoing monitoring of progress and project risks. Any project to develop a marketing or customer information system requires a project manager who understands the management mechanisms of deadlines, milestones, progress reports, progress meetings, escalation procedures for issues which cannot be immediately resolved at his level, and steering groups to monitor overall progress.

■ *Establishing a 'project office'*. On large projects, the establishment of a 'project office' is an important consideration. A project office contains all the project plans, files, notes, deliverables and any other relevant material relating to the project. It is usually run by a project administrator, who not only maintains the library of documents but also acts as overall controller for the project costs and project schedule. If the project starts to run behind schedule or over budget, the project administrator informs the project manager and senior management within the organisation. On smaller projects, a formal project office is not required and the project administrator role is often carried out by the project manager.

The involvement of marketing and sales users

For any computer system it is important to involve the eventual users in its development; this is particularly true of sales and marketing systems. User involvement in all stages of the development will ensure that the system will meet the needs of the users. All too often, computer systems are developed and 'handed over' to the users without their full involvement or 'buy-in'. It is also important that users are involved very early on in the process, particularly in the design phase which has a major impact on the rest of the project.

CONCLUSION

Typically, IT systems are developed in five phases: feasibility study, requirements analysis, design, implementation and maintenance. Within each phase, there are many different steps and tasks which are usually carried out sequentially. For example, within the implementation phase, the main steps are programming and configuration, testing, conversion and installation. Many people might envisage that most of the implementation phase would be devoted to programming. In fact, the testing step may require as much effort as the programming step. Marketing and sales information systems can be developed from scratch (custom built) or developed using one of the growing number of marketing and sales software packages that are available today. Software packages can be cheaper, less risky and quicker to implement, but have their drawbacks as well. The primary drawback is that the vast majority of software packages will require modification before they can meet all the requirements of a particular marketing department or salesforce. The development of any marketing or sales information system can be a time-consuming, complex and difficult undertaking. Senior management sponsorship, good project management and the involvement of marketing and sales (especially in the design phase) will increase the chances of the development being successful.

ASSIGNMENT QUESTIONS

1 What is the systems development life cycle and what are its five key phases?
2 Choose one of the five phases and discuss its steps and tasks in more detail.
3 Describe the pros and cons of using packaged software.
4 Is senior-level sponsorship important in the development of a sales and marketing system and, if so, why?
5 Discuss why it is so important to have the final users of a system involved in the early design phases.

Case study

THE LONDON STOCK EXCHANGE

It might have been a scene in Bombay, or Moscow. Hundreds of workers, many of them middle-aged women, sitting huddled over long lines of wooden desks. Their job? To sift through an avalanche of paper (they got through more than 1 million pieces in a busy week) in a giant game of snap, matching cheques from buyers of company shares with receipts from those who have sold them. But this was no ramshackle emerging stockmarket. It was how share trades were settled on the London Stock Exchange (LSE), the world's third busiest, prior to July 1996. Similarly, in a vault in Islington, north London, sat a pile of paper representing £120 billion of share certificates held in custody on behalf of large investors by the Royal Bank of Scotland. Since July, that pile started dwindling as shares were dispatched from the vault, never to return. This was because London's much-awaited paperless share-settlement system, known as Crest, had been plugged in and switched on. Even the crustiest of British institutions, it seems, cannot resist change. Along with the 300 settlement jobs which disappeared when Crest was turned on, the exchange said it would cut a further 90 jobs by the end of 1997, leaving it with 550 staff; in 1991 the LSE employed nearly four times this number. 'In five years' time, 95 per cent of the settlements will be electronic, and the other 5 per cent may create 25 per cent of our costs,' says a broker. The introduction of Crest was long overdue. Other European exchanges had been investing heavily in building electronic share-settlement systems for years.

In 1993, the LSE's previous attempt to build one, called Taurus, collapsed after the exchange had spent four years and £75 million on it. The collapse had been devastating for the Exchange. Despite the fact that rumours had been circulating for weeks, few people believed that the Taurus development would actually be binned. Thus, when the official announcement was released by the LSE on the afternoon of 11 March 1993, it was met by widespread incredulity, followed by anger. Those reactions were easy to understand. If, as the Exchange claimed, the problems stemmed from the original design laid down in 1989, why was this only realised at the testing stage? That design became unmanageable as soon as it tried to meet all of the requirements of the large number of brokers, banks and other institutions involved in the complex process. How then could things have been allowed to go on for so long, and why were the participants forced to spend so much time and money chasing an ideal which was apparently unattainable from the outset? There were a lot of knee-jerk reactions in the immediate aftermath of the debacle but what were the actual reasons behind the failure?

As the recriminations began to fly, registrars were being blamed for blocking the original proposals for a central register database. At the time, most companies used a service registrar, the market for which was dominated by three banks: Barclays, Lloyds and NatWest. A few companies still kept their register in-house, often for historical reasons or particular organisational requirements. But the registrars denied that they should shoulder the blame for the way Taurus became such an unwieldy beast, and questioned whether the removal of competition in registrar services was in the interests of their customers, the listed companies. Once regarded as something of a backwater, share registration was shaken up by the big privatisations of the 1980s, when systems had to be updated to cope with the volumes involved in those flotations. Taurus threatened yet more change to the registrar business. Dave Wilcox, director of Barclays registrars, hit back at criticism of registrars. 'Registrars have been working very hard trying to make sure that companies and their shareholders were properly protected – I don't think we have been obstructive. We helped to develop a system where companies knew who their shareholders were, and to protect shareholders' rights.' John Hutchinson, controller of IT projects at NatWest, thought that Taurus was conceived without much thought for what a registrar, effectively at the back end of the process, needed to do. Out of the general despair following the scrapping of Taurus, there was at least one positive side. If the LSE had problems at the centre, then it was good that they acted then rather than struggle on with more testing. It would be nice to be able to salvage something from the software developed for Taurus, but it was more important to look at the roots of the problem afresh.

Altogether, the less-ambitious Crest project cost £29 million and was delivered in 1996 on time and to budget, which was a major achievement for an IT project of its size. In addition to securing the LSE's position as a leading European stockmarket, paperless settlement has brought additional benefits. First, dealing has become more efficient. A certificate previously moved through an average of 25 pairs of hands each time it was traded. Second, share dealing has become cheaper. Talisman, the previous paper-based system owned and operated by the LSE, charged the industry around £55 million a year for its services. Crest costs less than £30 million a year.

Source: Adapted from 'Silencing the bull' and 'The crying game', *Banking Technology* (April 1993); 'Select and settle', *The Banker* (January 1996); 'Settled at last', *The Economist* (13 July 1996); and 'Farewell to mounds of paper', *Financial Times* (15 July 1996).

Questions

1 Why did the Taurus project fail?

2 Could anything have been done in 1991, 1992 or 1993 to save it?

3 What lessons can be learnt from the failure of the implementation of Taurus?

4 What do you believe were the main reasons the implementation of Crest succeeded?

5 What is the impact (both positive and negative) of information technology on the LSE?

Case study

BLOOMINGDALE'S BY MAIL

'Bloomingdale's Retail Marketing Services database consists of the customer charge card master file. This file includes more than one million active charge customers who are concentrated in our 14 trading areas. This file forms the basis from which all of our efforts are generated to target and segment our customers, as well as to identify our new prospects. Originally this file was simply a mailing list developed for billing purposes. But in the early '80s, the direct marketing experts were charged with forming Bloomingdale's By Mail. Our mail order catalogue counterpart is a free-standing business within the Bloomingdale family. It's an $80 million business. But the people at Bloomie's By Mail recognised the potential value of the customer list. The Bloomingdale's customer database was neither easy nor inexpensive. It involved a major commitment on the part of management to spend the time and money necessary to turn literally millions of bits and bytes of disorganised information about our customers and their transactions at our stores, into a comprehensive collection of interrelated data. The commitment involved moving the credit and transactional files out of the store to a computer service bureau so that the raw data could be made both manageable and accessible.

'Four years ago, the Bloomingdale's customer database was returned from mail order to the retail side to be used primarily as a mailing tool by Sales Promotion, enabling us to distribute 40 catalogues a year through direct mail promotions, more than 250 individual store and department events via solo mail, as well as mail plans for 100 cosmetic events, not to mention the potential for hundreds more promotions. The original aim was to significantly reduce our in-the-mail advertising costs. Since that time, the role of our customer database has continued to expand, turning this proven mailing tool into an effective guide to targeted marketing. The creation of a database is within the reach of all companies and is not limited just to those with the prestige and resources of Bloomingdale's. It is a way of marketing that in many ways must be easier to implement in a more timely fashion by the smaller volume retailer or vendor that may not be as encumbered by bureaucracy or the political minefields of larger volume stores. An additional payoff is that the cost of creating a database from a smaller amount of data is significantly less, although of course there is some leverage to be exercised in the manipulation of massive amounts of data found in files the size of mine.

'THE FIRST STEP: The creation of a database of course is the first step in developing a database marketing programme. At Bloomingdale's, the raw data for the database was originally culled from information from our point-of-sale files, the information that comes off the register in the store that becomes the base for the customer's credit history and, of course, that same information is then passed onto the merchants to enable them to do their reordering and their merchandise planning. In other words, I'm recycling information that the store already owns.

'STEP TWO: Getting all this data into working shape involves commitment, time, expense and staffing. The data in a company's files needs to be put into a workable format, which requires the combined professional expertise of an information systems expert and a savvy detail-oriented retailer. Through their dialogue the two delineate the specifications for a database that's uniquely formulated to meet their specific needs.

'THE THIRD STEP: But having armed ourselves with some fairly substantial information about our retail customers, we decided it was definitely worthwhile to add even more data to our files in order to fill in the detail. The information obtained from consumers who apply for accounts and credit cards is invaluable as a database enhancement. We also enhanced our database with geo-demographic information available from outside vendors. It's relatively inexpensive and contains, for example, statistics on age and income, presence of children, home ownership, hobbies, other interests and phone numbers.

'THIRD-PARTY PARTNERSHIPS: Knowing the age, income and demographic profile of our customers positions us for partnerships. For example, we tied in with Nissan and launched the Infiniti car in the Bloomingdale's markets. Without the data that we had from our enhanced file, we never would have been able to convince Infiniti that we were a valid outlet for them to market the very high-end car. Infiniti even gave us some cars to use as give-aways. So the cross-marketing capabilities are amazing when you have a well-developed enhanced file.

'CUSTOMER LOYALTY: Unfortunately, we occasionally close a store. But that doesn't necessarily mean losing the customer. They are your customer: you can still maintain them.

'I think that if you don't use database marketing, you're going to find yourself in the dinosaur room at the Retail Museum of History. I think all marketing executives should join associations like the Direct Marketing Association, read the trade papers, consult many books, set long-term and short-term goals for yourself and your company and talk to the experts. Benefit by mistakes that experts know their clients have made, so you don't make the same mistake. Also add database experts to your staff; make sure there are database people, introduce yourself to your credit people and MIS people. You might find you like each other. And I think if you're like Bloomingdale's, be comfortable with the fact that you need to go outside for services. Lastly, follow the inspirational message: Long journeys start with small steps.'

Source: Adapted from F. Smith, 'Bloomingdale's By Mail', *Direct Marketing*, September 1992.

Questions

1 Describe how the customer database had developed since Bloomingdale's By Mail was formed in the 1980s. Based on what you have learnt in previous chapters of this book, and from your own experiences, is this typical?

2 Compare and contrast the three steps outlined in the case study above with the seven steps describing the development of a customer database in Chapter 4.

3 'I think that if you don't use database marketing, you're going to find yourself in the dinosaur room at the Retail Museum of History.' Discuss.

References

[1] Lucas, H.C. (1985). *The Analysis, Design and Implementation of Information Systems*. 3rd edn, Singapore: McGraw-Hill.
[2] Flaatten, P.O., McCubbrey, D.J., O'Riordan, P.D. and Burgess, K. (1989). *Foundations of Business Systems*. Orlando: The Dryden Press.
[3] Gooding, C. (1995). 'A difficult sell to the sales staff', *Financial Times*, 1 November.
[4] Black, G. (1995). 'Flexible tracking system saves £5m a year', *Financial Times*, 1 November.

GLOSSARY OF TERMS

386/486   Earlier generations of microprocessing **chip** used in **PC**s. Manufactured by US company Intel.

3GL/4GL   *Third-generation/fourth-generation languages.* 'High-level' computer languages that enable programmers to program more quickly and more effectively.

ABC   *Activity-based costing.* A method of cost allocation which allows marketing managers to obtain a more accurate and realistic view of how much a product costs to manufacture.

ACD   *Automatic call distribution system.* ACDs are sophisticated telephone exchange systems designed to handle and route large volumes of incoming calls to customer service representatives (**CSR**s) in a **call centre**.

ADSL   *Asynchronous digital subscriber line.* Emerging technology for sending video and high-**bandwidth data** across existing copper wire networks without the need to upgrade to **fibre-optic** cable.

advertising-on-demand   The term given to the increased control that **IT**-driven trends in television give viewers over the amount and type of advertising that they watch.

affinity cards   Loyalty schemes based on **applications** of **plastic card** technology.

AI   *Artificial intelligence.* The actions resulting from a computer program which, if carried out by a human, would be regarded as intelligent.

analogue   A signal that varies smoothly and continuously over time. For example, voice is an analogue signal and the output from a telephone microphone is an analogue voltage signal. Opposite to **digital**.

animation   The computer-assisted generation of animation sequences for **multimedia** advertising. Also see **virtual reality**.

application   Or *application program.* The **software** that fulfils a specific business or marketing function such as sales management, payroll, general ledger.

ATM (1)   *Asynchronous transfer mode.* Emerging **broadband** technology which allows high volumes of **data** to be transmitted across a network.

ATM (2)   *Automated teller machine.* Machines at banks and building societies which provide cash and allow account enquiries, but which are increasingly providing other functions such as bill payment. Also see **kiosk**.

BACS   *Bulk automated clearing system.* An electronic funds transfer (**EFT**) **application** for payment of salaries and other relatively low-value financial transactions.

bandwidth   Loosely used to describe the **data**-carrying **capacity** of a **telecommunications** system, usually measured in terms of bits per second (**bps**).

banner   A form of **Internet** advertising whereby an **icon** or logo is placed in the corner of the user's screen, usually with an invitation to click on the logo to obtain further information.

bar-code   A code in the form of a series of parallel lines of different widths which is used to enter **data** into a computer. For example, the bar-codes of items bought in a supermarket are scanned at the checkout, providing cost information immediately to the till and providing management, marketing and reordering information for store managers.

BBS *Bulletin board service.* A service for disseminating information and promoting discussion on a particular topic over a network such as the **Internet** or an **on-line service provider**.

bit An abbreviation of *binary digit*, the most basic form of digital information used by computers. Bits are either '0' or '1'. Eight bits make a **byte**.

bps *Bits per second.* The unit of measurement for the rate at which **data** is transferred, e.g. the fastest **modems** transmit **data** at 28 800 bps.

brand manager A marketing manager with responsibility for all aspects of a particular brand or group of brands.

broadband Loosely used to describe a high-**capacity** (or large-**bandwidth**) **data-transmission** system. Typically, speeds higher than 2 million **bps** are regarded as broadband. Opposite to **narrowband**.

broadcast A term used to describe a one-way signal sent indiscriminately to all receivers within range, such as a television, radio or cable.

browser The software that is required to navigate around the World Wide Web (**WWW**) and 'surf' the **Internet**.

bug Commonly used word used to describe a problem in the logic of a **software** program.

business analyst Member of the **IT** department who can analyse the business requirements of a company and translate them into practical technical requirements and sensible implementation plans.

byte Eight **bits** of **data**. The term byte is used for measuring storage **capacity** of computer disks, tapes or **CD-ROM**s.

cable The fixed-connection (as opposed to wireless) means of **telecommunication**. The three generic types of cable are **twisted pair**, **coaxial** and **fibre optic.**

cable modem A type of high-**capacity modem** used in conjunction with cable television to bring the **Internet** into people's homes.

CAD/CAM *Computer-aided design/computer-aided manufacturing.* Examples of **IT applications** used in manufacturing which are collectively known as computer-integrated manufacturing (**CIM**).

call centre A centralised facility for handling large numbers of customer calls, usually employing technologies such as **ACD, IVR, customer databases** and **CTI**.

capacity (1) The **transmission** capacity of a **telecommunications** system, sometimes referred to as **bandwidth.**

capacity (2) The **data**-storage capacity of a computer disk, tape or **CD-ROM**.

CBT *Computer-based training.* Interactive training programmes that are delivered through **PCs** or through the use of **multimedia**.

CD *Compact disk.* An optical storage device from which **digital data** is read by means of a laser. Usually refers to a disk that stores music.

CD-ROM *Compact disk – read-only memory.* A variation of the **CD** which is used in computers. The ROM refers to the fact that the **data** can not be changed once the CD-ROM has been created.

cellular The term used to describe a series of overlapping cells within which a base station relays signals to **mobile telephone** users. Also see **GSM**.

chip A computer chip, sometimes known as an **integrated circuit.** It is made from a thin wafer of semi-conductor material such as silicon, which has been chemically processed to give it particular electrical characteristics such as storage, circuits etc.

CIM *Computer-integrated manufacturing.* A manufacturing term used to describe IT applications such as **CAD/CAM, MRP** and **MRPII.**

client/server   The most recent wave of **software** computing which allows workload to be shared between a powerful central computer (the server) and a **PC** (the client). Typically, the server is a **mini-computer** but can also be another, more powerful, **PC**, **workstation** or **mainframe**. Sometimes referred to as **distributed computing**.

coaxial   A type of **cable** used for long-distance telephone lines and for carrying cable television signals, they have a higher **bandwidth** than **twisted-pair cable**.

compression technology   An **application** of **IT** for reducing the **capacity** required to store or transmit **data**, e.g. **MPEG**.

conference room pilot   A variation of **prototyping** which is carried out with all the key users of an **IT** system in a controlled environment.

contact management systems   **Software** modules which allow sales representatives to maintain all significant contacts with their customers.

convergence   The growing tendency for new technologies such as telephone, television and computer to merge.

conversion   The translation of paper-based information into electronic format for use in a new computer system. Also refers to the translation of all electronic information on old systems into the correct format for the new computer system.

credit card   A **plastic card** which allows the cardholder to make transactions against a credit account, up to an agreed limit.

CSR   *Customer service representative.* The name given to a human operator in a **call centre** who answers customer queries.

CTI   *Computer telephony integration.* CTI is the ability to retrieve customer **data** from a **customer database** and deliver it to an operator in a **call centre** while the operator is handling that customer's telephone call.

customer database   A **database** of customer information that can be used for operational purposes (e.g. customer service, billing) or for analytic purposes (e.g. **data mining**).

cybermarketing   A term used to describe the new forms of marketing in **cyberspace**.

cyberspace   The virtual world of the **Internet**.

data   Facts, concepts or instructions that are presented in a formalised way and which can be communicated, interpreted or processed by humans or computers.

data mart   A smaller, cheaper version of a **data warehouse** which is sometimes confined to a single department rather than the full enterprise.

data mining   A technique for sifting through huge amounts of **data**, using powerful computers, to find hidden nuggets of information in the form of statistical correlations.

data warehouse   A **database** which holds high-level operational, historic and customer **data** for the entire organisation and makes it available for decision-making purposes. Also see **data mart**.

database   A collection of interrelated **data,** stored and indexed in a particular fashion which allows users to recall or analyse it easily.

database marketing   Refers to all uses of **databases** for marketing purposes. Includes, but is not confined to, the area of **direct marketing**.

debit card   A **plastic card** which is used to make transactions, the payment for which is immediately debited to the cardholder's bank account.

design   The third phase in the **systems development life cycle** when the functional and technical components of a computer system are designed.

dial-up   The use of telephone lines or **ISDN** to connect a computer to a service. The opposite to a permanent connection such as a **leased line**.

digital   The representation of **data** by means of binary digits, or **bits**. Modern computers and high-speed **telecommunications** are based on the manipulation and **transmission** of digital **data**. Opposite to **analogue**.

direct mail   The issuing of advertising material directly to prospective customers by mail.

direct marketing   The term used to describe marketing which is targeted at specific individuals. Includes **direct mail**, **direct-response advertising** and **telemarketing**.

direct-response advertising   A form of **direct marketing** which involves the issue of marketing messages by any means other than by mail, requiring the prospective customer to respond by mail, telephone or other means.

distributed computing   See **client/server**.

document image processing   A technology for replacing paper files by scanning and storing electronic images of documents. Often used as part of a **workflow** system.

DOS   *Disk operating system*. A proprietary set of programs, from Microsoft, that operates most PCs.

DP   *Data processing*. **IT** departments used to be referred to as DP departments in the past, as this term reflected more accurately the type of work that the department carried out.

DSS   *Decision support system*. A subset of the broader category of **MIS** which applies to the analysis and resolution of semi-structured problems.

DVD   *Digital video disk*. An emerging technology which has eight times the **capacity** of a **CD-ROM** and which can be re-recorded.

e-cash   *Electronic cash*. Another term for **electronic money**. Also a proprietary digital money scheme pioneered by the Dutch software company DigiCash.

e-mail   *Electronic mail*. A means of sending text messages to individuals or groups using a computer network such as the **Internet**.

ECDL   *European computer driving licence*. An EU initiative to train and qualify people in the basics of computer **applications.**

EDI   *Electronic data interchange*. The use of computer networks and predefined message standards for the automatic (computer-to-computer) exchange of trading data. EDI is used for tasks such as ordering and invoicing.

EFT   *Electronic funds transfer*. The transfer of funds by electronic means, using predefined standards such as **SWIFT** or **BACS**. Also see **electronic payment systems** and **EFTPoS**.

EFTPoS   *Electronic funds transfer at point of sale*. Refers to the transfer of funds by electronic means in a retail outlet or shop, usually through the use of a **plastic card** and associated card-reading technology. Also see **electronic payment systems** and **EPoS**.

EIS   *Executive information system*. Management information systems designed for use by senior executives. Also see **DSS**.

electronic commerce   General term for a variety of different methods of conducting business by electronic means. Also see **electronic payment systems**.

electronic money   The replacement of traditional cash by electronic means. Also see **electronic payment systems**, **electronic purse** and **e-cash**.

electronic payment systems   The collective term for **IT applications** to support payment, including **EFT**, **EFTPoS**, **EDI** and **electronic money**.

electronic purse   A form of **electronic money** for making low-value purchases in the form of a pre-paid **smart card**. Also referred to as change card, cash card, electronic wallet, pre-paid card and stored value card.

EMV   *Europay Mastercard VISA*. An emerging international standard for **smart card** payments.

EPoS   *Electronic point of sale*. Point of sale refers to the location at which payment transactions are captured by card-reading devices and product information is captured using bar-code-scanning equipment. Also see **EFTPoS**.

fax-on-demand   A telephone and **IT application** which enables requested information to be faxed automatically to the customer.

feasibility study   The first phase in the **systems development life cycle**.

fibre optic   A type of cable made from very fine fibres of glass which are used for transmitting **data** in the form of pulses of light. Fibre-optic cables have a very high **data transmission capacity** or **bandwidth**.

floppy disk   Portable electronic storage device for use with a **PC**. Also see **hard disk**.

FMCG   *Fast-moving consumer goods*. FMCG products are those items typically found on supermarket shelves.

functional specification   A document that is produced during the design stage of an **IT** project which describes the functional workings of the computer system, including workflows, processes etc. Also see **technical specification.**

fuzzy logic   An **application** of artificial intelligence (**AI**).

geo-demographic segmentation   A traditional approach to customer segmentation based on geographic variables such as country and postcode, and demographic variables such as age, sex and marital status. Also see **psychographic segmentation**.

GIS   *Geographic information system*. An integrated system designed to capture, manage, manipulate, analyse, model and display **data** geographically. The three major categories of GIS are true GIS, **mapping systems** and **presentation graphics systems**.

groupware   Software that helps a group of workers to share the knowledge needed to do their jobs. One of the leading groupware products is *Lotus Notes*. Often used in conjunction with an **intranet**.

GSM   *Global system mobile*. A European (and increasingly global) **telecommunications** standard for **mobile telephones**. Also see **cellular**.

GUI   *Graphical user interface*. Pronounced 'goo-ey'. The 'look and feel' of old computer screens was not very appealing – white or green text on a black background. GUI is the term used to describe the new 'look and feel' of modern computer systems. This includes the use of **WIMPs** as well as colour.

hard disk   The storage device on a **PC**. Also see **floppy disk**.

hardware   The electrical and mechanical components of an **IT** system including disk drives, monitors, processor etc.

HDTV   *High-definition television*. A new television technology characterised by its very high picture resolution.

helpdesk   The term given to any central, telephone-based support facility.

home banking   Conducting banking transactions such as electronic funds transfer (**EFT**) from home or work by using a **PC**.

home shopping   The use of **interactive television** (or **PC**) to purchase goods from home.

HTML   *Hypertext mark-up language*. The computer language used to create documents and pages on the World Wide Web (**WWW**). Also see **hypertext**.

HTTP   *Hypertext transfer protocol*. The standard method of transferring files across the World Wide Web (**WWW**). Also the first four letters of any **Internet** address.

hybrid marketing   The term which refers to the management of marketing through a number of different distribution channels, usually supported through **IT**.

hypertext   A body of text where some or all the information is linked. Also see **surfing**.

icon   A small pictorial representation of an action or a command on a computer screen, e.g. a wastepaper basket (meaning delete) or a filing cabinet (meaning file). Also see **WIMPS**.

implementation   The phase in the **systems development life cycle** when the computer system is programmed, tested and installed.

infobahn   Another term for the **information superhighway**.

information society   The phrase used to describe the new society that is beginning to emerge today which is based on the wide availability and usage of information, across an **information superhighway**.

information superhighway   The **hardware**, **software** and **broadband telecommunications** infrastructure that will allow universities, businesses, government, communities and individuals to share information. Also see **infobahn**.

integrated circuit   A complete electronic circuit comprising transistors, resistors, diodes etc. which is constructed on a single thin piece of semiconductor material such as silicon. See **chip**.

intelligent agent   A software program designed to take on the time-consuming work of searching the World Wide Web (**WWW**), **intranet** or other electronic location for specific items.

interactive television   A two-way service that offers **digital multimedia applications** on a television set, e.g. **home shopping**, **home banking** and **video-on-demand**.

Internet   The 'network of networks'. A series of inter-linked networks spanning the globe which are used by both companies and individuals for **e-mail**, transferring files and a multitude of other functions. The **multimedia** version of the Internet is known as the World Wide Web (**WWW**).

intranet   A private, or internal, version of the **Internet** which uses the same language and standards. Also see **groupware**.

ISDN   *Integrated services digital network*. An integrated **digital** network used for more than one service, e.g. telephony and **data** transfer.

ISP   *Internet service provider.* An organisation that provides a range of **Internet** services to businesses and individuals. Also see **on-line service providers**.

IT   *Information technology.* A generic term encompassing a range of technologies to capture, store, process and transmit information. Includes the three main technology groups of **hardware**, **software** and **telecommunications.**

IVR   *Interactive voice response.* See **VRU**.

JIT   *Just-in-time.* A production or manufacturing technique which minimises the levels of raw materials, inventory and finished goods held by the company and maximises the ability of the company to respond rapidly to changes in demand.

kiosk   *Or multimedia kiosk.* A **multimedia** self-service outlet operating up to 24 hours a day, providing value-added services and information. May also include live video access to a human operator in a **call centre** for more complex queries.

knowledge worker   A new breed of professional who utilises the knowledge captured electronically by his or her information-based employer, to carry out work more productively than a counterpart in a traditional organisation.

LAN   *Local area network.* A computer network for connecting **PCs** within a limited distance of each other, e.g. within a building or within the same floor of a building. Also see **WAN**.

lead management systems   Software modules which allow sales representatives to capture all information relating to the development and management of a sales lead.

leased line   A means of buying **telecommunications bandwidth** in bulk. Instead of paying the **PTT** or network provider by the minute, a fixed amount of **capacity** is provided and a flat annual fee is charged regardless of usage.

legacy systems   A commonly used, if somewhat pejorative, term used to describe the old, inflexible (but often extremely reliable) systems that operate in many organisations today.

loyalty card   A **plastic card** used to support a loyalty programme.

magnetic stripe card   A type of **plastic card** which has information encoded onto a black magnetic stripe on the back of the card. Credit and **debit cards** are typically magnetic stripe cards.

mainframe   A large computer which requires its own large air-conditioned room. IBM was the first, and is still the largest, manufacturer of mainframe computers. See **mini-computer** and **micro-computer**.

maintenance   The final phase in the **systems development life cycle** when computer systems are maintained and enhanced.

mapping systems   A form of **GIS** which is less sophisticated than a true GIS but more sophisticated than **presentation graphics systems**.

massively parallel processors   See **supercomputer**.

memory   The memory of a computer is the storage area which is used to store the software that operates the computer.

memory card   A type of **plastic card** which has information encoded into a **chip** which is embedded into the card. The chip is not a **micro-processor** and therefore the memory card is not regarded as a true **smart card**.

micro-computer   Small computer which is designed to be used only by a single person at a time. The first micro-computer was not portable. A later version, known as the personal computer or **PC**, could be carried around by its user. Also see **mini-computer** and **mainframe**.

micro-processor   A **micro-computer** with all its processing facilities on a single **chip**. Typically refers to the central processing unit in a **PC** or the **chip** on a **smart card**.

mini-computer   A medium-sized computer, larger than a **PC** or **micro-computer**, but smaller than a **mainframe**. Capable of supporting tens of users who were attached to the mini-computer by means of terminals, or **PC**s. The first mini-computer was invented in 1960 by Digital Equipment Corporation.

minitel   A generic term for the range of terminals provided by the French (or other) **PTTs** to telephone subscribers to access a **videotex** service.

MIS   *Management information systems*. Information systems for helping management to understand how their company is performing and to make better-informed management decisions. Also see **DSS**.

MkIS   *Marketing information system*. A formal system designed with the objective of creating an organised, regular flow of relevant information for use and analysis by marketing decision makers.

mobile telephone   The increasingly popular form of the telephone which does not rely on a fixed connection to the telephone exchange. Also see **cellular** and **GSM**.

modem   *MODulator-DEModulator*. A device which transforms a **digital** signal to an **analogue** signal (so that computer **data** can be transmitted across a telephone line, for example) and back again.

mouse   A navigation device attached to, or part of, a computer which the user moves to make the cursor on the screen move.

MPEG   *Motion Picture Expert Group*. The consortium of **hardware**, **software** and publishing interests that creates international standards for the **compression** of video and other **digital** signals.

MRP   *Materials requirement planning*. The use of **IT** to plan the type of materials required in the production process. Also see **CIM**.

MRPII   *Manufacturing resource planning*. The integration of **MRP** with other manufacturing processes such as production scheduling and shop floor control. Also see **CIM**.

MSP   *Marketing and sales productivity systems*. An extension to the concept of **database marketing** and **MkIS**.

multimedia   The combination of text, charts, drawings, sound, animation, voice or motion pictures in a single medium such as a computer demonstration or high-impact presentation.

narrowband   Loosely used to describe a low-**capacity** (or low-**bandwidth**) **data-transmission**

system. Typically, speeds up 2 million **bps** are regarded as narrowband. Opposite to **broadband**.

neural network   A type of computer technology whereby the computer is 'trained' to solve a problem in a similar fashion to a human brain. Often used synonymously with artificial intelligence (**AI**).

node   The access point to a computer network such as the **Internet**.

object-oriented   A type of computer programming which allows small programs or blocks of computer code, known as objects, to be reused, thereby increasing the productivity of the programmers.

OCR   *Optical character recognition.* OCR scanners are used to read characters (letters, numbers) from paper into a computer system.

OLAP   *On-line analytical processing.* A term used to describe the type of analysis that is carried out using modern **DSS** and **data-mining** techniques.

on-line   Direct access to computer-based **data** files and operations systems via a **PC** or computer terminal. Also see **real-time**.

on-line service provider   An organisation that provides commercial on-line services such as financial information to businesses and individuals. These services may be through a dial-up facility or across the **Internet**. Also see Internet service provider (**ISP**).

operating system   The control software on a computer that runs the **application software** on the computer.

parallel processing   A special type of computer design which allows very large numbers of numerical calculations to be carried out simultaneously. Used extensively in **data mining** and similar **applications**.

pay-per-view   Cable television programmes that are charged on a viewing subscription basis.

PBX/PABX   *Private branch exchange/private automatic branch exchange.* Telephone exchange systems which are the forerunners of the more modern **ACD** systems.

PC   *Personal computer.* Also known as **micro-computer**. The most powerful PCs are known as **workstations**.

Pentium   The latest generation of microprocessing **chip** used in **PCs**. Manufactured by US company Intel.

PIN   *Personal identification number.* A password which is used in conjunction with **plastic cards** such as **credit cards**, **ATM** cards etc.

plastic card   A form of storage device that can be used for a variety of functions including money withdrawal, loyalty schemes, entry to secure buildings and electronic payments. The four main types of plastic card are **bar-code** cards, **magnetic stripe cards**, **memory cards** and **smart cards**.

platform   Computer jargon that refers to the **hardware** on which **software** runs.

POTS   *Plain old telephone service.* Refers to the traditional, low-**capacity**, **telecommunications** medium of **twisted-pair cable** provided to homes and businesses by the **PTT**.

predictive dialling   A telephone **application** for automatically dialling customers or prospective customers using a list of telephone numbers stored on a **customer database**.

presentation graphics systems   The least sophisticated form of **GIS**. Also see **mapping systems**.

project office   A facility on major systems implementation projects for centrally managing all project plans, files, notes and other relevant project-related material.

prototyping   The production of a working model of an information technology system. Prototyping is carried out during the **design** stage of the **systems development life cycle**.

psychographic segmentation   A newer form of customer segmentation based on variables such as lifestyle, attitude and personality. Also see **geo-demographic** segmentation.

PTT *Post, telegraph and telephone* companies. A name used to describe the main telecommunications companies such as BT, Deutsche Telekom, etc.

real-time Refers to the immediate processing of a transaction carried out by a computer user. Opposite to batch. Also see **on-line**.

relational database A form of **database** where the information is held in tables which are linked to each other. **Customer databases** are typically relational databases.

relationship marketing The use of customer information and **database marketing** techniques to enhance a company's knowledge of its customer base, with the ultimate objective of increasing their lifetime value to the company.

requirements analysis Phase in the **systems-development life cycle** when the high-level needs of the marketing or business users are gathered prior to the **design** phase of a new computer system.

server A computer that links a **PC** to a network such as a **LAN** or the **Internet**, or acts as the main computer in a **client/server** operation.

SFA *Salesforce automation.* A variety of computer and **IT applications** for improving the productivity of sales representatives.

smart card A type of **plastic card** which has a **chip** embedded into it which allows it to hold more information and carry out many more functions than the more common **magnetic stripe card**.

software The **programs** used in a **data**-processing or information system.

STM *Simulated test marketing.* A quicker, cheaper, IT-enabled form of test marketing.

supercomputer A special type of computer designed to carry out hundreds of millions of instructions per second. Used in **data mining applications**. Also known as **massively parallel processors**.

surfing The popular term given to the movement around different pages of the World Wide Web (**WWW**) using **hypertext** links.

SWIFT *Society for Worldwide Interbank Financial Telecommunications.* An international financial transaction network, as well as the standard for such transactions. SWIFT is an example of electronic funds transfer (**EFT**).

systems development life cycle The sequence of phases, tasks and steps that are followed when an information technology system is developed. The five phases in the life cycle are **feasibility study**, **requirements analysis**, **design**, **implementation** and **maintenance**.

systems integrator A consulting or **IT** company that is hired to implement an integrated software solution for a customer.

technical specification A document that is produced during the design stage of an **IT** project which describes various technical specifications for the computer system, including **database**, file structures, input and output devices, computer processor, networks, security etc. Also see **functional specification.**

telecommunications Refers to the wide variety of communicating via electronic and electromagnetic means and covers applications of **IT** as diverse as telephone, television, computer and satellite.

telemarketing A type of **direct marketing** conducted by telephone. Telemarketing can be inbound, for example in response to a direct-response advertising campaign, as well as outbound.

teletext A one-way broadcast information service accessed through a television using a special keypad. Examples of teletext include Ceefax and Oracle in the UK. Also see **videotex**.

teleworking Working remotely from home using computer and telephone technology. A person who teleworks is known as a teleworker.

tracking software Software for recording and tracking all customer interactions with a company, or for tracking customer service problems from initial logging to final resolution.

transmission   In **telecommunications**, transmission is the act of sending information in an unchanged form, from one place to another, by electronic means.

twisted pair   A type of cable using two pieces of insulated copper wire. Twisted-pair cables are typically used in telephone systems and have a relatively low **data-transmission capacity**.

UNIX   A type of **operating system**.

VCR   *Videocassette recorder.* A device used for recording, playing and storing video information such as television programmes and movies on tape.

videoconferencing   A method of holding teleconferences using a **telecommunications** network, where both parties can see and hear each other.

video-on-demand   An interactive (two-way) facility which allows users to select and play videos which are held on a central system, as opposed to on a local **VCR**. A cheaper and easier service to deliver is near-video-on-demand.

videotex   A two-way information service, such as Prestel in the UK and Teletel in France, which is provided over a specialised terminal. Also see **teletext**.

virtual reality   The use of interactive three-dimensional multimedia to create a realistic, but computer-generated, world for computer users. Can be immersive (using headset and gloves) or non-immersive (using 3D modelling techniques on a computer screen).

voicemail   A technology for leaving voice messages for individuals or groups of individuals. The voice equivalent of **e-mail**.

voice-response systems   A collective term for any telephone-based response system such as **IVR** or **VRU**.

VRU   *Voice-response unit.* Sometimes known as **IVR** (interactive voice response). VRUs are used to automate certain customer service tasks such as obtaining customer account numbers or dispensing account balances.

WAN   *Wide area network.* Network that links users across a wide geographic area. Also see **LAN**.

WIMPs   *Windows, icons, mouse and pull-down menus.* The main components of a graphical user interface (**GUI**).

Windows/Windows 95   The **GUI** operating system from Microsoft which is used in the vast majority of **PCs** that are bought today. Also see **WIMPs**.

workflow   The term used to describe the incorporation of processes and procedures into a computer system.

workstation   Another name for a powerful **PC** at the top end of the market. Usually refers to a **PC** with good graphical capabilities.

WWW   *World Wide Web.* Also know simply as the Web. It is the **multimedia** version of the **Internet** and is rapidly becoming synonymous with it.

yield management   An **IT**-enabled means of pricing which allows marketing managers to maximise profits by charging different prices for different product offerings. Used extensively in the airline industry.

INDEX